The Big Picture

The Big Picture

A Short World History of Religions

by JOHN D. LOFTIN

McFarland & Company, Inc., Publishers
Jefferson, North Carolina, and London

Library of Congress Cataloguing-in-Publication Data

Loftin, John D., 1955–
    The big picture : a short world history of religions / by John D. Loftin.
        p. cm.
    Includes bibliographical references and index.
    ISBN 0-7864-0635-6 (illustrated case binding : 50# alkaline paper)
    1. Religions — History.   I. Title.
BL80.2.L64   2000
200'.9–dc21
                                                                99-44357

British Library Cataloguing-in-Publication data are available

©2000 John D. Loftin. All rights reserved

No part of this book may be reproduced or transmitted in any form or by any means, electronic or mechanical, including photocopying or recording, or by any information storage and retrieval system, without permission in writing from the publisher.

Manufactured in the United States of America

McFarland & Company, Inc., Publishers
    Box 611, Jefferson, North Carolina 28640
        www.mcfarlandpub.com

To Dad
and
in Memory of Mom

Preface

One day in September 1995, while I was eating lunch with Lowry Betts, a distinguished judge, and Lonnie Coleman, then a senior lawyer and now a judge, the subject of human weakness came up. At that time I had completed a couple drafts of this manuscript, but had not figured out a good way to begin. Judge Betts helped me out. After exchanging some recent courtroom war stories that accented the general sorriness of the human condition, Judge Betts spoke up, "People should have never stood up on two legs. That was original sin. We should have remained on all fours where we belonged." We all laughed. Later on I thought about his words and realized that he had summed up the book, for, surely, standing was the original human act.

Religion is a fascinating subject. Moreover, religious experiences have expressed themselves throughout human history and in every corner of the globe. Literally thousands of books have been written about the religions of various times and places and there are a large number of books today that discuss religion on a global scale. The great historian of religions, Mircea Eliade, in *The History of Religious Ideas*, charted the religious history of the world in three volumes. His work in many ways will remain the standard for years to come.

There are a number of shorter, one volume books dealing with the religions of the world. Here Huston Smith's *The World's Religions* stands out as the most readable and lasting. But Smith's book omits important chapters in the world history of religions. For example, he does not deal at all with the religious orientation of the Paleolithic (Old Stone Age) peoples. Neither does his book address the religious dimensions of the Neolithic revolution, and Mesopotamia and Egypt are not discussed at all.

Moreover, Smith's book does not wrestle with the religious significance of the discovery of the New World.

I have taught the world history of religions more than twenty times over a period of fifteen years. This book is an attempt to distill my thoughts on the world history of religions in a single, readable volume — hence the title, *The Big Picture: A Short World History of Religions*. The book is divided into four major segments: Prehistoric, Neolithic, the Axial Age, and the Discovery of the New World. Those four eras, in many ways, are the defining moments in the world history of religions and thus they are the basis around which this work is organized.

There are some obvious omissions in a short book such as this. Most notable is the lack of discussion of Greek and Roman religion. However, in addressing the Neolithic period, I decided to focus on the four earliest Neolithic cultures: Mesopotamia, Egypt, India and China. There are many other missing topics, such as Japanese religion and folk religion. Therefore, the book does not purport to be a comprehensive world history. Rather, it is one person's effort to see the religious forest amid the trees.

I want especially to thank my mentor, Charles H. Long, who is a retired, independent scholar living in Chapel Hill, North Carolina. His course, "Religious Orientations in World History," was probably the greatest learning experience I ever had and gave me the foundation on which to build this book. To him I owe a debt of gratitude that I can never repay. Many of the ideas in this work belong to Professor Long, or were influenced by him to a large degree. I, of course, remain responsible for the book's shortcomings.

Special thanks are also extended to my long-time legal assistant, Kathy Lawrence, who typed (and retyped) the manuscript, and to Loren Estes who typed the final draft.

I also want to recognize my wife, Angela, and my son, John. They give me love, support and a sense of perspective on life that words cannot express.

Contents

Preface		vii
ONE	Prehistoric and Primitive Religions	1
TWO	The Neolithic Revolution	31
THREE	Mesopotamia — Between the Rivers	51
FOUR	Egypt — Land of the Nile	67
FIVE	India and Hinduism	83
SIX	Ancient China	101
SEVEN	Judaism	117
EIGHT	The Axial Age	131
NINE	Buddhism	147
TEN	The Three Religions of China	167
ELEVEN	Christianity	189
TWELVE	Islam	215
THIRTEEN	The New World	235
Index		255

Chapter 1

Prehistoric and Primitive Religions

When one considers cosmic and geologic time, human history pales by comparison. While debate rages on concerning the age of the universe, most scientists agree that the universe is somewhere between 25 billion and 8 billion years old. The planet earth seems to be about 4 billion years old. Because humans did not emerge until about 7 million to 35,000 years ago, depending on who you talk to, it is clear that they are comparative newcomers. This realization alone occasions feelings of humility and wonder.

"When I was ten years of age I looked at the land and the rivers, the sky above, and the animals around me, and could not fail to realize that they were made by some great power"; thus spoke Brave Buffalo, a Dakota Sioux, in 1918 (quoted in Densmore 77). The perception of the world for the earliest peoples was itself a religious experience. Without going into the problem of the origin of religion, it should be said that the apprehension of the world was first and foremost a revelation of the sacred. The most significant aspect of primeval human experience was its humble passivity and quiet receptivity. The rhythms and forms of the world were first experienced as creating human beings before humans were able to project their wills onto the world. Humans did not discover the world; the world revealed itself to them. The primordial perception was a world that humans neither created nor controlled, and it was with that understanding that religion and the human way of life began. That apprehension of the world revealed the passivity of human existence — that humans are not in charge.

By contrast, the Western world's arrogance is nowhere better shown than by the famous American saying "Where there's a will, there's a way."

Even in the mighty United States old folks rarely invoke such self-certainty when describing their plans. Instead they generally say, "I'll see you tomorrow if the good Lord's willing and the creek don't rise." One is reminded here of the powerful words of James 4:13–16:

> Come now, you who say, "Today or tomorrow we will go into such and such a town and spend a year there and trade and get gain"; whereas you do not know about tomorrow. What is your life? For you are a mist that appears for a little time and then vanishes. Instead you ought to say, "If the Lord wills, we shall live and we shall do this or that."

In performing the oldest of the Sioux rites, *inipi*, the rite of purification, or sweat lodge, the participant bends low to enter the lodge and remembers that he is nothing compared to *wakan tanka* ("Great Mystery"); "it is you who have placed us upon this island" (quoted in Brown 35). The world strikes one as already there which, for original people, was contrasted with the human body. With this experience came religion.

The primordial perception of the world paralleled the experience of creation. The creation of the world is the most fundamental human perception and all other experience stems from it. It is also the most significant experience, for as the historian of religions, Henri Frankfort, stated, cosmogony is the only real change; that is, the transformation from nothing to something.

The sacred reveals the world and thus makes orientation possible. Orientation is always from a sacred center that establishes the world around it. For the Achilpa, an Australian tribe, the high god created a sacred pole and gave it to them in the "dream time." It represents the cosmic axis or center and makes the territory around it habitable. With it the tribe is oriented. The anthropologists Spencer and Gillen report that once the pole broke and the whole group lay down on the ground and waited for death to come because their lives had no bearing (388).

But it would be too simple to say that humans are merely passive. Among others, prehistorians Carleton Coon and Grahame Clark, and paleontologist Richard Leakey argue that erect, bipedal posture was the definitive act that separated hominids from the apes. As the social anthropologist Pierre Bordieu has shown, the human standing body functions as a geometer or axis around which the six cosmic directions were revealed (116–118). Up, down, right, left, front, and back are all revealed by movements or postures of the upright human body. The geographer Yi-Fu Tuan notes that the human body is unique in that it easily maintains an upright position. An upright position is more than a postural achievement; it is a new orientation to the world. A standing human is no longer simply a passive receptor within the world, but is ready to act upon the world. Space opens out before him and is immediately broken into the six directions. The six directions of the world are extrapolated onto the human body, which becomes a microcosm of the world around him. The Kwakiutl initiate exclaims, "I am at the center of the world," revealing at once one of the deepest meanings of sacred space (quoted in Eliade *The Sacred* 36).

Sky God

According to the historian of religions Mircea Eliade and the archaeologist Alexander Marshack, the experience of the sky was primary. The perception of the vault of the sky above struck earliest humanity as eternal, transcendent and majestic simply by being "up there" beyond the terrestrial realm of human beings. The primordial realization of the inaccessible "otherness" of the sky above revealed to human beings the eternal universality of the divine and simultaneously the mortality and finitude of human beings bound by time and space. For many religions the divine is linked inescapably with notions of height, sky and heaven. Simply seeing the sky above was, for earliest humanity, a profound revelation of a mysterious power upon which their very existence depended. Almost universally, for archaic peoples, the sky revealed itself as sacred and often as the most powerful of the gods. The Mongol name for the supreme god is *tengri*, which means "sky." The same is true for other Ural-Altaic tribes like the Tatar, Tangar, Chuvashes, Ostyaks and Voguls. Those tribes, Eliade notes, have best preserved the primeval character of their sky gods. They are also the tribes which best exemplify shamanism, a topic we shall come to shortly. For now, let us note that the shamanism and sky gods represent very old religious structures.

For humans life is simultaneously active and passive. Human awareness of the eternal and sacred nature of sky, earth, stone and water paralleled consciousness of their own power and their ability to impose themselves upon the world. The earliest peoples were hunter-gatherers and among hunter-gatherers men did the vast majority of the hunting of animals, while women gathered wild plants. Calling upon archeological and ethnological studies of hunting-gathering peoples over the last two centuries, it can reasonably be estimated that the earliest human communities ranged in numbers from twenty to fifty people. These small human communities migrated across and through space according to the seasons.

For almost all living hunting cultures, a key god is the Owner of the animals. Indeed, the god of the animals played so central a part in the religion of hunting-gathering peoples, that diverse scholars such as Raffaele Pettazoni, historian of religions; Alfred Kroeber, anthropologist; and Paul Radin, anthropologist, argue that the Owner of the animals was the first god, the sky god being of secondary origin and development. The Cherokee Indians of North Carolina traditionally made prayers to Little Deer every time they prepared to hunt deer, and they rendered prayers of thanksgiving and apology to Little Deer upon the completion of a successful deer hunt to avoid being inflicted with disease and scarcity of game.

It would seem that the sky god and the Owner of the animals are coexistent and coterminous and that each presupposes the other. The sky god and Owner of the animals correspond to two separate but interrelated modes of religious experience. The passive gaze of human beings upon the earth and sky and all of its forms reveals to human beings the power and majesty of the sacred. By simply looking out at the world human beings experience the rhythmical activity of the sacred. The quiescence of human experience is primary. It is this sense of receptivity that Edward Kennard referred to when he noted that the Hopi Indians speak as though they do not act autonomously to control their own destinies, "even when speaking English, a Hopi does not say, 'I guess I'll have to change my way.' Instead he says, 'I guess I'll come to that'" (470).

Hunting

At the same time, by engaging the world through everyday activities like hunting, tool making, fire making and house building, the earliest humans experienced the sacred because all human creations were ultimately recognized as given by the gods. Prehistoric hunters considered a successful hunt to be dependent upon the blessing of the Owner of the animals. No matter how talented or gifted a particular hunter was, everyone recognized that there could be no successful hunt unless the gods willed it. First of all, the Owner of the animals created game. As a Cree Indian once put it, animals could not be hunted if they were not created. Second, the Owner of the animals ultimately allows game to be killed. The Central Eskimo make it clear that the goddess Sedna may withhold game if she so desires. Thirdly, the human ability to hunt was itself seen ultimately as god-given. If someone in the group was an especially accomplished hunter, it was because the gods had decided that he would be so gifted.

Upper Paleolithic men often practiced encircling techniques, joining together to surround herds and drive them off of cliffs. This technique was also used among the Blackfoot Indians of Montana who would drive large buffalo herds off the cliff where they would be slaughtered by hunters in the valley floor below.

Blackfoot mythology tells of the time when the buffalo would veer right or left as they ran to the edge of the cliff, which caused the Blackfoot to be hungry. The god of the buffalo showed a father and daughter how to do the Buffalo Dance, and when the dance was over, the bull instructed the Blackfoot to go home and teach the dance and song to their people. The father and daughter returned to their camp and called a council of the chiefs and taught them the dance and the song of the bulls. In this way the All Comrades Association of the Blackfoot was organized.

Hunting is what might be called part and parcel of the active experience of the sacred, which is essentially male in character. In hunting cultures men did the hunting. It is interesting to note that, for the Hopi Indians, only four cultural implements form clan names. Those implements all relate to the process of hunting: the bow and arrow, the throwing stick, the fire spindle and the carrying strap. Furthermore, they all relate especially to male concerns and roles through which the sacred is experienced.

Women give birth to babies through their own internal space, the womb. The ability to give birth links women very closely to the earth mother. Women are homologous to the earth because they embody the most powerful and basic manifestation of the sacred, birth. For example, the ability of Hopi women to be mothers is highly prized and confers on them a sense of worth that, in one sense, is more fundamental than that of men. Men do not participate directly in the birth process as do women, but they can participate in other creative processes symbolically through the hunt. In the hunt men shed blood external to themselves in external space in order to create new forms such as meat, skins and other cultural artifacts (Long). Through the language of the hunt men seek a relation with the creative forces of the world which women express through birth in almost mute form.

Thus, men and women embody very different modes of sacrality. For the Hopi, men are likened to hawks, fierce hunters, who feed upon prey, and Hopi youth imitate hawks when they are initiated into manhood. Hopi women, on the other hand, are likened to butterflies, fertility and fecundity, and unmarried Hopi women traditionally wore their hair in butterfly whorls to depict this association.

There are a number of taboos which surround hunters and women (Frazer 241,252,694). For example, Nootka Indians, to catch whales, had to abstain from any contact with their women for a week. They often blamed unsuccessful whale expeditions on the failure of one of the fishermen to remain chaste during this period. Similarly, among the Aleuts of Alaska, a hunter who struck a whale with a spear would not throw again, but would return at once home and separate himself from his people in a hut especially constructed for this purpose. There he stayed for three days without food or drink or without touching or looking upon a woman.

Menstruating women were considered to be especially powerful and thus a ceremony usually followed a young girl's first menstruation. Among the Indians of California a girl at her first menstruation was secluded from her family, the community, and, indeed, the world around her. She was, for instance, forbidden to see the sun, the sun being linked with men and hunting. This seclusion of menstruating women from the sun was also practiced among the Chinook, the Nootka, Bella Coola and Tlingit. Among the Tlingit a menstruating woman had to wear a sort of hat with long flaps so that her gaze might not pollute the sky, and it was thought that her look would destroy the luck of any hunter or fishermen. The anthropologist Marla Powers has shown us that when an Oglala Dakota girl reaches her first menstruation, her hair is parted on the right side, her forehead is painted red and she is told red is a sacred color: "Your first menstrual flow was red. Then you too were sacred. This is to show that you are akin to the buffalo god and are his woman. You are now a buffalo woman" (69).

Moreover, taboos often surrounded husbands whose wives were pregnant. For example, a Cherokee was expected to refrain from hunting while his wife was pregnant because his prayers and thoughts should be directed towards the lifegiving powers of his wife's blood, not toward the shedding of an animal's blood (Mooney). The Mbuti Pygmies of Africa say that there are two types of blood: female blood of life and the male blood of death. The two types of blood are to be kept separate and they correspond roughly to what we might call male and female modes of sacrality. The cultural anthropologist Victor Turner found that the Ndembu of Africa also distinguish two forms of blood; "the blood of huntsmanship" must not be brought into presence with "the blood of motherhood." Therefore, when a hunter's wife is about to give birth, the husband must remove all of his hunting weapons from the vicinity of the house or risk its being rendered powerless. As Turner puts it, "for a child to be born, the maternal blood must coagulate around the fetus. Hunters shed blood and cause it to gush and flow. Again, women give life, while hunters take it. The two functions are antithetical"(363). Moreover, the men in some groups in Australia practice sub-incision of the penis or the arm. They explain that the hole produced is the same as a woman's vagina, and that the blood that flows from it is the same as the menstrual blood of a woman. An Australian told anthropologist Lloyd Warner, "[t]he hole in the man's arm isn't that hole anymore. It is all the same as the vagina...that had blood coming out of it" (quoted in Gross 288).

The anthropologist Lucién Levy-Bruhl was one of the first scholars to note that primitives are above all attentive to mystical connections which are felt rather than thought. Furthermore, he states that primitives perceive the natural world as manifesting spiritual forces and powers imperceptible to the senses. The ability to see or feel the invisible, to feel the sacred force that is within the material forms of the world, is denoted in the Sioux culture by the term *cante ista*—"the eye of the heart." As Professor Alfonzo Ortiz, an anthropologist and Tewa Indian puts it, "All things are thought to have two aspects, essence and matter" (143).

Language

Primitives do not separate themselves from the world that they perceive around them. Furthermore, the world around them has a spiritual essence which manifests itself by and through the physical. The spiritual dimension of the world is not deduced intellectually but is felt and lived. Maurice Leenhardt, who did missionary work in Melanesia from 1902 to 1927, developed this idea further, noting that the Melanesian is unaware that his body is an element which he himself possesses. The Melanesian has not differentiated himself from the world around him and this can be seen through his discussion of his family relationships. Whereas Westerners will say "my mother" and "my father," Melanesians will say "mother me," "father of me" (13). Not only does their language scrap the "I" for the "me," but the "me" has two different levels of significance. Because such an organic bond unites a Melanesian with his mother, there is no preposition to separate a Melanesian from his mother, thus "mother me." Fathers are connected to Melanesians, but more symbolically. Therefore, the relationship of a Melanesian to his father is denoted by the term "father of me." In contrast to Western language Melanesians use reflexive rather than possessive pronouns to describe parental relationships.

Similarly, the historian of religions Werner Müller has shown that the Dakota Indian language also prefers the reflexive over the possessive pronoun. Therefore, a Dakota will normally say, "The horse has died in regard to me," rather than "my horse has died" (230). The passive, receiving and feminine structure of Dakota language indicates an attitude which is quite distinct from an active, dominating will. As Müller says, "the I imposes itself on the world, the me adapts itself to the world; the I wants to act, the me wants to absorb; the I wants to change, the me wants to preserve" (231).

In the silence of birth, women embrace the sacred. Doranne Jacobsen has shown how Hindu women of Central India remain silent during the ritual of giving birth. Birth is performed without any particular verbal expressions or prayers. All formalized rituals are done by the male priests. For these Hindu women, with the exception of a few songs, religious activity is a matter of doing, rather than talking.

There also seems to be an ancient connection between language and hunting. It is instructive to note that the !Kung women of the Kalahari Desert speak in a hunting idiom. For example, they hunt both for nuts and for their children; dyes and roots are chased down; and when referring to sexuality, they say that their husbands chased them (Marshall). Language, one might say, is an attempt to express symbolically a relation with the world that women inhabited simply by being women. Men address the sacred through symbolic prayers and ritual activities, such as the hunt, precisely because they did not embody that power as did women. This helps us to understand the taboos that surround male hunters with menstruating and pregnant women.

Paleolithic people inhabited certain sacred centers along their landscape. Again, these centers were not discovered; they were manifested by the gods. The earliest human communities subsisted by hunting and gathering; therefore, they moved across and through space hunting wild animals and gathering wild plants. Several sacred centers disclosed themselves to these communities and provided orientation points for these communities as they made their seasonal rounds in search of food. Evidence gathered from prehistoric and historic hunting-gathering cultures indicates that the earliest humans did not form permanent structures and did not attempt to control space, as do the later agriculturists. The earliest humans apparently lived in wind screens and simple grass huts, similar to those of the Paiute Indians of America or the !Kung Bushmen of Africa, or they would live in caves that were discovered along the way. Space was something that prehistoric humans inhabited and made their way across, but did not dominate. The Paiute and Shoshoni Indians of the American Southwest traditionally migrated through a fairly well-defined area which corresponded to the availability of certain food stuffs according to the seasons. Thus, a number of different seeds were gathered in the spring, fruits in the summer, nuts in the fall, and hunting was emphasized in the winter.

Human Origins

When did humanity emerge? This is a question that has puzzled philosophers, anthropologists, archeologists and historians of religion for centuries. With the advent of radiocarbon dating and the scientific method, most modern scholars would deny that the world is only about six thousand years old, as Christian fundamentalists would have it. Archeologists today tell us that the earth itself is at least four billion years old and that human beings have only been around for a fraction of that time. But when did the human mode of being emerge? We do not wish here to recount the controversy surrounding evolutionary theory and the quest for the discovery of the beginning of the human way of life. Archeologists tell us that fully biped hominids (*Australopithecus*) walked the earth from about 4.1-3.7 to 3.18-2.5 million years ago (Burenhult, Leakey). However, the earliest humanlike creatures discovered around East and South Africa were not clearly human. No stone tools have been found in the earliest sites in Laetoli, Tanzania; Hadar and Kanapoi, Ethiopia; and two sites in South Africa, Sterkfontein and Makapansgat. Some archeologists think that that is because the earliest remains were not found near village sites, but among remains in the dens of hyenas that had dragged in the bones of the earliest hominids.

Most scientists agree that our own genus, *Homo*, appeared about 2.5 million years ago and includes at least three major species: *Homo habilis* (2.5–1.5 million years ago), *Homo erectus* (1.8 million–100,000 years ago) and *Homo sapiens* (100,000 years ago to present). However, research continues to uncover new finds that many scholars think point to at least six different species and maybe more. It may very well be the case that humans represent a twig on a hominid bush rather than a limb on a family tree.

Tools

In the Olduvai Gorge, Tanzania, and Koobi Fora, Kenya, two types of hominids had been found together with crude stone tools that have been dated at about 2.5 million years old. Crude choppers, flakes and scrapers roughly chipped from small cobbles are found among these remains. The discovery of tools in the Olduvai Gorge sparked tremendous curiosity among scholars as to what definitively separates human beings from the rest of the zoological kingdom. For awhile most scholars argued that only humans used tools and that the discovery of tools marked the beginning of the human way of life. However, subsequent observations by other anthropologists and naturalists prove that chimpanzees can pick up sticks and use them to fish termites from nests and sea otters can use rocks to break open mussels for feeding. These discoveries brought into question the simple notion that only human beings use tools.

However, it would seem that only humans make or manufacture tools. The chimpanzee who picks up a stick to fish termites is using a tool, but one that is found at his disposal. The same is true of the otter who picks up a rock and breaks open a mussel shell. About 2–2.5 million years ago hominid creatures in the Olduvai Gorge were manufacturing crude choppers from cobblestones. As prehistorian Johannes Maringer showed, the use of cobblestones to make other tools carries with it a recognition of time and consciousness of the future that does not seem to be present among animals who simply pick up tools and use them for their immediate needs (11). Furthermore, the evidence seems to indicate that these early hominids actually carried tools considerable distances for use at some future, unspecified time and this seems to show an awareness of time that is simply not clearly present among animals. The discovery of Paleolithic tools shows that these creatures thought, and that they were, as Marshack put it, "time factored." In other words, tools show the emergence of a reflective consciousness.

Hand axes similar to those found in Olduvai Gorge from 1.5 million years ago are found all over Africa, Europe and parts of western and southern Africa. Significantly, while the style of these axes changed very little, whenever the styles changed, they seemed to change everywhere within a short time. Professor Coon first noted that such widespread modifications and similarities in pattern show that these human beings were teaching tool-making styles to their children, who in turn were passing them on to their offspring (55–56). This teaching technique requires both speech and a discipline and is not unlike the teaching techniques of the !Kung Bushmen and Australian Aborigines. Coon concludes that human society was already formed when the hand-ax choppers of the world became uniform products (I).

During the Neanderthal period, that is, between 200,000 and 35,000 B.C.E. (230,000–29,000 B.C.E.?), crude stone tools were supplemented with more sophisticated hand axes, scrapers and cutters. The earliest tools were core tools shaped by knocking off bits from a large lump, or core. Prehistoric people must have felt the resistance of stone to their efforts to shape it. Stone is hard — it resists. By working stone, the passivity of stone's sacrality manifested itself. Eventually, however, the core would yield its fruit.

By the development of the late Cro-Magnon Gravettian period,

28,000–24,000 B.C.E., we find in the limestone-cave carving known as Venus of Laussel a pregnant woman holding a bison antler. Bison antlers were apparently used during Cro-Magnon times to make flake tools. This connects tool making with bone and the rebirth of game animals. Bone was only rarely used for the manufacture of tools by Neanderthals, but was utilized often by Cro-Magnons to make flake tools. Flake tools are made by detaching chips through the use of pressure points. One core stone gives birth rather easily to several smaller stones; thus stone reveals itself as fertile. In pressing a stone or bone against a larger stone, one gives birth to little "baby" stones which become points, flakes, choppers and axes (Long). Furthermore, this activity concretely links stone with eternity because stone may always give birth from itself to another smaller stone.

An important link here between tool making and fire making through the use of the fire stone is depicted in a story among the Kaska Indians of British Columbia who state that, in the beginning, Bear, the most sacred of all animals, was the only person who had the fire stone. Humans had no fire and the bear guarded the fire stone jealously. Eventually, a number of animals got together and stole the fire stone from Bear. In the end, Fox, on top of a mountain, broke up the fire stone and threw a fragment of it to each tribe. That is how the many tribes all over earth got fire (Teit).

Beginning about 50,000 years ago, Cro-Magnon communities heated flint between 400 and 1100 degrees Fahrenheit to make the stone work more easily. This also connects fire, stone and birth. As we have seen, the act of tool making ultimately pointed back to its passive character. The use of fire to heat flint by Cro-Magnons in order to make easier the production of tools represents an increased willingness to exercise one's specifically human power over the sacred in order to obtain a desired result. As we will see later, the use of fire to accelerate human production and the rhythms of the world carries with it meanings of pollution and taboo that are important religiously.

Fire

A more definitive break with the animal kingdom seems to have occurred somewhere between 430,000 and 230,000 B.C.E. The famous Choukoutien (Zhoukodian) caves in northern China contain skeletal and other remains of people indicating that they were successful hunters of deer, that they used fire, and that they perhaps engaged in cannibalism. It is also clear that they made very crude choppers and simple flakes from stones in the area. These people have also been named Homo Erectus and

Peking Man. At camp sites near Terra Amata, in France, traces of fire have been found that date back to between 300,000 and 200,000 years ago. Some of the hearths are found on arrangements of pebbles, while others are located in shallow pits. Only human beings directly use and control fire, and it appears that for all human communities fire was originally perceived as sacred. Fire defines the paradoxical character of human existence. As Van der Leeuw said, "Fire is a phenomenon in which man participates, though does not activate, recognizes as superior, yet handles at will" (Vol. I 60). The making of fire is likened to creation and birth.

The earliest fires were made by either the use of a fire stone or fire stick. For example, the Kaska Indians of British Columbia make fire by striking one stone, a flint, against another larger stone, thus generating sparks. The striking of one stone against another is compared to human sexuality and the sparks that result are symbolic of birth itself. The Hopi Indians of Arizona traditionally made fire by rotating a fire stick in a fire board (Loftin 23). This creates friction which eventually brings about fire. Among the Hopi Indians, and many other peoples throughout the world, the stick is called male and the board female. The union of the male spindle and the hole in the female board brings about birth. The homology between birth and fire perhaps helps us to understand why some people say that women produced the first fire from their genital organs (Frazer 220).

It is significant that among many peoples the origin of fire is linked with the origin of death. According to Pygmy mythology, in the beginning the god Tore had fire, and the Pygmies did not. A Mbuti Pygmy stole fire from Tore's old mother and she died from the cold. Tore, unable to catch the thief, proclaimed him to be his own equal, but added that human beings would thereafter die as punishment for this haughty act (Maquet 54). Only human beings possess fire, and its acquisition parallels the origin of human awareness of time and space. To gain fire is also to become aware of death, and thus fire and death have been linked since the beginning.

Jacques Maquet discusses a myth collected by the anthropologist P. Schebesta, in which the Mbuti Pygmies state that, in the beginning, they had no fire and that the chimpanzees of the forest had fire. A Mbuti was once a guest in the chimpanzee village and managed to steal the fire from the chimpanzees. Since that time it is said that the chimpanzees retreated to the forest where they live without fire. Thus, for the Mbuti Pygmies, fire is the distinguishing difference between animals and themselves. The Pygmies traditionally had no knowledge of how to generate fire by either the fire spindle or the fire stone, or it may be the case that they had the knowledge to make fire, but considered fire to be an act of the gods and, thus, refused to do it. The Mbuti carry embers of a fire and leaves with them wherever they go. They say that without fire they would die (Maquet).

During the Molimo ritual, an old woman appears, sometimes assisted by a younger married woman and some virgins who invade the sanctity of the Molimo hearth, which is the province of the men. They assert their power over the men by literally tying all the men together with the twine used for making hunting nets, and they also attempt to stamp out the sacred fire. The efforts of the old woman during an elaborate dance are encountered by the men, who gather up the scattered embers and rebuild the fire, fanning it into life with a wild erotic dance that imitates the act of copulation. Mbuti mythology says that women had fire before men, but that men stole it from the women. This ritual follows the death of a tribal member and shows the important link between fire and death, as well as the male character of fire (Turnbull, Teit).

Animals

On the one hand, for hunting peoples all over the world, animals symbolize the sacred, and animal symbolism seems to be extremely widespread among Paleolithic finds. Van der Leeuw once said that animals are wholly different from humans, yet intimately attached and familiar (76). As such, they symbolize the sacred because the sacred is experienced as intimate, yet strange, immanent, yet transcendent. Animals thus represent the paradoxical nature of the sacred. They do not cause religion; they serve as a mode of its expression. To primitive peoples the sacred reveals itself through concrete and material modalities and animals manifest the sacred quite powerfully for Paleolithic hunters. Killing game was thus a ritual act for ancient hunters.

On the one hand, hunting revealed human autonomy and power over the sacred. Therefore, hunting evoked feelings of guilt linked with the exercise of human will over and against the sacred — thus the Cherokee's apologies to Little Deer for slaying deer. In some tribes a successful hunter will say that a member of another tribe actually killed the animal with hopes that any retribution on the part of the animal's spirit will be directed to an enemy. At the same time, a successful hunt ultimately reveals the passivity of the hunt, for the Owner of animals allows game to be killed if proper prayers and ritual preparations are performed. Because bones were often linked with the eternal nature of the sacred, Paleolithic hunters many times would dispose of the bones in a proper manner as directed by the gods to ensure future successful hunts.

Death

There can be no serious question about the fully human status of Neanderthal peoples about 60,000 (100,000?) years ago as evidenced by their practice of interment of the dead (Burenhult, 70–73; Leakey, 125–26, 155–56). While some Neanderthal burials are controversial, three graves seem obvious. In La Chapelle aux-Saints a skeleton was found in a steep-sided, square-cut pit. A mature male was buried on a bed of flowers at the entrance of a cave in the Zagros Mountains of northern Iraq. More recently, another pit grave was unearthed at Kebara Cave in Israel. Red ochre was sprinkled on some of the corpses in the Paleolithic period; for certain Australian Aborigines, red ochre symbolizes the blood of birth, and thus painting a corpse with red dye is a prayer for rebirth into the next life. In some of the Neanderthal graves there are necklaces and implements and other burial goods. This shows them to be similar to burial practices among other primitive peoples all over the world. Some of the corpses were found in the fetal position. For a number of American Indian tribes a dead person is buried into the womb of mother earth in a fetal position as a prayer that they be reborn as a baby into the next life.

In some primitive tribes, the deceased are bound in a bent huddle position to ensure that they do not come back to haunt the living. This idea is perhaps even older than the idea of burial to ensure rebirth into the next world and harks back to an archaic way of looking at the relationship between body, death and God. The idea of rebirth into another world may involve a later stage of religious thinking than that of recognizing the continuity between the living and the dead. Or it may be that the binding of the dead to prevent the dead from coming back to the living simultaneously emerges with the hope that the dead are reborn into the next life and that the two meanings coincide with one another.

Among the Melanesians there is no fear of the dead returning to the living because the differentiation between life and death is not absolute. Therefore, it is not until the dead are feared that there is simultaneously a separation between the spheres such that there are prayers for life after death. Maurice Leenhardt's work among Melanesians showing the lack of differentiation between notions of corpses and God may help illuminate prehistoric humanity's understanding of the dead. At the most archaic level of religious understanding Melanesians do not differentiate between corpse and god. Their language has a single notion which refers to both. Funeral rites do not separate the living from the dead but rather signify the enrichment of the sacred world through the incorporation of a relative's spiritual essence, upon which the human world depends. Death does not denote nothingness for Melanesians. When someone lies dying, the Melanesian understands that only the person's skin is ultimately sick because the spiritual aspect of the person springs eternal. Thus, strictly speaking, the visible and invisible aspects of existence do not correspond strictly with what we call life and death, but rather with incarnate life and purely spiritual life. These two states participate in the same reality and are not in opposition to one another. When someone dies in Pygmy society, there is a great mourning which takes place, but there are no accusations of witchcraft or sorcery. Burial consists of simply pulling down the grass hut around the body and then vacating the camp. The emphasis is on restoring the normality of society as soon as possible.

Perhaps that kind of understanding explains why there is no evidence of burial for Paleolithic hominids until the Neanderthal period (100,000?–60,000 B.C.E.). Perhaps that also helps to explain the apparent cannibalism that took place in the Choukoutien caves in China between 430,000 and 230,000 years ago. There dead were eaten rather than buried, and in eating marrow from the bones of the dead Peking man incorporated within his being the essence of the deceased which itself was not distinct from God. In other words, cannibalism, if it occurred, was sacrament, and, because there was no clear distinction between the living and the dead, there was no burial.

Because cannibalism is generally found among farmers and not among hunter-gathers, Johannes Maringer argued that Peking man more likely practiced dual burial like the Andaman Islanders, who were traditionally hunters. The Andaman Islanders would bury their dead and, after a period of mourning which lasted several months, would dig up the corpse. The bones were then cleaned and the skull in particular was preserved and actually carried around. The opening at the base of the skulls (*foramen magnum*) was enlarged in order to remove the brain which was slow to decompose.

Similarly, the skulls of Peking man showed artificial enlargement of the *foramen magnum*, and it may be that the brains were removed but not eaten, as has been commonly assumed. Peking man may have preserved the skulls of the deceased out of reverence for the spiritual essence which was understood to be seated in the skull. The skull represented the locus of the person's divinity, which merged with the sacred power at death. By maintaining contact with the deceased's skull, Peking man may have been able to draw up the spark of eternal life that dwelled inside for protection, good health and long life. Because ancient people perceived close homologies between the dead and the divine, the skull, because it lasted "forever," was perceived to embody and symbolize the sacred essence of the cosmos. On the other hand, recent studies of Peking man have raised serious questions about cannibalism. A number of archaeologists have postulated that Peking man did not eat human brains and bones. At Choukoutien there is abundant evidence that scavenging hyenas may have eaten human remains.

Bear

In the Alps bones of cave bears have been found which date to the last interglacial period. Deposits of bones, especially skulls and long bones, were often grouped together and placed along cave walls. At Regourdou, in the Dordogne, a pit containing over 20 cave bear skulls was found covered by a large stone slab. Nearby a complete bear skeleton and part of a Neanderthal skeleton was uncovered. While some scholars have argued that these bear-bone deposits are the result of geologic processes or the bears themselves, others feel that these were the intentional acts of human beings. The significance of the bear as the most sacred of all animals among hunting peoples throughout the world is very clear. For numerous tribal peoples the bear is considered the preeminent animal of creation who knows everything.

Among the northern Saulteaux, special procedures were carefully followed in hunting the bear (Hallowell). A hunter could not kill a bear unless he had first addressed it using a specified name or kinship designation. The hunter would apologize for having to kill the bear, explaining to it that it was only because of his great hunger and the people's need for food. After killing the bear, the hunter would immediately dress it in fine clothing so that it took on the appearance of a human. The Saulteaux explained that bears had to be treated thus because there was a chief of the bears who must be obeyed or he would be offended and withhold bears in the future. A small piece of the heart was taken from a slain bear and offered to the spiritual Owner of the bears, and the rest was consumed so that one might acquire the cunning and courage of the bear. The bones had to be properly buried so that they might not be eaten by the dogs, and it was perhaps this type of understanding that helps us to understand the alignment of bears' skulls and bones found in some upper Paleolithic caves.

Among the Ainu, a traditional hunting-fishing community of the northern islands of Japan, the bear is the most sacred of all animals (Kindaiti, Munro). When a young black bear cub is caught, it is raised as a child until it becomes big enough to be dangerous, then it is caged for two years. The bear is then ritually killed to return its spirit to his parents. In fact, the name of the ceremony is *iyomande*, "to send away." When the Ainu kill a wild bear, its body is taken into the hunter's house through an entry way known as "god's window," and its arrival is called "god's arrival."

Among the Cherokee Indians the bear is said to be the most sacred of all of animals. There was once a bear clan among the Cherokee, but the bears decided to return to a life in the wild so they would not have to work and so they could live naturally in the world. Still, the Cherokee say that bears can occasionally be heard singing Cherokee lullabies to bear cubs from their homes in mountain caves (Mooney).

Bear ceremonialism is perhaps the most characteristic complex of hunting religion practiced in both America and the Old World as part of a circumpolar culture that seems to go back to the Paleolithic times. Evidence of this ceremonialism exists throughout North America, and remains of an old bear ceremonialism may even be found in the Pueblo Southwest among groups such as the Hopi which hold that the bear clan is the most important of the clans.

Given the significance of the bear among hunting cultures all over the world, it would seem that the formations of bear skulls and bones in various caves during the Paleolithic period was a ritual activity related to the sacredness of the bear. Some have argued that the Owner of the animals was offered the bears' brains and marrow as a prayer that more animals would be sent in the future. Others argued that the skull and long bones of the slain bear were preserved so that the Owner of the animals could resuscitate them the following year. Whatever the interpretation, there seems to have been a very close link between the hunters and the bears.

Finally, the significance of the performance of Paleolithic rituals and artwork within caves deep below the surface of the earth cannot be overlooked. Pueblo Indians say that human beings emerged from the womb of the earth and there seems to be a primordial femininity to the earliest experiences of the sacred. The underworld is the origin of everything. It is that which gives birth to all life and forms.

The first experience of the sacred was its otherness which transcendence ultimately pointed back to the primal immanence or relation and unity of the sacred. One might say that the initial experience of separation from the sacred occasioned in humans the recognition of a prior unity with the sacred that was lived at an unconscious level. Thus, it seems that the significance of the womb of the earth is occasioned by and points back to the transcendence of the sky. With the performance of rituals in caves, Paleolithic humans perhaps returned to the primeval unity that was lived prior to human awareness of the sacred through the revelation of the sky. By returning to the womb of mother earth, Paleolithic humans demonstrated their knowledge of the unity that was once inhabited at an unconscious level. The womb of the earth is a realm of life and death. Women produce death through life. That is to say, when someone is born, he is doomed to death. The Maori of New Zealand recognized the connection between birth and death. They note that "what destroys men is the...female organ which they call by a name that means 'the location or origin of death and misfortune'" (Van der Leeuw Vol. I 207). Van der Leeuw noted that the snake is the animal par excellence in symbolizing the sacred and it is interesting that the earliest artwork found in Paleolithic caves included serpentine symbols (76). The snake, of course, is intimately connected with the chthonic world which is the world of death, water and also life.

Art

A lot of Paleolithic art is found in the form of cave paintings. These date primarily to the Cro-Magnon period, and a number of the findings are especially significant. The first question that arises in the context of the religious interpretation of Paleolithic art is the background on which the art was drawn, namely caves. Many of the most spectacular paintings were done during the Magdalenian period, between 17,000 and 12,000 B.C.E., on walls deep in caves in France and Spain. Some of the pictures portray, with a great deal of realism, deer, bison, horses, rhinoceros and other animals that served as important sources of food. Many observers think that cave paintings were part and parcel of religious activities that included dancing and singing. Looking for connections between sight and sound, the French anthropologists Iegor Reznikoff and Michel Dauvois surveyed three caves in the Ariege region of southwest France. Singing as they went, they tested the resonance of each cave section. They found what they were looking for; those areas with the highest resonance were also those most likely to house a painting or carving (Scarre).

Other important Paleolithic art finds include the famous Venus statuettes. We have already mentioned the Venus of Laussel, who held a bison antler in her hand. Numerous four to six inch statues of women with enlarged breasts, stomachs and buttocks are found throughout the Cro-Magnon period between 28,000 and 24,000 B.C.E. These small statues are made of stone, bone and ivory, and in some way seem to emphasize the fertility of women. The fact that they are often made of stone is perhaps significant in that stone struck prehistoric peoples as eternal and as fertile. In other words, stone was eternally fertile, a realization that was prompted passively by simply perceiving stone formation and actively by the making of stone tools, in which a smaller stone was extracted from a larger mother stone. The Venus statuettes were perhaps a prayer that women be fertile as stone is fertile.

For many primitive peoples the sky and the sun are seen primarily as male, earth as female. One Hopi myth says that when the sky father and the earth mother united, their union brought the fertilizing rains. Mbuti Pygmies perceive the rays of the sun as spears which penetrate to the earth just as their spears penetrate game animals. Thus, the sun is male for the Pygmies and is related to the hunt. Similarly, for a number of primitive peoples, the earth is seen as female.

Perhaps this helps us to explain why many Paleolithic paintings are drawn deep in the womb of the earth. Caves are female and are likened to the womb of the earth from which comes all life. Yet the underworld is also the realm of the dead, from which life comes. Thus perhaps hunting rituals were performed deep in the womb of earth as a prayer that game be created for successful hunts. We have already mentioned how the hunt is a symbolic birth activity for men and thus perhaps the historian of religions E.O. James was correct when he stated that what we see in Paleolithic paintings of the hunt are death and fertility rites side by side. Perhaps the drawings of male buffalo chasing female buffalo and of hunters chasing buffalo are prayers both for game increase and successful hunts in order to sustain life for the community. In Montespan there is a painting of a bear who is covered with dart holes. At the Cavern of Niaux a bison is covered with rudely painted outlines of spears. These paintings seem to depict prayers for successful hunts and seem to typify what Professor E.A. Hooton has said was "art for meat's sake." That these prayers for successful hunts were done deep in the womb of mother earth seems to imply that they were simultaneously prayers for the rebirth of slain animals so that there could be plenty of food for the group in the future.

Alexander Marshack found a number of bone engravings dated back to the upper Paleolithic period (30,000 B.C.E.). In France he found several bones with minute lunar engravings depicting one lunar year (Marshack 1972). The bone markings also revealed a meandering pattern that perhaps served as a map to orient people through space according to the lunar calendar. A historic parallel is perhaps found in western Australia in the Oldea Region where *Inma*(dream time) boards are said to contain the original migration path laid down in the dream time by Iguana. The Australian Aborigines say that the migration path is also mapped out in the marks found on the back of the Iguana.

Lunar symbolism appears to be quite old among humans. In fact, the moon was perhaps one of the oldest religious symbols depicting life of human beings. Human beings are born, they grow, mature, decline and then they die; so does the moon. But the moon after three days is reborn in the sky and the perception of the rhythms of the moon perhaps occasioned in Paleolithic humanity an understanding that life comes out of death and from death comes more life. Thus the perception of the rhythms and vicissitudes of the moon itself evokes in human beings understanding of both time and timelessness.

The moon also seems inextricably bound up with the tides and with water and, of course, with the menstrual cycle of women. Thus the Pygmies of Africa celebrate *Pe*, the feast of the new moon, which takes place a little before the rainy season. Pygmies call the moon *Pe* and say that it is the principle of generation and the mother of fecundity. For the Pygmies the feast of the new moon is reserved exclusively for the women, just as the feast of the sun is celebrated exclusively by men. Leo Frobenius noted that Pygmy men liken their hunting spears to the rays of the sun, and women associate themselves with lunar rhythms. The moon is also associated with water and with the underworld and hence with women, and therefore ultimately with snakes, which are also tied up with fertility.

In the Dordogne region of France an ox bone was found with some markings on it that have been dated to about 135,000 B.C.E. Marshack calls these curvy lines a "macaroni-meander" image and argues that they point to the antiquity of a serpent-rain-water-storm-clouds symbolism (Marshack 1977). They also arguably point to the meandering orientation to the world which characterized prehistoric humanity. This early link between water, life, female and the sacred is interesting and is perhaps the earliest evidence of a definitive religious symbol system.

Dance

Dance is sacred for primitives, and we may assume that it was sacred for Paleolithic people. As R. R. Marrett stated, religion is first of all emotional, not logical, and was first danced, not intellectualized (xxxi). Dance was prayer and expressed the complexities of human religion more profoundly than could speech. Lorna Marshall notes that the !Kung Bushmen of Africa danced quite frequently, at least two or three times a month and sometimes more often. Most importantly, dance is "one concerted religious act of the !Kung and it brings people into such unison that they become like an organic being" (271). As the cultural interpreter Lame Deer notes when talking about the religion of his people, the Sioux Indians, "All our dances have their beginnings in our religion.... They were sacred.... Dancing and praying—it's the same thing" (233). At Montespan Cave there is a floor of clay in which marks were left by the feet of young men. Curt Sachs has no doubt that this was ritual choreography and is an example of the circular dance which is extremely widespread among hunting peoples from Europe to Asia, and Melanesia to America (Eliade 1978). The purpose everywhere is either to pacify the soul of the slain animal or to ensure the multiplication of game. This dance is also the primary ritual dance of the Shoshoni Indians, one of the last hunting-gathering tribes in native North America. Evidence of ritual dance was also found at the cave of Le Tuc d'Audobert where the footprints of six children were discovered. Aligned in six rows, the prints reveal a distinct dance pattern. In the big cave at Niaux, archaeologists have found more than 500 footprints in a sanctuary located more than 3000 feet deep in the mountain. Made mostly by 13- to 15-year-olds, they are found among flutes and other possible musical instruments, perhaps showing that music accompanied dance.

Shamanism

In the Neanderthal period religious specialists began to emerge within the human community. One prehistoric painting from the cave of Les Trois Frères at Ariège, France, has been entitled the Dancing Sorcerer. This painting depicts a human-like figure who is possessed of certain animal attributes such as antlers. While we do not know what the dancing sorcerer meant, it is arguably a painting of a shaman who is dancing to ensure the abundance of game animals, something that is seen quite frequently in hunting cultures all over the world.

Shamanism is a phenomenon found fundamentally among hunter-gathers in which a particular person has the gift of ecstatic experience. Ecstatic experience is the capacity to exit the soul from the body or to be voluntarily possessed by a god (Eliade). In shamanistic cultures, shamans receive the gift of ecstasy and then undergo traditional forms of teaching from elder shamans in order to learn all of the methods of healing, finding lost people, dancing for rain and helping to secure successful hunts. The anthropologist Knud Rassmussen recounted a Caribou Eskimo shaman's first vision and subsequent training. He noted that spirits visited the man and spoke to him so clearly that the man could relate the details to his fellow shamans. An old man was appointed his mentor and his formal education began. Rasmussen goes on to tell of the severe training that followed, which included long fasts and subjection to bitter cold.

Among the Central Eskimo it is understood that the sea animals are controlled by a goddess named Sedna (Boas). Sedna lives at the bottom of the ocean and has no fingers because her father cut them off years ago and from them created the sea animals upon which the Eskimo live. Periodically, Sedna becomes frustrated because she cannot comb her hair and begins to withhold the sea animals. Then the Eskimo become hungry. At that point the shaman goes into a trance and his soul leaves his body and goes to the bottom of the ocean where he finds Sedna and combs out the tangles of her hair. Thus satisfied, she then returns the game animals to the Eskimo.

Ceremonialism

Hunting peoples all over the world have dreams or visions of animals, plants or other objects which serve as their guardian spirit and help them through life with various tasks, especially hunting. Most guardian spirits are animal in form. Among the Plains Indian tribes of North America the vision quest is commonly practiced. In the vision quest a young man seeks a secluded, sacred spot and fasts for one to four days in hopes of obtaining a vision of a guardian spirit. This practice seems to have existed around 30,000 B.C.E. in various caves in southern France. Among the Crow Indians of North America vision questers would often sacrifice the joint of a finger in seeking a guardian spirit in order to demonstrate the earnestness and sincerity of their prayer. Professor Robert Lowie wrote that, during the period of his visits to the Crow from 1907 to 1916, he saw very few of the old men with their left hands intact. This practice of sacrificing joints of the finger was perhaps practiced by Paleolithic people around 30,000 B.C.E. On the walls of many of the caves silhouetted hand prints of participants have been painted and many of these show the same loss of finger joints that Professor Lowie found among the Crow.

If myths are the dreams of a society, then perhaps myths inspire totemism and clanship just as individual dreams inspire a notion of the guardian spirit. It would seem that the guardian spirit was first revealed to Paleolithic humans through dreams. The seen and the unseen worlds were but one reality for Paleolithic peoples. Dreams and visions were communication between sacred forces and the concrete world. Communication with the sacred was most completely brought about in dreams where humans passed from one world to the other without being aware of it. For many primitive peoples the soul leaves the body for a time during a dream in order to commune directly with the spirits and the gods. Upon awakening, the soul returns to the body.

Thus, through dreams, primitive peoples were able to communicate directly with the gods. This does not mean that all dreams were sacred. For example, the Indians of New France clearly distinguished between dreams that were false and dreams which were true. Among the Crow there were four grades of dreams (Nabokov 61). Some were considered meaningless and others referred only to wishes and to the acquisition of certain items. However, there were also medicine dreams or visions, those words being used almost interchangeably. It is not clear whether the quester is actually asleep or awake when he receives such a dream, but it would seem that for hunting peoples the guardian spirit was originally received in dreams. Later, however, as is the case among Plains Indians, vision questers would actively seek guardian spirits through fasting at some secluded spot, and thus arises the vision quest.

While we do not know which came first, it would seem that totems are somehow related to the guardian spirit. It may be the case that those people who envisioned the same guardian spirit perceived themselves to be related, and thus formed a clan. In other words, if several people envisioned a eagle, an eagle clan might be formed. Or it may be that the very notion of clan embodied a notion of a totem or spirit which defined the clan's identity and that these clan totems were given at birth through the line of the mother or the father. In that case the individual vision quester would simply receive a vision from a totem that he acquired at birth by virtue of being born to a particular mother or father. One will never really know the answer, but there does seem to be some close connection between guardian spirits and totems.

In a Magdelenian layer at Dordogne, a richly decorated oval object some six and one-half inches made of reindeer antler was found. It was perforated at one end so that a cord could be inserted through it. It is remarkably similar in shape and design to the bullroarers of American and Australian aborigines. For some Australians the bullroarer is used to conjure up the voices of the ancestors or the supreme being. For the Pueblo Indians of the Southwest the bullroarer is used to imitate, microcosmically, the wind and thunder that accompanies rain. Rain is sacred and manifests the sacred so that the bullroarer is used to invoke the presence of a deity. The Magdelenian hunters covered their bullroarers with red ochre which may have been a chromatic prayer for a successful hunt.

The Problem of the Prehistoric New World

The history of Native American peoples is problematical to say the least. The West tends to look to the origins of American Indians in the Old World, perhaps a carry over from the days of Columbus when it was felt that all people came from the Old World, from the Garden of Eden. Perhaps westerners still cannot conceive of human life originating in the New World. Archeologists still tell us that no simian remains have been found in the New World, and since evolutionists argue that human beings evolved from simians, they say that there is no independent origin of human beings in the New World. Furthermore, the oldest human remains that have been found in the New World have been dated back no older than about 10,000 years. We do have evidence of human habitation that is about 12,000 years old in North America. Scientific evidence indicates that Native Americans migrated to the New World during the Wisconsin glacial period about 15,000 to 8,000 B.C.E. The Indians who came here during that period would not have recognized the new continent as distinct, for they were simply following big game across the frozen tundra. To them the New World would have been simply an extension of the old.

The debate over origins is controversial and brings to light some of the real tensions and relationships between religion on the one hand, and science and history on the other. Archeologists today are trying to reconstruct the history of the inhabitation of the New World. However, their theories almost invariably conflict with the theories of the Native Americans who have their own versions of how they came to live in North and South America. For example, the Hopi Indians of Arizona by and large refute the Bering Straits theory of migration to the New World (Loftin 1996). They do have a theory of migration, but they say they crossed the sea on rafts in the long ago, a migration that is ritually enacted in the flute ceremony. Furthermore, for the Hopi, the migration to this land is fraught with religious values of pilgrimage and purification, leaving a corrupt world behind and heading to a new sacred world. As such, they have no scientific theory, although some have said the same is true for archaeologists. Perhaps the problem originates because the Hopi and other Native American Indians seek religious meaning and significance in their stories of origin, whereas Westerners study history in an attempt, as Professor Ranke said, to find out "the way it really was."

Prior to 1850 there were a number of theories concerning the origin of Native Americans, all of which were related in some way to Christianity and the Bible. Sometimes the Indians were called "anti-polar" men which means that they were not of Adam and Eve's descent. Some people said that Indians were one of the ten lost tribes of Hebrews; the *Book of Mormon* still says this. Even as late as 1930 some professional anthropologists felt that native North Americans could not have been in the New World for longer than 3,000 years.

But in 1926 in Folsom, New Mexico, several scholars found some manmade lance points that were associated with 23 now extinct bison. These points have been dated between 8900 and 8300 B.C.E. and again brought into question in a very fundamental way the old Christian theories of American Indian origin. In 1932 in Clovis, New Mexico, another type of stone point linked with extinct elephants was found and these were dated even older than the Folsom finds, about 10,000 to 9000 B.C.E. Richard "Scotty" MacNeish has studied archaeological finds all over the New World, and because he has radiocarbon dated a site in Peru to be about 22,000 B.C.E., he argues that people have been in the New World between 40,000 and 100,000 years. The fact of the matter is that we really do not know, and the dating of human remains in the New World is so emotionally charged with ideologies related to evolution and Old World superiority that the issue may never be resolved.

Furthermore, our evidence is very limited and there is no telling what we might find tomorrow. Moreover, interpretations of evidence are also subject to change. At one time archaeologists dated bone tools at Old Crow Basin in Alaska at about 27,000 B.C.E. using the carbon assay test on bone apatite, which is now considered an unreliable carbon source. Today those finds are thought to be less than 3000 years old (Jennings and Norbeck).

Still it does seem clear that between 10,000 and 8000 B.C.E., humans were occupying parts of southeastern Arizona and southwestern New Mexico, and this culture has been termed Cochise. By 7000 B.C.E. we have evidence of the mortar and pestle in the Southwest, and these mortars and pestles are not unlike those that are still used today by Pueblo Indians in the area. A number of Great Basin Indians, such as the Paiutes, the Supai and the Shoshoni, apparently lived very much like the hunting gathering Indians of the Cochise period. The Cochise community seemed to involve more gathering and small-game hunting than did the big game hunters of the Folsom and Clovis areas.

About 2,000 years ago grass hair brushes, eagle bone whistles and rabbit fur blankets were made. The significance of these finds is that they are almost identical in form to hair brushes, bone whistles and rabbit fur blankets that are still manufactured and used today by the Hopi Indians of that region (Loftin 1991). This region is what is called the Four

Corners area and is north of the Cochise area. The first period has been called Basketmaker II and the culture that seems to be the earliest forerunner of the Pueblo Indian culture. Basketry was made during the Basketmaker II period and also yucca shifters which are very much like those still made by the Hopi Indians.

In eastern North America we get a somewhat different development in the prehistoric period. By 8000 B.C.E. we find the development of hand axes and what has been called the earliest Archaic period. There was no pottery, and hunting was accomplished by the spear thrower, or atlatl. At first, atlatl blades were small stone points but over the course of time they become large and thin. The Archaic period continues for some 7,000 years in the east and develops into the Woodland period about 1000 B.C.E. with the introduction of agriculture and the bow and arrow. Interestingly, the oldest pottery in the New World was fiber-tempered and was found at the Puerto Hormigaste on the Northern Caribbean coast of Columbia. It has been dated 3000 B.C.E. On the mainland the oldest New World pottery shows up along the Atlantic coast of Georgia and Florida around 2500 B.C.E.

Agriculture did not arise in the east until about 500 B.C.E. with the development of squash, but it does seem that these early Woodland cultures gathered nuts and perhaps cultivated a number of wild plants, such as sunflower and marshelder, goose foot and amaranth. The most famous of the early Woodland cultures is the Adena culture (1000–500 B.C.E.) which was characterized by double post permanent houses and burial mound complexes. These people also apparently used tablets for printing and stone pipes were found for the first time in the east. Elaborate grave goods have been found in some burials which suggest that there may have been some class distinctions among the Adena peoples, and a kind of reptilian bird symbolism is prominent among these people. Whether the Adena was the result of Mesoamerican migration or diffusion of ideas is unknown, but the Adena did develop burial mounds and temple mounds very similar to those found in Mesoamerica.

From about 500 B.C.E. to C.E. 500 the Hopewell culture developed in the east, replacing the Adena. Pottery became more elaborate, and exotic raw goods were imported from all around North America. This culture was first located in Illinois and then moved to Ohio. Imported goods include conch shells from the Gulf Coast, mica from the North Carolina mountains, obsidian from the Rockies and copper from the Great Lakes. All of these indicate vast trade routes. Burial mounds were extremely elaborate and squash was developed at the beginning of the period. Corn was developed about 200 B.C.E., and it was cultivated until about

C.E. 400 Corn then basically disappeared until about C.E. 900. During the Hopewell period a specialized priestly class arose. Bird symbolism was still prominent and especially common was a symbol of a falcon that was cold hammered on copper. Clay figurines abound with fancy hair styles and slanting foreheads, not unlike the Mayans. These figurines often depict earspools. Hopewell houses were single post houses, rather than double post as in the Adena, and the Hopewell peoples mined much more metal than did the Adena. The Hopewell culture peaked when it moved into the Ohio Valley, and this move paralleled great increases in population and the development of organized villages. Hopewell influences radiated throughout the east into central Georgia, west Florida, western North Carolina, Michigan and Wisconsin. By C.E. 500 the Hopewell culture began to decline, and by C.E. 750 the Hopewell had abandoned the Valley sites for the hilltops in the Ohio Valley. Between 700 and C.E. 900, around St. Louis, the Cahokia culture developed. Building the largest earth mound in the New World, this culture seems to have been influenced by both Hopewell and Mesoamerica. Corn farming became very prominent, and this culture seems to have affected various cultures along the Gulf of Mexico which began to develop. Temple plazas with stockades developed and flat top mounds bearing temples or chiefs' houses were also built. In C.E. 1000 the Missouri Valley declines and new cultures develop in the south. From C.E. 1100 to 1400, the Southern Death Cult emerged in the southeast which seems to reflect a Mesoamerica overlay on Adena and Hopewell strata. The largest three sites are in Moundville, Alabama; Spiro, Oklahoma; and Etowah, Georgia. During this period the forerunner to the southeast Indian Green Corn ceremony may have developed. Pottery in this period was very distinctive as clay was mixed with fresh water shell. Furthermore, the Mississippian peoples, as they have been called, seemed to have been the only eastern Indians to have painted pottery. There was a lot of zoomorphic symbolism and a number of other prominent symbols developed. Widespread is the symbol of the weeping eye, the eye in the palm of the hand, and circles and crosses. The cross within the cross, as interpreted by later southeastern Indians, represented the world divided into four quarters. It is out of the Mississippian cultures that the historic Cree, Chickasaw, Cherokee and Choctaw Indians emerged, where DeSoto met them in 1540. Of all the southeastern Indians, only the Natchez carried on Mississippian culture into the historical period, as can be seen by their temple mounds and their rigid divisions of classes, as well as their practice of human sacrifices and slavery.

Bibliography
(Chapter 1—Prehistoric and Primitive Religions)

Boas, Franz. "The Central Eskimo." *Annual Report of the Bureau of American Ethnology.* Vol. 6. Washington, D.C., pp. 390–669.

Bordes, F. *Old Stone Age.* New York, 1968.

Bordieu, Pierre. *Outline of a Theory of Practice.* Trans. Richard Nice. Cambridge, 1977.

Breuil, H. *Four Hundred Centuries of Cave Art.* Montignac, 1952.

_____, and R. Lantier. *The Men of the Old Stone Age.* Trans. B.B. Rafter. London, 1965.

Brown, Joseph. *The Sacred Pipe: Black Elk's Account of the Seven Rights of the Oglala Sioux.* Norman, Oklahoma, 1953.

Bryan, Allen. "Early Man in America and the Late Pleistocene Chronology of Western Canada and Alaska." *Current Anthropology* 10 (1969):339–65.

Buckley, Thomas. "Menstruation and the Power of Yurok Women: Methods and Cultural Reconstruction." *American Ethnologist* 9 (1982):47–60.

Burenhult, Göran. Editor. *The First Humans: Human Origins and History to 10,000 B.C. The Illustrated History of Humankind.* Vol. I. San Francisco, 1993.

Campbell, Joseph. *The Masks of God: Primitive Mythology.* New York, 1976.

Capps, W.H. Editor. *Seeing With a Native Eye: Essays on Native American Religion.* New York, 1976.

Clark, Graham. *The Stone Age Hunters.* London, 1967.

_____. *World Prehistory—An Outline.* Cambridge, 1961.

_____, and Stewart, Piggott. *Prehistoric Societies.* London, 1965.

Coon, Carlton. *The Story of Man.* New York, 1950.

Dart, Raymond. "The Birth of Symbology." *African Studies* 27 (1968):15–27.

Eliade, Mircea. *A History of Religious Ideas.* Vol. 1. Trans. Willard R. Trask. Chicago, 1978.

_____. "Notes on the Symbolism of the Arrow." *Religions In Antiquity: Essays in Memory of E.R. Goodenough.* J. Neusner. Editor. Leiden, 1968.

_____. *Patterns in Comparative Religion.* Trans. R. Sheed. New York, 1958.

_____. *The Sacred and the Profane: The Nature of Religion.* Trans. W. R. Trask. New York, 1959.

_____. *Shamanism: Archaic Techniques of Ecstasy.* Trans. W.R. Trask. Princeton, 1964.

Frazer, Sir James. *The Golden Bough: A Study in Magic and Religion.* Vol. 1. Abridged Addition. New York, 1922.

Greenman, E.F. "The Upper Paleolithic and the New World." *Current Anthropology* 4 (1963):41–91.

Grinnell, George. *Blackfoot Lodge Tales.* Lincoln, Nebraska, 1962.

Gross, Rita M. "Menstruation and Childbirth as Ritual and Religious Experience among Native Australians." *Unspoken Worlds: Women's Religious Lives in Non-Western Cultures.* N. A. Falk and R. M. Gross. Editors. New York, 1980.

Hallowell, A. Irving. "Bear Ceremonialism in the Northern Hemisphere." *American Anthropologist* 28 (1926):1–175.

Harris, Marvin. *Culture, Man and Nature.* New York, 1971.
Hultkrantz, Åke. *Native Religions of North America: The Power of Visions and Fertility.* New York, 1987.
_____. *The Religions of the American Indians.* Trans. M. Setterwall. Berkley, California, 1979.
Jacobson, Doranne. "Golden Hand Prints and Red Painted Feet: Hindu Childbirth Rituals in Central India." *Unspoken Worlds: Women's Religious Lives in Non-Western Cultures.* N.A. Faulk and R.M. Gross. Editors. New York, 1980.
James, E.O. *Prehistoric Religion.* New York, 1957.
Jennings, Jesse, and Edward Norbeck. Editors. *Prehistoric Man in the New World.* Chicago, 1964.
Kennard, Edward. "Metaphor and Magic: Key Concepts in Hopi Culture and Their Linguistic Forms." *Studies in Linguistics.* M.E. Smith. Editor. The Hague, 1972.
Kindaiti, Kyousuke. *Ainu Life and Legends.* Tokyo, 1941.
Lame Deer, John, and Richard Erdoes. *Lame Deer: Seeker of Visions.* New York, 1972.
Leakey, Richard. *The Origin of Humankind.* New York, 1994.
Lee, Richard, and Irven Devore. Editors. *Man The Hunter.* Chicago, 1968.
Leenhardt, M. *Do Kamo: Person and Myth in the Melanesian World.* Trans. B. M. Gulati. Chicago, 1979.
Leroi-Gourhan, André. *Prehistoric Man.* New York, 1957.
Lévy-Bruhl, Lucien. *Treasures of Prehistoric Art.* New York, 1967.
Levy, Gertrude. *The Gate of Horn: A Study of the Religious Conceptions of the Stone Age and Their Influence Upon European Thought.* London, 1948.
Livingstone, Frank. "Genetics Ecology and the Origins of Incest and Exogamy." *Current Anthropology* 10 (1969):45–61.
Loftin, John D. "A Hopi-Anglo Discourse on Myth and History." *Journal of the American Academy of Religion* LXIII (1996): 677–93.
_____. *Religion and Hopi Life in the Twentieth Century.* Bloomington, Indiana, 1991.
Lommel, Andreas. *Shamanism: The Beginnings of Art.* New York and Toronto, 1967.
Long, Charles H. "Lectures on Religious Orientations in World History." University of North Carolina at Chapel Hill, 1979–80.
Lowie, Robert. *Primitive Religion.* New York, 1924.
MacNeish, Richard S. "Early Man in the Andes." *Scientific American* 224 (1971): 36–46.
Makkay, J. "An Important Proof to the Prehistory of Shamanism." *Alba Regia* 2/3 (1963):5–10.
Maquet, Jacques. *Civilizations of Black Africa.* Trans. Joan Rayfield. New York, 1972.
Marett, R.R. *The Threshold of Religion.* New York, 1914.
Maringer, Johannes. *The Gods of Prehistoric Man.* New York, 1960.
Marshack, Alexander. *The Roots of Civilization.* New York, 1972.
_____. "The Meandor as a System: The Analysis and Recognition of Iconographic Units in Upper Paleolithic Compositions." *Form and Indigenous Art.* Peter Ucko. Editor. Canberra, Australia, 1977: 286–317.

Marshall, Lorna. "The Kung Bushmen of the Kalahari Desert." *Peoples of Africa.* J.L. Gibbs, Jr. Editor. New York, 1965.

Mooney, James. *Myths of the Cherokee and Sacred Formulas of the Cherokee.* Nashville, 1972.

Müller, Werner. "'The Passivity' of Language and the Experience of Nature: A Study in the Structure of the Primitive Mind." *Myths and Symbols: Studies in Honor of Mircea Eliade.* Joseph Kitagawa and Charles Long. Editors. Chicago, 1969: 227–239.

Munro, Neal. *Ainu Creed and Cult.* New York, 1963.

Nabokov, Peter. *Two Leggings: The Making of a Crow Warrior.* Lincoln, Nebraska, 1967.

Narr, Karl. "Approaches to the Religion of Early Paleolithic Man." *History of Religions* 4 (1964):1–22.

_____. "Approaches to the Social Life of Earliest Man." *Anthropos* 57 (1962):604–620.

Powers, Marla. *Oglala Women: Myth, Ritual and Reality.* Chicago, 1986.

Radin, Paul. *Primitive Religion: Its Nature and Origin.* New York, 1937.

Rasmussen, Knud. *Across Arctic America.* New York, 1927.

Scarre, Christopher. *Exploring Prehistoric Europe.* New York, 1998.

Spencer, Baldwin, and F.J. Gillen. *The Arunta: A Study of Stone Age People.* London, 1927.

Swadesh, Morris. *The Origin and Diversification of Language.* Chicago, 1971.

Teit, James. "Kaska Tales." *Journal of American Folk-Lore* 30 (1917):427–471.

Tuan, Yi-fu. *Space and Place: The Perspective of Experience.* Minneapolis, Minnesota, 1977.

Turnbull, Colin. "The Mbuti Pigmies of the Kongo." *Peoples of Africa.* J. L. Gibbs, Jr. Editor. New York, 1965.

Turner, Victor. *The Forest of Symbols: Aspects of Ndembu Ritual.* Ithaca, New York, 1967.

Van der Leeuw, G. *Religion in Essence and Manifestation.* 2 Vols. Trans. J. E. Turner. Reprint. Gloucester, Mass., 1967.

CHAPTER 2

The Neolithic Revolution

The historian V. Gordon Childe called the period of time from 9000 to 7000 B.C. the Neolithic Revolution. In some ways it may be said that the changes that took place in the human community during the Neolithic period were more dramatic and far reaching than those that occurred during the Enlightenment and the Industrial Revolution. For hundreds of thousands of years, if not millions of years, human beings lived in small communities which roamed across the land in search of wild game and plants. During the Paleolithic period, small communities traversed the countryside in a meandering pattern which took them to various sacred centers along the way. In the Neolithic period the ceremonial center underwent a transformation and the movement of human beings was no longer across space but to and from the center. The ceremonial center of the Neolithic period parallels sedentary life since the orientation of space is now in terms of centrifugal and centripetal patterns rather than a meandering pattern.

Inextricably bound up with the development of ceremonial center and this new orientation to space is the domestication of plants. About 12,500 B.C.E. a culture arose in the Levant that stretched from southern Turkey to the Sinai. Between 11,000 and 9,000 B.C.E. at Abu Hureya, on the banks of the Euphrates River in northern Syria near modern day Aleppo, people began to settle in small semi-permanent villages. They harvested a number of wild plants with flint and bone-bladed sickles and resided in circular houses up to 30 feet wide. Later, between about 9000 B.C.E. and 7000 B.C.E., at Abu Hureya, farming began. The first crops were barley, rye, lentils, chickpeas and two kinds of wheat. Immediately, a large village covering more than 30 acres sprang up.

Agriculture at Abu Hureya was probably "invented" by women who were already the primary gatherers of wild plants since Paleolithic times. Women had a special relationship with plants and, indeed, even in hunting cultures associations between women, plants and earth were very widespread. At some point women must have discovered that, if they left a certain number of plants in a particular gathering site, seed from those plants would generate more plants the next season. Eventually, women may have begun to experiment with planting seeds from various wild plants in order to propagate them, and it may be that the earliest forms of agriculture involved the reproduction of various wild plants. Human activity, coupled with genetic combinations and recombinations, as well as crossbreeding between cultivated and wild plants, resulted in the development of domestic plants, some of which, like corn, were completely dependent upon human intervention in order to live.

In *The Pivot of the Four Quarters*, Paul Wheatley, a geographer, examined the origins of the first seven urban communities: Mesopotamia, Egypt, China, India, West Africa, Peru and Mesoamerica. After studying each of these, he rejected the idea that cities ultimately depended upon irrigation, warfare, social differentiation or trade market developments. The constant factor that Wheatley found in all urban areas was the ceremonial center. The center of the Neolithic period was ambiguous; it was sacred and it oriented human communities to and from, yet it also allowed humans to control space in a way unknown to prehistoric peoples. Thus, Wheatley describes the ceremonial centers of the Neolithic period as metaphysical orderings of effective space.

Agriculture multiplies seeds at an incredible rate, thus generating a large surplus. The Paleolithic period knew of surpluses, but its character was very different. It was clear to prehistoric hunters that humans did not control the creation, production or maintenance of wild animals and plants and that they did not participate in the production of wild foods at all, except through ritual prayers. In the Paleolithic period people were obviously dependent on the gods for food and survival. The Master, or Owner of the animals, provided wild game to humans. But with the experimentation and handling of seeds a new orientation opened up and the question arose as to who controlled plants, God or humans?

Originally, agriculture was perceived as even more auspicious and sacred than hunting because of the way it was linked with women. Women were already perceived as being especially closely connected to the sacred lifegiving forces because they gave birth. Men gave birth to meat, fur and skin symbolically through the hunt, but women participated in creation more directly through procreation. Therefore, agriculture, because it was linked with women, was likely first seen by men as further evidence of the intimate relationship that women had with the creative forces of the universe. Eventually men took over, or at least assisted in, farming activities and began to develop consistently successful techniques which parallel an ambivalence concerning the powers that control plant growth and production. It is significant that in a number of agricultural communities there exist myths about the theft of agriculture from women. Pygmies say that they stole fire from women; other tribes have stories in which it is said that the men stole agriculture from the women, who had it first. Eventually, men basically took control of farming and the development of agriculture parallels an increased awareness and emphasis on the autonomy of human beings. This is perhaps especially true where irrigation techniques became widespread. With irrigation farmers became less dependent on the rains and, therefore, rain dances perhaps became less important. For example, the Hopi Indians of Arizona farm in a semi-arid region that receives only eleven inches of rain per year. For them, rain dances are critical life supporting events which are fundamental to their religious ceremonialism. The emphasis on rain prayers by the Hopi is contrasted with the Havasupai, who perhaps acquired corn horticultural from the Hopi, but who live in the Grand Canyon along rivers and streams which provide irrigation for their crops. Havasupai Indians have even said that they do not pray for rain, as do the Hopi, because they have no need for such supplications.

Almost all agricultural myths embody an emphasis on human activity that one does not find among hunters. Adolph Jensen classified agricultural myths into two types corresponding to two different types of agriculture, tuber and grain. Tuber agriculture developed about 7000 B.C. at Kuk in the Wahgi Valley, New Guinea; grain agriculture began in northern Syria about 9000 B.C. An interesting example of tuber agriculture comes from Ceram, one of the Islands off New Guinea. According to the Wemalmale tribe, there was once a goddess named Hainuwele. In the beginning, Hainuwele was surrounded in a spiral dance by the Dema who later became human beings. The Dema danced and danced until Hainuwele fell into a hole in the center where she was covered up. Later her father dug her up, cut her into pieces and planted her. This primordial murder created the various plants upon which the Wemalmale tribe later lived. After Hainuwele's death, however, another god became angry and made the Dema pass through a great gate which turned them either into humans or animals. By becoming human, the Dema also introduced sexuality, death, and religious and social institutions that are still in force.

For the Dogon of Mali, Africa, grain agriculture was acquired somewhat differently. In the beginning of time, Amma, the high god, controlled the distribution of seeds to the Dogon people. Ogo, the blacksmith, was chosen by the people to visit Amma and steal more seeds from Amma so that they could enlarge their yield. We will return to the significance of Ogo later, but for now note that Jensen designated this as a Prometheus type myth, typical of grain farmers throughout the world. Actually the distinction between tuber and grain agriculture is not absolute. Henry Schoolcraft recorded a myth about corn origin among the Ojibwa Indians that involves the killing of a deity. In that myth an ancestral youth wrestled with a god until the god was finally overcome, and the youth was then directed to strip off the garments of the god and bury him in the earth. From that burial came corn which is the staple food of the Ojibwa people (Schoolcraft).

If one compares the above myths with the Cherokee myth of the origin of game, one sees the vital difference between agricultural and hunting mythologies. In Cherokee mythology the sons of Kanati follow their father each day to find out where the game animals come from. Each day Kanati goes to a cave and rolls back a rock letting out a certain number of game animals which the people hunt. One day the sons go to the cave, roll back the rock and set free all of the animals. As a result, Kanati punished humans by making game scarce and more difficult to kill. In agricultural myths human intervention resulted in more seed, not less. Similarly, in the Eskimo myth of Sedna, sea animals were created by the amputation of the joints of her fingers by her father. However, Sedna the goddess still controls the amount of sea animals that will be successfully hunted by the Eskimo, and the Eskimo are dependent upon Sedna's goodwill for successful hunts. In the agricultural myths there seems to be less dependency on the gods. This, of course, is not an absolute distinction. For example, there are the Hopi Indians of Arizona whose agricultural surplus is extremely unpredictable and dependent upon the gods who may withhold the lifegiving rains so necessary for crop growth in a semi-desert environment. At the other extreme are the Northwest Coast Indian tribes whose land was so rich with wildlife that they were able to settle in permanent villages without the benefit of farming.

With the development of farming came village life and eventually urban development. Because of the tremendous surplus that can be produced by farming, food production was no longer the job of every single person. In successful agricultural communities various full-time jobs emerged, such as merchants, artists, warriors and priests. Initially each of these occupations was linked with a particular god, for everything in human history was first seen as a gift from the divine. Each new human activity carried a sacred significance and was seen as the manifestation of a new divinity. For example, in Rome, specialization of human life within the city occasioned the appearance of numerous gods, the *indigetes*, which have been called "flash of an eye" deities. These gods arise in relation to all major movements. In Rome, plowing manifested the god Insitor, cross plowing invoked Imporcitor, and the marking of property lines evinced Terminus. Actions did not, however, create the gods; they evoked the manifestation of the gods who were already there. The high god who was associated with the sky for Neolithic communities receded into the background and became a *deus otiosus* ("hidden god"). Recession of the high god paralleled the decline of the unity of community which, as we will see later, was overcome by the monotheism of the Semitic traditions. As cultural unity declined, each people began to emphasize those gods which were most closely connected with their own activities. Furthermore, there was a greater and greater emphasis on specifically human concerns and activities. Therefore, the sky god, who was basically neutral with respect to specifically human concerns, was rarely addressed. As the passive dimension of human religiosity began to give way, the human community gave more emphasis to those gods who were directly related to human needs, and since the various classes of people in the Neolithic had very different daily concerns, religious commonality was, to a degree, lost at first. The Neolithic's loss of unity paralleled the loss of awareness and concern with the god of the heavens.

This differentiation of the sacred contrasts markedly with the Paleolithic period in which everyone was involved in all major activities in the community, and therefore everyone worshipped the same gods. Furthermore, because Paleolithic peoples were so dependent on the gods for success in hunting and gathering, the sky god was not so dramatically eclipsed. The anthropologist Marshall Sahlins said this best in discussing the sacred economy of hunting cultures. He noted that wealth is largely in the eye of the beholder: "want not; lack not (11)." Paleolithic peoples did not want much; therefore, they did not ask for much. In other words, Paleolithic religion emphasized thankfulness for the gifts of life which were given by the gods, whereas Neolithic religion was characterized by an increase in human activity and desire which manifested itself in prayers for specific things.

At the risk of greatly oversimplifying, it can be said that Neolithic religiosity was characterized by an increase in greed for those things that humans wanted but did not have and ignorance of the presence of the high god. However, with this increase in human activity came a simultaneous sophistication of religious awareness for Neolithic peoples. On the one hand, it could be argued that Neolithic farmers addressed the little gods more than the big god out of greed. But on the other hand, the shift of emphasis may have been the result of a new-found humility with respect to the high god. The god of the sky for most cultures is a passive god who overlooks the workings of the entire cosmos. The high god is concerned with creation itself and not simply with specifically human concerns. Therefore, it is also true to say that Neolithic farmers did not address the high god regularly out of a sense of reverence because the high god should not be addressed except in times of critical desperation.

For example, among the Akan Ashanti of Ghana, Africa, the high god's name is Nyame. But Nyame is almost never addressed directly by human beings because of his aloofness with respect to specifically human questions and wants. If an Ashanti wants a particular thing, such as rain for his crops or a cure for illness, he will address the particular god who is concerned with that aspect of the cosmos. That god is seen as an aspect of Nyame or, as Evans-Pritchard put it, a "refraction" of the high god which is very limited and concrete in scope (Evans-Pritchard *Nuer Religion*). No right-thinking Ashanti would indiscriminately invoke the presence of Nyame for a given situation because to do so would be considered somewhat arrogant. Therefore, rather than invoking Nyame, he would call upon that aspect of Nyame who has a separate name and is concerned with the particular aspect of life that is brought into existential focus at that time.

One is reminded here of the story of Job where Job questioned God for all the personal tragedies which he had suffered, including loss of wealth, loss of family and, finally, loss of health. Yahweh, the high god of the Hebrew tradition, in response to Job's interrogation, asked Job, "Where were you when I laid the foundation of the earth?" (Job 38:4). Therefore, the Neolithic's increase in the number of gods parallels an increased sense of humility and sophistication with respect to the addressing of the high god. The emergence of agriculture is only half the story of the Neolithic.

Pastoralism

In addition to the domestication of plants there occurred also in the Old World, especially in the Near East around Palestine, the domestication of animals: the dog about 11,000 B.C.E.; sheep in Iraq, Iran, and the Levant coast about 8000 B.C.E.; the goat in the Zagros Mountains, Iraq, about 8000 B.C.E.; the pig in southwest Asia about 7,000 B.C.E. and cattle about 8,000 B.C.E. also in southwest Asia (Liljegren). At Catal Huyuk, a fertility cult paralleled the domestication of cattle as shown by a goddess who is represented as a young woman giving birth to a bull. One sanctuary, dated 6200

B.C.E., has a place where four human skulls are situated under the heads of bulls.

While pastoralism and agriculture developed side by side in a number of areas, there also emerged in the Neolithic a pastoral way of life that was not sedentary. Melville Herskovits, an anthropologist, was the first to talk about the cattle complex, whose greatest example is found in East Africa among the Nuer, Dinka and Masai tribes. As the anthropologist E.E. Evans-Pritchard put it, their social idiom is bovine (Evans-Pritchard *Nuer Religion* 19). The historian of religions Bruce Lincoln later amplifies this idea by noting that cattle also provide tribal religious language. For these tribes, cattle are the basis of life, economically and religiously, just as reindeer are among many circumpolar peoples.

God is transcendent and is associated with the sky, although he is not hidden. It is easy to understand how pastoral peoples did not lose sight of the sky god as did farmers. Pastoralists have a transhumant life style, not unlike that of hunter-gatherers, which takes them across space. Some pastoralists in the Sahara Desert of Northern Africa liken their land to the sea, and because land forms change so rapidly and dramatically as a result of wind erosion, the sky orients them much the same way that the sky guides seafaring peoples.

God

For pastoral people the sky god receives prayers regularly, and above all during the sacrifice of an oxen. Sacrifice, the central rite for pastoral peoples, returns to god that which is really his. Like hunter-gatherers, pastoral peoples do not control the land like farmers. The Nuer high god's name is *Kwoth*, which means "spirit," although sometimes the term is expressed *Kwoth a nhial*, or "spirit in the sky." The Dinka term is *nhialic*, which translates "in the sky." For the Masai, the high god is called simply *ngai*, meaning "rain."

It is tempting but wrong to reduce religion to economics for pastoral peoples by saying that they worship their means of food production. Economics does not create their religion; rather, it is the lens through which they see the sacred. Put differently, they worship the divine through the medium of cattle. Cattle are god's gift to these people, and thus the worship of cows is the worship of that which creates and sustains life. Furthermore, among the Masai there are two main breeds of cattle. One gives more milk and the other has longer horns and is considered more beautiful and more valued. Thus, it is clear that the religious orientation of those peoples cannot simply be reduced to economic concerns. Furthermore, among all three tribes oxen are more highly prized for sacrifice than are cows, which are much more economically valuable.

Raiding

The mythology of these people is interesting, saying that humanity emerged when the people acquired cattle. The gaining of cattle was the beginning of the human way of life. A Masai myth tells how another people, the Dorobo, did not act properly in the beginning and thus lost the right to cattle. Therefore, the Dorobo must hunt for a living, a state which the Masai people view with disdain. Each of the East African pastoral peoples claim that their god gave them cattle in the beginning of time, noting that the other groups tricked god into letting them have cattle also. But when God found out what had happened, he gave each of the pastoral people the right to raid the others in order to reclaim that which is really theirs by divine decree. Thus, warfare is sanctioned by these people and warriors receive high prestige by successfully raiding for cattle. According to the Nuer version of the myth, the Nuer and the Dinka were both considered chosen sons of God who had promised to give an old cow to the Dinka and a young calf to the Nuer. One night the Dinka came by and deceived God by imitating the voice of a Nuer and thereby received the calf. Once God found out that he had been tricked, he authorized the Nuer to raid the herds of the Dinka until the end of time.

Raiding is a sacred act among pastoral peoples since it was performed in mythical times and taught by the gods. The raids are strictly for cattle, no other booty being taken. The only status and religious meaning obtained through raiding is the acquisition of cattle.

Sacrifice

Ultimately, all oxen are to be sacrificed, returning the ox to its creator. Periodically other animals are offered but they are still called oxen, although they, in reality, do not have quite the same status. Sacrifice of oxen takes place on a number of occasions, all significant, such as spring and autumn, rainy and dry seasons, during all rites of passage, and for all serious illnesses. Sacrifice shows the reciprocity between god and humans. Just as god gave humans cattle, so humans must reciprocate this gift, which, in return, obliges god to give them more cattle. In this way, sacrifice is a world renewal rite because it helps keep the world going. The sacrifice of the ox and the feast that follows serves, as anthropologist Godfrey Lienhardt says, to reaffirm social solidarity between warriors and priests. But the ox symbolizes more than society, or, to put it another way, society includes more than people.

The Masai interchanged the term cattle with "everything on earth," for cattle symbolizes their world. Thus, the destruction of the ox and its consumption at a ritual feast symbolizes the destruction of the old world so that god can create it anew with a creation of a new ox. The feast symbolizes unity with the world, or with god, so there is also a mystical dimension to cattle sacrifice. In one sense, the cattle sacrifice involves both sacred and social dimensions. The celestial sovereign gives cattle to his people which are stolen by traditional enemies. Warriors recover cattle in a raid which are then sacrificed by priests, thus returning them to the celestial sovereign. A cycle is thus created which reveals a two-fold social structure involving warriors and priests, each of which complements the other. But on another level these groups are very different.

Priests see the sacrifice as the chief means of acquiring prosperity; warriors see raiding similarly. Sacrifice is strictly the role of priests, while raiding is the domain of warriors. In one sense neither party needs the other to do its work; therefore both groups see themselves as the most important. Priests see the celestial sovereign as the most important god, and warriors, especially among the Nuer, worship primarily spirits of the air that are associated with warfare. But, in the end, priests are perceived as the most important, for they must give permission for the raids and must pray for success. Without the help of the gods, the warriors could not be successful. Ultimately, warriors are subservient to the priests with the exception of perhaps the Nuer, for whom warriors acquire a special significance. This situation creates a certain amount of resentment and, indeed, this tension between them was perhaps instrumental in the break of the Nuer people from the Dinka tribe. The Nuer were originally a warrior clan of the Dinka who broke away because they resented being less important.

But in either case cattle remain central to the religion of the people. Significantly, pastoralism may accompany urban development but cannot support a city as can farming. Still, there is an emphasis on human activity through the raiding and stealing of other cattle from other peoples, all of which seems very Neolithic. Hunting-gathering peoples were not traditionally very warlike, and while it is true that ritual warfare takes certain themes from hunting, it is also very distinct from hunting. Hunting-gathering peoples were extremely dependent upon the gods for their existence.

Moreover, their communities were so small that widespread warfare was virtually unknown. However, pastoral peoples such as the Dinka are able to maintain rather large tribes, and there is a great deal of raiding and warfare. Thus, warriors are elevated in a way that was unknown to hunting-gathering peoples. In a sense, the taking of a human life by another human through warfare represents a decline in the passive nature of religious experience. Killing another human being in war involves a level of human volition and power that was little known to prehistoric peoples.

And yet, there is something especially sacred about the taking of another life. It is, in a sense, the ultimate human activity which ultimately reflects back on itself and is seen quite passively and religiously. Among a number of native North American tribes, successful warriors carried special significance. The Hopi Indian who killed an enemy from another tribe had to seclude himself for over twenty days, during which time he fasted and asked forgiveness from both the god of his slain enemy and of his own tribe. For Cherokee Indians a warrior who killed an enemy tribesman had to seclude himself for three days, during which time he fasted while the women of the tribe circled his hut singing various purification charms which were designed to discharm the pollution that surrounded this intensely human act. Still, among warrior tribes, raiding and stealing were considered more sacred than the actual taking of human life. Thus, for the Plains Indians, such as the Crow, the Sioux and Cheyenne, who herded great numbers of horses, stealing horses from an enemy tribe was considered a more honorable act than killing an enemy. Even in warfare a Sioux Indian acquired more prestige and status within his group by racing down upon an enemy warrior, striking him with a stick and retreating, than he did by actually taking his life. In counting coups a Sioux warrior would ride upon an enemy facing death courageously. He would then tap the enemy on the shoulder with a club and ride off, thus showing the enemy that he could have killed him but did not. For this act he received the highest honor that a warrior could receive. But the Sioux, while incorporating some of the mythology of pastoral peoples through their mythology which sanctioned raiding enemy tribes for horses, remained, in the end, primarily a hunting people.

For true pastoralists like the Masai, the Nuer and the Dinka, warfare was more widespread and honorable, but even among those people priests were considered more important. Again, the exception was the Nuer for whom the status of warriors was considered to be equal to that of the priests. Therefore, it may be fair to say that the Nuer represented the most developed of the pastoral peoples of East Africa.

It is well known that pastoral peoples and agricultural peoples often do not get along very well. Agricultural peoples tend to settle around a particular place and to farm fields which they soon begin to claim as their own. For pastoral peoples, their land generally includes a larger area which they do not own and possess like farmers. It seems that where there are herders and farmers, there have been conflicts over land. It is not unusual for herding people to graze their animals on the crops of farmers, which of course creates hostilities. The best modern example of this would be the ongoing dispute between the Navajo and Hopi Indians of Arizona. The Navajo are predominantly sheep herders while the Hopi are dry farmers. The two tribes have been engaged in land disputes for many centuries and these disputes have finally culminated in protracted court litigation which has been some of the most costly in human history. Navajo sheep herders follow their sheep and feel very strongly that they have a right to graze their sheep wherever they go. Hopis, on the other hand, have a strong sense of ownership of the fields around their villages and resist and resent Navajo incursions and raids upon their lands. The tensions and conflicts between herders and farmers were also discussed in the Book of Genesis. The differences between herding and agricultural peoples is a theme that runs throughout the Hebrew religion, as we shall see shortly. It is significant that pastoral peoples emerge in areas that are peripheral to agriculture. Thus, the Huns and the Mongols who lived in the Eurasian steppe come to mind. In the steppe there existed vast areas in which hardy grasses grew, sustaining large herds of animals.

Herding Symbolism

Apart from milk, meat and blood, the staple foods for the Nuer, cattle furnish a number of household necessities. Their skins are used for trays, beds, cord; for carrying fuel; for leather collars for oxen and the skin of drums. Skins are used in the making of pipes, spears, shields and snuff containers. Scrota of bulls are made into bags to contain tobacco, spoons and other small objects. Tail hairs are made into tassels used as dance ornaments by girls. The bones are used for armlets and as beaters, pounders and scrapers. The horns are cut into spoons and are used in the construction of harpoons. Cattle dung is used for fuel and for plastering walls, floors and the outsides of straw huts in cattle camps. Dung is also used to protect wounds. The ashes of burnt dung are rubbed over men's bodies and are used to dye and straighten the hair, as a mouthwash and tooth powder and in preparation of sleeping skins and leather bags. Cattle urine is used in churning and cheese making and the preparation of certain utensils for tanning leather and for bathing face and hands (Evans-Pritchard *The Nuer* 28–29).

But it would be too simple to describe the symbiotic relationship between eastern African pastoral peoples and their cattle in purely economic terms. For cattle provide the lens through which they perceive all aspects of the world. The same is true for the Dinka. As Godfrey Lienhardt put it, "the Dinka's very perception of color, light and shade in the world around them is in these ways inextricably connected with the recognition of color configurations in their cattle" (12–13). If their cattle-colored vocabulary were taken away, they would hardly be able to describe visual experiences in terms of color and light. The Dinka's perception of color and shading in nature and cattle creates a world in which cattle are linked with features of the natural and social environment through perceived similarities of color and shading. This color symbolism is also important for understanding Dinka religious thought and practice. Cattle and humans are furthermore linked because the Dinka state that their own lives and the lives of cattle are in many ways the same. Divisions of the day are reckoned with respect to activities related to cattle. Rather than referring to the position of the sun and the sky, the Nuer will refer to time on a daily basis by reference to cattle activities. Times of the day for a Nuer are: taking of the cattle from byre to kraal, milking, driving of the adult herd to pasture, milking of the goats and sheep, driving of the flocks and calves to pasture, cleaning of the byre and kraal, bringing home the flocks and calves, the return of the adult herd, the evening milking and the enclosure of the beasts in byres. Men in particular imitate cattle, and it is a common sight in western Dinka land to see a young man with his arms curved above his head identifying himself with his herds.

But perhaps the clearest example of the way in which cattle represent not only human beings but all human relationships within the community can be seen in the division of the sacrificial meat once the beast is killed. A Dinka chief once said, "the people are put together as a bull is put together" (Lienhardt 23). Different parts of a sacrificial beast represent the various classes or social units within the community. Thus the sacrifice has many meanings. It returns the sacrificial beast to God and reestablishes all kinship and social relationships within the community through distribution of meat. In so doing the people reaffirm the relationships that were laid down to them by divinity in the beginning of time. Among the Dinka, the preeminent clan is the spear-masters. The clan descends from the mythical ancestor Aiwel Longar. The functions of the masters of the fishing spear are many. They sacrifice for the cure of the sick and the vitality of their people, they drive away lions and other dangers of the forests and of the river, and they are considered the peacemakers or the mediators between warring factions. But most importantly, at least in the past, were their prayers for victory in war and raiding. In Dinka eyes the ability to pray for success in war is considered more significant than rain. Again, the Nuer elevate war even more than do the Dinka. Raiding the Dinka for cattle is one of their principle pastimes. Nuer boys look forward to the day they will be able to accompany their elders on raids against the Dinkas, and all of them try to establish their reputations as warriors.

Nuer prophets invoke the spirits of the air, for raids on the Dinka are considered the most important. Prophets also participated in healing, stopping epidemics, and exorcism of troublesome spirits. They are also credited with the power to foretell events. The pastoral way of life makes possible much larger human communities than was the case for hunter-gatherers. For example, the Nuer number over 200,000 people, and the Dinka, from whom the Nuer branched, number some 900,000 people.

Pottery, Mining and Metallurgy

The first extensive human settlement that approaches a city was found in Palestine at Jericho where inhabitants had domesticated barley and sheep around 7000 B.C. The residents at Jericho also engaged in weaving. Significantly though, the people at Jericho did not make pottery. The invention of pottery occurred somewhere in the Near East, probably around 7000 B.C. By 6000 B.C. pottery was plentiful at Catal Huyuk as well as at a farming settlement in Macedonia. Pottery spread slowly and was still not known in Jericho and other sites in the Near East centuries later. Its use became universal only during the sixth millennium.

Around 6500 B.C.E. copper was mined and cold hammered into trinkets and later into weapons. Copper was clearly a superior material to use for weapons because it was less likely to break off and shatter. In Mesopotamia and Egypt between 4000 and 3500 B.C. copper was smelted and mixed with tin to form bronze. Copper was mined, and mining is an activity that was initially fraught with religious meaning and significance. In mining one digs into the womb of the earth to extract a precious substance. We have already seen how the womb of mother earth was seen as an especially auspicious place for Paleolithic hunters who would retreat deep into the recesses of caverns in order to perform sacred ceremonies for the rebirth of game animals. But there is something inherently polluting or taboo about the miner because the miner goes into the earth to take away something that has required an unfathomable amount of time to produce, and he leaves nothing in return.

With farming, which represents an increased amount of human activity in contrast to hunting and gathering, humans still inhabit the rhythms of the world. Human activity is aligned with the rhythms of planting, weeding and harvesting, and humans take only as much as the earth gives. In fact, farming many times produces more surplus than humans can consume, and thus reciprocity between the sacred and the human community is maintained. Not so with mining. The earth takes millions of years to produce copper and obsidian. These materials were not replenished at the rate that they were extracted; therefore, the activity of mining carried with it a sense of haughtiness and arrogance that was unprecedented in human history. A miner dared to take something from the earth at a much faster rate than the gods could replenish it. Thus the miner, in a real sense, stole from the sacred.

As late as the twentieth century, the Hopi Indians of Arizona engaged in mining operations for sacred clay, salt and coal. The Hopi traditionally undertook a migration periodically to a place within the Grand Canyon which is said to be the place of their emergence to this world from the underworld in the "long ago." A special yellowish clay used for ritual purposes is found under the ground near the original sacred center of the Hopi and must be dug. Don Talayesva, a Hopi Indian, noted in his autobiography that he was "required to keep his mind and heart full of good wishes to ward off death," and he makes it clear that the entire operation was perceived passively or receptively because the Hopi acquired only as much as the sacred wished to give (242). Therefore, Talayesva noted that after a couple of attempts to dig the sacred clay out, he dug no more for his father "remarked that the spirits had decided we had enough for this time" (242). Those same thoughts of entering a sacred area where humans had no right to be or had only a limited right to be were arguably present at Catal Huyuk, where obsidian was first mined.

The Hopi Indians also used to mine coal in and around Second Mesa. Ernest Beaglehole found that some men from the village of Mishongnovi stopped mining coal from the north side of Second Mesa after a man was killed there by falling rocks while mining (57). The villagers interpreted this as a sign that no more coal was to be taken from that place. Mining was an activity that was conducted with great caution for Neolithic peoples. Because mining stripped the womb of mother earth quicker than she could gestate and reproduce, it was an activity fraught with religious taboo.

Pottery adds still another element of autonomy to Neolithic humanity. Pottery represents the first artificial product of human beings because it is made up of clay, minerals, earth and straw or grit to keep it from cracking. Thus, in making the potter's clay, Neolithic humans actually created a product not found in nature, thereby participating symbolically in the creative act of the gods. It would seem that pottery was likened to creation and was also seen as a very significant ritual activity. But the potter does not stop there. The potter bakes the clay and thereby transforms it into something else. With the firing of pottery humans utilize that element which most clearly distinguishes them from the animal kingdom in order to speed up the natural rhythms of the world and to transform a substance into a new product. Heated, the potter's clay becomes plastic. Upon cooling it retains not only its shape, but becomes hard, like stone. Indeed, it is interesting that in Sumer, where the land had no stone or metal, the Sumerians were able to fire clay at a temperature of 1200 degrees in order to create clay blades which could be used as sickles to cut and harvest crops. Therefore, pottery may have represented the decisive step in the development of Neolithic urban communities, and it is perhaps the lack of pottery that has prompted historians V. Gordon Childe and R. J. Braidwood to reject the idea that Jericho was the first city in the world. They argue that since Jericho had no pottery, it was not truly urban.

Metallurgy, which developed between 5000 and 4500 B.C.E., took the use of heat still another step. The Mesopotamians added tin to copper in order to make bronze. The technology employed in metallurgy is even more sophisticated than that used in agriculture or even pot making. Conversion of metallic ores into tough red copper or bronze is an authentic transubstantiation or transmutation. The metamorphosis from solid to liquid and back to solid again which takes place in metallurgy strikes humans as even more auspicious and awe-inspiring than weaving or pottery making. Thus, with the beginning of metallurgy, smiths and miners employ skills that link them with the chthonic mysteries. It is interesting to note that, for the Dogon of Mali, Africa, the blacksmith was chosen to steal seeds from the Supreme Being, Amma, to gain an oversupply of food. The blacksmith was a spiritual daredevil who took ores from the earth and, like the gods, transformed them into something else. Because he was willing to deplete nature's reservoir and duplicate creation, the Dogon chose him to steal seeds from Amma. In some ways the smith was considered to be even more powerful than priests and shamans. Among the Yakuts it is said that "smiths and shamans come from the same nest." However, the Yakut also say that while "the wife of a shaman is worthy of respect, the wife of a smith is worthy of veneration" (Eliade *The Forge* 81). Furthermore, the knowledge acquired by smiths and miners was not known to all members of the community; not every clansman was trained as a smith. The knowledge required to do this kind of work required intricate training, and thus metallurgy became a full-time job. After the priests and religious specialists, the metallurgists in the Neolithic urban communities were probably the first to be removed directly from food production. But smiths and miners were distinguished even from priests because in the Neolithic community priests were tied to a particular community in which they lived. Miners and smiths, on the other hand, had a market for their skills which transcended the local community, and these people might be employed to work throughout a large region. Their ability to migrate between communities allowed them to pool their experience and to spread their discoveries; this probably explains the comparative uniformity of the very earliest metal products. Indeed, the spread of similar metal implements was coextensive with the urban revolution. In other words, metallurgy was perhaps the first international trade. Copper was not common everywhere and was often imported from various sites. Thus a trade network was established in the Neolithic period between communities for the importation of copper. Tin was even rarer, and the unavailability of tin has been listed as one of the reasons that Samaritan tools were made of pure copper rather than bronze. Bronze did reappear in Mesopotamia after Sargon's time, ca. 2350 B.C.E., but tin had to be sought from as far away as central Europe. Bronze equipment requires a great deal of social labor and hence a great agricultural surplus. Bronze was expensive, and, as we shall see later, the international nature of trade that took place along the Silk Road during the Axial period paralleled dramatic changes in religious history and helped bring about what we now know as the world religions. Religion never became a global matter in the Neolithic period, but it would seem reasonable to think that the smiths and miners who were traveling back and forth between the various communities were exchanging more than just their skills and products. We have reason to believe that at least the religious experience of metallurgy was similar everywhere during the Neolithic period.

Bibliography
(Chapter 2 — The Neolithic Revolution)

Adams, Robert McCormick. *The Evolution of Urban Society*. Chicago, 1967.
Altekar, A.S. *A History of Village Communities in Western India*. Bombay, 1929.
Anderson, J. Gunnar. *Children of the Yellow Earth*. London, 1934: 184–187.
Beaglehole, Ernest. *Notes on Hopi Economic Life*. New Haven, Conn., 1937.
Bishop, C.W. "Long-Houses and Dragon-Boats." *Antiquity* XII (1938): 411–424.
Braidwood, R.J. "The Agricultural Revolution." *Scientific American* CCIII (1960):
    130–148.

_____. *The Near East and the Foundations for Civilization.* Eugene, Oregon, 1952.
Brenneman, Jr., Walter L. "Serpents, Cows, and Ladies: Contrasting Symbolism in Irish and Indo-European Cattle-Raiding Myths." *History of Religions* 28 (1989): 340–354.
Briffault, Robert. *The Mothers.* London, 1927.
Cameron, D.O. *Symbols of Birth and of Death in the Neolithic Era.* London, 1981.
Childe, V. Gordon. *Man Makes Himself.* 2nd Ed. London, 1941.
_____. *New Light on the Most Ancient East.* London, 1935.
_____. *Prehistoric Migrations in Europe.* Cambridge, Massachusetts, 1950.
_____. *Social Evolution.* London, 1951.
_____. *What Happened in History.* New York, 1946.
Clark, J.G.D. *Prehistoric Europe: The Economic Basis.* New York and London, 1952: 241–281.
Cole, Sonia Mary. *The Neolithic Revolution.* London, 1963.
Curwen, E.C. "The Furrows in Prehistoric Fields in Denmark." *Antiquity* XX (1946): 38–39.
_____. *Plough and Pasture: The Early History of Farming.* New York, 1953.
Deevey, Edward S. Jr. "The Human Population." *Scientific American* CCIII (1960): 195–204.
Dumezil, Georges. *Archaic Roman Religion.* 2 Vols. Trans. Phillip Crapp. Chicago, 1970.
Eliade, Mircea. *The Forge and the Crucible.* Trans. Stephen Corrin. New York, 1962.
_____. *A History of Religious Ideas.* 1 Vol. Trans. Willard R. Trask. Chicago, 1978.
Embree, John F. *Suye Mura, A Japanese Village.* Chicago, 1939.
Ercker, Lazarus. *Treatise on Ores and Assaying.* Trans. A.G. Sisco and C.S. Smith. Chicago, 1951.
Evans-Pritchard, E.E. *The Nuer.* Oxford, 1940.
_____. *Nuer Religion.* New York and Oxford, 1956.
Fei, Hsiao-Tung. *Peasant Life in China.* New York, 1939.
Firth, Raymond. *Malay Fishermen: Their Peasant Economy.* London, 1946.
Forbes, R.J. *Metallurgy in Antiquity.* Leiden, 1950.
Garraty, John, and Peter Gay, Editors. *The Columbia History of the World.* New York, 1972.
Gimbatus, Marija. *The Goddesses and Gods of Old Europe, 6500-3500 B.C.: Myths and Cult Images.* Berkeley, 1982.
Gordon, D.H. *The Prehistoric Background of Indian Culture.* Bombay, 1958.
Hall, A.R., E.Y. Holmyard, and Charles Singer. *A History of Technology.* Oxford, 1955.
Hawks, C.F.C. *The Prehistoric Foundations of Europe to the Mycenaean Age.* London, 1940.
Homans, George C. *English Villagers of the Thirteenth Century.* Cambridge, Massachusetts, 1941.
Hose, Herbert. *Ancient Roman Religion.* London and New York, 1950.
Jensen, Adolph. *Myth and Cult Among Primitive Peoples.* Trans. Marianna Choldin and Wolfgang Wiessleder. Chicago, 1963.
Kroeber, A.L. *Anthropology.* New York, 1948.

Lamberg-Karlovsky, C.C. *Introductions to Hunters, Farmers, and Civilizations: Old World Archaeology.* San Francisco, 1979.

_____, and Jeremy A. Sabloff. *Ancient Civilizations: The Near East and Mesopotamia.* Menlo Park, California, 1979.

Lienhardt, Godfrey. *Divinity and Experience: The Religion of the Dinka.* Oxford, 1961.

Liljegren, Ronnie. "The Domestication of Animals." *People of the Stone Age: Hunters, Gathers and Early Farmers.* Vol. 2. *The Illustrated History of Humankind.* Goran Burenhult. General Editor. New York, 1993: 68–69.

Lincoln, Bruce. "The Indo-European Cattle Raiding Myth." *History of Religions* 16 (1976): 42–65.

_____. *Priests, Warriors, and Cattle: A Study in the Ecology of Religion.* Berkeley, California, 1981.

Linton, Ralph. *The Study of Man.* New York and London, 1936.

Long, Charles H. "Lectures on Religious Orientations in World History." University of North Carolina at Chapel Hill, 1979–80.

Lowie, Robert H. *The Origin of the State.* New York, 1927.

Maine, Henry S. *Village Communities in the East and West.* 3rd Ed. London, 1907.

McNeill, William. *The Rise of the West: A History of the Human Community.* Chicago and London, 1963.

Mellaart, James. *Catal Huyuk: A Neolithic Town in Anatolia.* New York, 1967.

Miner, Horace. "The Folk-Urban Continuum." *American Sociological Review* XVII (1952): 529–537.

Mooney, James. *Myths of the Cherokee.* Bureau of American Ethnology. 19th Annual Report. Part I. Washington D.C., 1900.

Moris, Norval, and David J. Rothman, Editors. *The Oxford History of the Prison: The Practice of Punishment in Western Society.* New York and Oxford, 1995.

Mumford, Lewis. *The City in History.* New York, 1961.

Neugebauer, O. *The Exact Sciences in Antiquity.* Princeton, New Jersey, 1952: 161.

Parrinder, E.G. *African Traditional Religion.* London, 1962.

_____. *West African Religion.* London, 1961.

Piggott, Stuart W. *Prehistoric India to 1000 B.C.* Harmondsworth, 1950.

Polanyi, Karl. *The Great Transformation.* New York and Toronto, 1944.

_____. "Our Obsolete Market Mentality." *Commentary* III (1947): 112.

Ray, Benjamin. *African Religions: Symbol, Ritual and Community.* Englewood Cliffs, New Jersey, 1976.

Redfield, Robert, and Alfonso Villa Rojas. *Chan Kom, A Maya Village.* Washington, D.C., 1934.

Rickard, T.A. *Man and Metals: A History of Mining in Relation to the Development of Civilization.* New York, 1932.

Robins, Fredrick W. *The Smith: The Traditions and Lore of an Ancient Craft.* London, 1953.

Rowley-Conwy, Peter. "Abu-Hureyra: The World's First Farmers." *People of the Stone Age: Hunter-Gatherers and Early Farmers.* Vol. 2. *The Illustrated History of Humankind.* Goran Burenhult. General Editor. New York, 1993: 27–29.

Sahlins, Marshall. *Stone Age Economics.* New York, 1972.

Sauer, Carl O. *Agricultural Origins and Dispersals*. New York, 1952.
Schoolcraft, Henry R. *Information Respecting the History, Condition and Prospects of the Indian Tribes of the United States*. Philadelphia, 1853–57.
Settegast, Mary. *Plato Prehistorian: 10,000 to 5000 B.C. in Myth and Archaeology*. Cambridge, Massachusetts, 1986.
Smith, Arthur H. *Village Life in China*. New York, 1899.
Snell, Daniel C. *Life in the Ancient East, 3100–332 B.C.E.* New Haven, Connecticut, 1997.
Srejovic, Dragoslav. "Neolithic Religion." *Encyclopedia of Religion*. Vol. 10. Mircea Eliade. Editor in Chief. New York, 1987.
Talayesva, Don. *Sun Chief: The Autobiography of a Hopi Indian*. New Haven, Connecticut, 1942.
Tax, Sol. Editor. *Evolution After Darwin*. Chicago, 1960.
_____. "Revolution and the Process of Civilization." *Human Origins, An Introductory General Course in Anthropology, Selected Readings, Series II*. 2nd Ed. Chicago, 1946.
Ucko, Peter J. *Anthropomorphic Figurines of Predynastic Egypt and Neolithic Crete*. London, 1968.
_____, and G.W. Dimbleby, Editors. *The Domestication and Exploitation of Plants and Animals*. London, 1969.
_____. *Man, Settlement and Urbanism*. Tringham Ruth, and G.W. Dimbleby. Editors. Cambridge, Massachusetts, 1972.
Wheatley, Paul. *The Pivot of the Four Quarters: A Preliminary Inquiry into the Origins and Character of the Ancient Chinese City*. Chicago, 1971.
Wheeler, Robert. *Early India and Pakistan to Ashoka*. London, 1959.
White, J. Peter. "Pacific Explorers: Highlanders and Islanders." *People of the Stone Age: Hunter-gatherers and Early Farmers*. Vol. 2. *The Illustrated History of Humankind*. Goran Burenhult. General Editor. New York, 1993, 145–149.
Wilson, Peter, Jr. *The Domestication of the Human Species*. New Haven, Connecticut, 1988.
Wyckoff, Dorothy. "Albertus Magnus on Ore Deposits." *Isis* XLIX (1958): 109–122.

CHAPTER 3

Mesopotamia — Between the Rivers

Mesopotamia means "between the rivers." The Tigris and Euphrates rivers refracted Mesopotamian religious life in a profound manner. It would be fair to say that the Mesopotamian people mirrored the rhythms of the Tigris and Euphrates rivers. As S.N. Kramer wrote, "history begins at Sumer." By 5500 B.C.E. small scale irrigation farming produced the first permanent villages in Mesopotamia. People migrated between and around the lower reaches of the Tigris and Euphrates rivers. We do not know who these pioneers were, but their neighbors in the north called them Sumerians.

Sumer was a land only recently raised above the waters of the Persian Gulf by the silt carried down by the two rivers. It was an area of vast swamps with towering reeds that was periodically flooded. The waters were full of fish and the reeds were alive with wild fowl, wild pig and other game, and on every bit of soil grew date palms which were very nutritious and were the basic stock food in Mesopotamia. We know that farmers erected mud walls around the trees and tended them for up to five years, long before they began to yield fruit. Thus, in Mesopotamia, the need for a sophisticated calendaring system arose, and, indeed, throughout the Neolithic period, human communities developed calendars that were more sophisticated than the crude lunar carvings which oriented Paleolithic humanity.

Sumer was an oasis surrounded on either side by desert. The soil was incredibly fertile, and by 2500 B.C.E. an average yield of a field of barley was 86 times the amount of seed sown. While food production was bountiful, raw materials were scarce. Wood and metals had to be imported from other areas, and thus trade became a necessary and essential aspect of Sumerian civilization. Copper was soon chosen over stones and flints for tools since it was as readily available and was much more dependable and durable. Sumerian civilization apparently had no older traditions out of which to grow. And yet, in Sumer, we find the earliest written documents, jails, wheeled vehicles, cylinder seals, animal drawn plows and potters' wheels, despite the fact that growth was very slow and unsteady. A number of small independent agricultural communities farmed along the rivers in Mesopotamia. The remains of most of these earliest villages have been found on the sites of the best known later cities — Erech, Eridu, Lagash, Ur and Nippur. Each city had a sacred center on top of which was built a temple with mud and sun dried brick. These temples (ziggurats), which involved the manufacture of bricks and the importation of pine wood and metals, presuppose a fairly substantial labor force, and hence an urban population. Priests, who formed collective groups that represented the gods, ran the temples. Each particular city had a central god, and that god owned the most extensive plots of land in the area. The priests also administered the lands of the gods.

The Tigris and Euphrates rivers were very unpredictable and could flood at a moment's notice. Therefore, Mesopotamian agriculture and the stability of these early communities were dependent upon a system of planned canals by which irrigation was carried out. With large scale irrigation came a population explosion and villages expanded into cities. Early on, political power rested with a general assembly of elders. But in times of crisis absolute powers might be conferred on one particular member who was temporarily designated king. Kingship, however, was held initially for a limited period of time and the assembly could revoke it when the crisis was over.

One Sumerian myth says the farmer was "a man of dikes and canals." Sumerian farmers did not fear drought because they did not depend upon the rain. The canals of Sumer served both as waterways and fish ponds and they watered the palm groves and rich grasslands which furnished feed for the sheep and cattle. Grain could be harvested as often as two or three times a year.

But life was very uncertain along the Tigris and Euphrates rivers. Even though Mesopotamians intervened in nature and directed her with a sophisticated series of dikes and canals, Mesopotamians never felt in control of the rivers. Indeed, they again and again stressed their frailty and weakness before their gods and the powers of the world. Rarely does one find Mesopotamian mythology or poetry that trumpets the Mesopotamians' power over nature or the gods.

Mesopotamians were warlike and militant in contrast to the Egyptians. There were a number of nomadic, warlike peoples who migrated into Mesopotamia, bringing conflicts and small scale war. Indeed, the Akkadians, who conquered Sumer, appear to have been a Semitic people. They were, in turn, conquered by the Gutians, a nomadic people from the Upper Tigris. In addition to this almost constant human conflict, the unpredictable and uncontrollable rhythms of the Tigris and Euphrates rivers also struck fear in their hearts. This turbulent environment occasioned a religious response which the historian of religions Thorkild Jacobsen notes stressed the "mysterious *tremendum*," the awesomeness of the sacred (*Towards the Treasures*). Mesopotamians emphasized their distance from the gods in a way which portrayed humans as servants for powerful and dominating gods. This experience of god as distant and awesome contrasts very sharply with the Egyptian experience of the sacred. There, god was experienced as close and serene, evoking a very different religious response. God in Egypt was experienced as attractive, as *fascinans*. A creative mystery which sustained life in an orderly and harmonious manner, the Nile River, was, relatively speaking, a very predictable river that flooded annually from June to October. Furthermore, until the Hyksos came between 1674 and 1570 B.C.E., the Egyptians had no outside enemies to battle as did the Mesopotamians.

It is interesting to note how Mesopotamian and Egyptian artwork refracts their very different religious sensibilities. Mesopotamian sculptures often show priests with very large eyes, eyes that reveal a sense of awe and uncertainty about the world. By contrast, Egyptian statues generally depict pharaoh as serene, calm and bold, reflecting a quiet sense of confidence that the gods supported their way of life.

The construction of Sumerian temples was a cooperative effort that required the labor of hundreds of people. The outlines of the temple were marked out with a red colored string, the marks of which have actually been uncovered at Erech. Sumerian architectural ingenuity was credited to the gods, who were believed to have been the actual designers of temple plans. God revealed these blueprints to priests through dreams.

In a temple belonging to the Uruk at Erech phase, clay tablets turned up scratched with short-hand pictures and numerals. The priests were administrators of the temple's estates and had to give accountings to the gods of the cities. They agreed upon a conventional form of recording receipts and expenditures so that their successors could read them, and thereby invented writing around 3300 B.C.E. Writing, therefore, began with the recording of the production, receipt, and distribution of an agricultural surplus. For Paleolithic people surplus was granted by the gods and was something over which human beings had very little, if any, control. Paleolithic humans did not control the production or acquisition of wild plants and wild animals in the way that Neolithic societies did domestic plants and animals. Once humans began producing their own food and creating a surplus through agriculture and animal husbandry, they made their own world in a manner unprecedented in Paleolithic times. The significance of this cannot be over emphasized. It is interesting to note that the earliest forms of writing were farm records. And yet, this was still a religious activity because each Sumerian city was ultimately considered the domain of a central god whose estate was administered by temple priests. Ultimately, Sumerian control over food production and the administration and distribution of an agricultural surplus was perceived as the work of the gods who owned the temples.

It is significant that writing emerges after Sumerian cities develop out of villages. The city represents a quantitative and qualitative change over its precursors. With the development of Sumerian cities, human beings, for the first time, find themselves in a world of their own making, relatively secure from the immediate pressures and rhythms of the cosmos. Sumerian cities were artificial landscapes of gardens, fields and pastures created out of a swamp through a complex system of irrigation canals. The city of Ur with its canals, harbors and temples occupied some 220 acres. The ruler of Lagash, one of the smaller cities of Sumer, claims to have ruled 36,000 people, and this number perhaps applied only to adult males. Ziggurats were the most dominant feature of Sumerian cities, but also important were the granaries and workshops. The gods owned the farmland. Lagash seems to have been divided into estates owned by some 20 different deities, with one god being the chief god of the entire city. The temple functioned as a divine household of sorts from which a number of different job activities were singled out. Thus, there were bakers, brewers, weavers, spinners, smiths, artisans, officials, clerks and priests. Jobs became specialized in contrast to the Neolithic village where a single household might fulfill all or most needs to a degree.

It is the division of labor that perhaps most clearly distinguishes Sumerian cities from the earlier villages and with each specific job activity came a plethora of new gods. It has been said that Mesopotamia at one time contained over two thousand different gods. As religion became more complex and differentiated, so did social life. This is a phenomenon well known in the history of religions of urban communities, and Mesopotamia depicts this process very well. One of the things that comes out of this is the possibility of class distinctions, which is related to the access to surplus.

The priests in Mesopotamia represented the highest social class because they controlled the granaries and the allocation of surplus. They also controlled writing.

This conscious effort by Mesopotamians to produce highly regulated surpluses represents a significant development in religious history. Paleolithic and primitive peoples did not attempt to generate the kinds of surpluses that make urban societies possible. For example, among the Northwest Coast Indians of North America, potlatch ceremonies were held at different times of the year so that surpluses in animal skins, and later blankets, might be given away periodically to avoid their stockpiling by any one person (Vertovec). In the nineteenth century, the potlatch culminated with the burning of very finely woven blankets in order to destroy surplus. Among southeastern Indian tribes such as the Cherokee and the Chickasaw, at the annual Green Corn ceremony the food surplus from the previous year was eaten up. Moreover, all transgressions and wrongs except murder were forgiven so that following the new year ceremony the past was forgotten and everyone started out anew on equal footing (Perdue).

The idea of destroying a surplus seems to be related to the very ancient view of time as cyclical. For primal people, every year there was a new year ceremony in which the past was abolished and the world was created anew. As we shall see, this idea continued and was even emphasized in Mesopotamian cities, but a new idea of time also emerged corresponding to the production and allocation of agricultural surplus — history. It is true that historical time was not viewed as sacred until the emergence of the Hebrew tradition (Eliade *The Myth of the Eternal Return*). But it is also true that Mesopotamians did recognize historical time. The recognition of time as linear seems to be further developed in Mesopotamia with the arrival of kingship, and a number of scholars, including Ian Cunnison, have shown that the notion of divine genealogies parallels a historical reckoning of time. It is instructive to note here that even among a predominantly hunting culture, such as the Lakota, Plains Indians of North America, the acquisition of large surpluses of horses, along with strong war chiefs during the eighteenth and nineteenth centuries, paralleled historical records of certain major events. Warfare among Mesopotamian cities was commonplace, perhaps demonstrating how the Mesopotamian peoples mirrored the violent rivers upon which they depended.

Other than the account tablets, the oldest legible documents from Mesopotamia describe wars between the adjacent cities of Lagash and Umma for the possession of strips of territory. As warfare became more commonplace, a new political institution emerged, kingship. The earliest city governors are kings who generally call themselves *ishakku*, which means "tenant farmer" (of the god). Only rarely is the term *lugal* or "king" used. Thus, even with the early development of royalty and urbanity among Mesopotamians, the link with farming remained strong. As the representative of the tribal god of the city, the *ishakku* received the largest plot of the clan lands. At Lagash he enjoyed the use of 608 acres. The king still did not rule absolutely. Priests remained in power despite dynastic changes. Each of these city-states seemed to remain independent in Mesopotamia until about 2375 B.C.E., when Lugalzaggizi of Umma conquered a number of cities. Still, even his kingdom was transient. It was not until about 2340 B.C.E., when Sargon of Akkad conquered Lugalzaggizi, that a true kingdom which unified the various city-states emerged in Mesopotamia. Sargon's assent to power paralleled a couple of important changes in Sumerian mythology which we shall discuss very shortly.

As cities emerged, more exact sciences were developed to direct the large amount of manpower needed to keep the city going. Sumerians were not interested in the abstract qualities of mathematics. Their math was related to very practical questions such as the amount of seed needed to sow a god's field, the number of bricks needed for a temple wall, how much earth must be dug for a dike, and how many men were needed to finish a job by an appointed time. Mathematics developed from the "imagination of matter" and was directly related to everyday activities (Long). The word "volume" for Mesopotamians meant literally "mass of earth." One is reminded here of the story Barre Toelken tells of an old Navajo Indian whom he once showed a picture of the Empire State Building in New York City. The old man's question was "How many sheep will it hold?" Barre Toelken then displayed to the old man a picture of a large airplane and again, the question was "How many sheep will it carry?" Similarly, the world for Mesopotamians was not a place that they thought about abstractly, but rather lived according to the tasks that were laid down for them by their gods.

Sargon's conquest seems not to have worked any major changes on the old cities in Sumer. Temple communities continued as before, but in Akkad very important transformations took place. For one thing, temple communities were not as important as they were in Sumer. Tribal and clan leaders, rather than priests, managed most of the Akkadian agricultural and pastoral lands. Through time, something similar to individual land ownership began to evolve. Temples continued, but the god of the temple became only one land holder among many, and his temple depended heavily upon the support of the king. Such changes only lasted about a century.

Myth and History

To a large degree, Mesopotamian history is refracted through its mythology and ritual calendar. For Mesopotamians, as for archaic peoples everywhere, the new year ritual was the most important. Every year the cosmogony was ritually reenacted, thus recreating the world. In Sumer the new year ritual was called *A-ki-til*, which means "power making the world live again." This ritual was performed during both the spring and autumn equinoxes and represented both the creation and the destruction of the world. The ceremony culminated with the king and the queen copulating to symbolize creation and fructification.

In Sumer religion centered around the cult of Dumuzi (Tammuz). Dumuzi was a cult of women who venerated life and young men. The god Dumuzi was revealed in four places, all associated with life — dates, milk-shepherd, grain and tree sap. All of the above were linked with young men, for young men were loved by all women. Warfare was common in Sumer. Mesopotamia lacked the geographical barriers of Egypt and thus was subject to attack from the outside. Furthermore, inter-city warfare was widespread. In Mesopotamia young men, like grain, were cut down in the prime of their lives. Because men were killed in their prime, they were mourned by women. Man cuts grain and man kills man.

Thorkild Jacobson says that the god Dumuzi was an "intransitive provider" because he manifested himself by being acted upon by humans (Toward the Image of Tammuz). The idea that god manifests himself by his submission to man's activity is very different from the revelation of god in the Paleolithic period. Because Dumuzi was killed by man, the cult of Dumuzi was associated with guilt. Dumuzi reflected the warlike environment of Mesopotamia. In his various forms Dumuzi was linked with separate experiences of the sacred. As palm dates, Dumuzi represented the security and eternal presence of the divine, for dates were stored year around. As milk-shepherd, Dumuzi was associated with brevity and loss, for milk was not easily stored for very long, and the young shepherd men did not live very long. Finally, *damu* or sap corresponded with the Mesopotamian experience of anxiety and rebirth that occurred every spring. Ethically, Dumuzi was neutral. He was not a teacher or a prophet, and he was defenseless, immature and possessive. He was not brave. In short, Dumuzi corresponded socially to a society oriented by custom rather than ethics. Dumuzi expressed early Sumerian religion and was often associated with other myths.

One early cosmogonic myth in Sumer told of humans growing from the earth like plants with help from Enlil's hoe. Thus, initially, Mesopotamian religions stressed the relationship between god and humans. Two other early myths even mentioned the link between humans and gods. Enki was said to breathe the vital life into humanity and Dumuzi was associated with the king. By the third dynasty of Ur (2150–2050 B.C.) all five kings were called Dumuzi and were linked with the myth of Dumuzi and the *A-ki-til* ceremony.

Mythically, Dumuzi is said to have married Inanna, the goddess of procreation. Dumuzi becomes king and Inanna visits the netherworld and dies. When Inanna dies, all life dies. To restore life, Dumuzi and Inanna's sister sacrifice themselves annually, with each dying for one-half of the year. Dumuzi's life corresponds with the growing season. In another version of the myth Dumuzi is killed by demons at the end of the lambing season, or spring, and Inanna tries to restore him and is killed. Theodor Gaster says that Dumuzi was part of a broader structure of Ancient Near Eastern rituals of filling and depletion. Gaster notes that all over the Ancient Near East, there were rituals of filling which celebrated the joy of spring planting and of the return of life. In the autumn there were rituals of depletion, mourning a god who was no longer present. As noted above, true Mesopotamian kingship began when Sargon conquered Lugalzaggizi in 2340 B.C. He became the first ruler of Mesopotamia, founded Akkad, and ruled about a century. The Gutians followed and dominated for a brief while, and then came the Third Dynasty of Ur, which lasted about another 100 years.

During the time of Akkad, the central new year ritual for Mesopotamians was the *zagmuk* ritual, which is a Sumerian term meaning "beginning of the year." It was called *akitu* in Babylon. This ritual was associated with the *enuma elish*, which means "when on high." Reenacted each year during the new year ritual, this myth begins with two bodies of water, Apsu, "fresh," and Tiamat, "salt," mingling. Associated with Apsu and Tiamat is Mummu, who probably represents clouds and mist. From the mingling of these waters comes Lahmu and Lahamu, the powers of silt. Born from their union are Anshar and Kishar, the powers of the horizon. The powers of the horizon come together and engender Anu, the sky, and he creates the god of the waters, Ea, or Enki.

The birth of these gods is coextensive with a new principle, movement or activity. Activity contrasts sharply with the primeval, vaporous chaos which stood for rest and inactivity. Apsu becomes upset because the new gods are disturbing his rest and sleep. The gods hold a council and Ea/Enki is chosen to place a spell over Apsu. Ea places Apsu into a deep sleep, kills Apsu, and establishes his realm above him. Then Ea locks up Mummu and passes a string through his nose.

In the land which Ea has established Marduk is born. He becomes the real hero of the story. In earlier versions it was Enlil who was born at this time. But in later versions Marduk replaces Enlil for reasons that will be discussed soon. Tiamat is chided by her associates for allowing Apsu to be killed, and thus she prepares to do battle with the gods. At the head of her army is her second husband, Kingu. Because Ea was victorious over Apsu and Mummu, he is chosen at first to do battle with Tiamat, but the gods realize that he is not powerful enough and so they choose Anu, the sky god. Even Anu realizes though that he does not have enough authority to face Tiamat.

Then, finally, it is proposed that young Marduk, "whose strength is mighty," should be chosen to do battle with Tiamat. Marduk is a young god with abundant strength who looks ahead to his contest. But Marduk has no authority because he is such a new god; therefore, all of the gods get together, hold counsel, and decree upon Marduk "destiny," which gives him a seat of honor and new powers. As they tell Marduk, "Thy rank is unsurpassed and thy command is Anu's. Marduk, thou art of consequence among the elder gods; thy rank is unequaled and thy command is Anu's. From this day onward, shall thy orders not be altered.... Among the gods known none shall encroach upon thy rights" (Jacobsen "Mesopotamia" 178).

Thus Marduk becomes the king of the gods and establishes the archetype of Mesopotamian kingship. As the other gods tell Marduk, "We give thee kingship, power over all things." Seven terrible storms and great winds overpower Tiamat. This myth originally involved Enlil, who is associated with the force of wind. Marduk slays Tiamat and Kingu and cuts Tiamat in half in order to create the heavens and the earth. He punctures Tiamat's eyes and from them flow the Tigris and Euphrates rivers. Human beings emerged from the blood of Kingu.

On one level this story represents the annual spring floods in the Mesopotamian plain. Each spring the waters rise and flood the land until the wind eventually pushes back the waters and dries them, allowing the inundated land to reemerge. With the emergence of Marduk in the myth, the divine sanctioning of Mesopotamian kingship emerges. Marduk becomes equal to all of the senior gods in the assembly and sets the stage for the emergence of a king on earth who is the leader of the army in war, and, with the assent of the assembly, the leader of all matters of internal organization. Marduk is appointed king and ruler of heaven and earth. In Mesopotamia, the king comes to be called the "King of Four Regions." It is said that a supernatural light shown from the king's head who was born of earth yet was the son of god. Kings in Mesopotamia represented god and yet were not worshipped as gods as were Egyptian pharaohs.

Importantly, in the *enuma elish* ("Epic of Creation") human beings are seen as demonic, as they are essentially of the nature of Kingu. Furthermore, the story reflects the emergence of kingship over kinship as the basis of the social structure in Mesopotamia (Long). With the establishment of Sargon's kingdom, tribal and clan relationships were superseded in importance by the king's overarching influence. But it was not until Hammurabi emerges in 1792 B.C.E. from the small city state of Babylon that a king succeeded in conquering all of southern Mesopotamia.

Marduk is said to have been chosen by the divine assembly to administer the functions traditionally held by the god Enlil. As Marduk took over Enlil's functions, so Hammurabi was executive for Marduk on earth. However, given that myths are often embodied before they are articulated, it is fair to say that the myth of Marduk's ascension as king of the gods paralleled the unification of Mesopotamia under Sargon. Then, under Hammurabi, Babylon became a truly urban society which was administered by written laws. The primary myth of this period, the *Epic of Gilgamesh*, also embodied the history of the people at this time.

The *Epic of Gilgamesh* begins with the king of Uruk who was the son of a mortal man and the goddess Ninsun. He becomes a great leader whose knowledge and great works of construction set a good example. But soon afterwards he begins violating women sexually and forcing men to work as slaves. The people pray to the gods to send them someone who can confront him, and the gods create Enkidu, a wild man, a half-savage creature who lives in peace with the wild beasts. Gilgamesh hears of this giant and wondrous creature from various hunters and sets out to find him. Enkidu is seduced by a woman, and once he has contact with her the animals flee him. Shunned by his former friends, he follows her back to the city. There he engages in a great wrestling match with Gilgamesh, who eventually emerges victorious. The two become friends. They then set out for the distant Forest of Cedars, which is guarded by a monstrous fire giant called Huwawa. They defeat the fire giant and on their way back the goddess Ishtar asks Gilgamesh to marry her, but he turns her down. Humiliated, Ishtar gets the god of the sky, Anu, to create a giant bull to destroy Gilgamesh and his city. Enkidu and Gilgamesh fight the bull as he charges down on the walls of Uruk and vanquish the bull. After ripping off one of his legs and throwing it at the feet of Ishtar, Enkidu dreams that he is condemned by the gods and dies soon thereafter. The death of Enkidu in the prime of his life affects Gilgamesh terribly, and he tries everything to bring Enkidu back to life. Wandering through the desert, Gilgamesh complains that he does not want to die like Enkidu. The thought of death terrifies him, and nothing that he does can comfort him.

As a consequence, Gilgamesh becomes consumed with the quest for personal immortality. Gilgamesh knows that Utnapishtim, who survived the flood in mythical times, is still alive and he decides to search for him. His journey to find Utnapishtim is full of ordeals. He comes to the mountains of Mashu and finds a gate through which the sun passes daily. Gilgamesh is paralyzed by fear at the sight of the Scorpion Man and his wife, but they allow him to pass by. He meets the nymph Sidure and asks her where he can find Utnapishtim. She tries to make him change his mind: "When the gods made men they saw death from men; they kept life for themselves. Thou, Gilgamesh, fill thy belly and make merry by day and night. On each day make a feast and dance and play, day and night" (quoted in Eliade *A History* 78–79). In other words, Sidure advised Gilgamesh to eat, drink and be merry for tomorrow he may be dead. But Gilgamesh holds fast to his decision to seek immortality, and goes on to visit the boat man, Urshanabi. In one version he crosses the Sea of Death with Urshanabi as his ferryman, and in another version, he carries with him 120 poles, each 60 cubits long, which he uses as stilts to avoid death. He finally finds Utnapishtim, the only mortal ever to reach immortality. After hearing that Gilgamesh seeks eternal life, Utnapishtim tells Gilgamesh that he was given the gift of immortality because he had built an ark according to the directions of the gods. Utnapishtim does, however, tell Gilgamesh about a sacred plant that grows at the bottom of the sea which Gilgamesh dives for and finds. Carrying the plant back with him towards Uruk, Gilgamesh takes a swim in a lake. As he bathes, a snake comes out, carries off the plant, and sheds its skin. Heartbroken, Gilgamesh arrives back at Uruk and invites Urshanabi to go up on the city walls in order to admire its foundations.

Thus, even the mighty Gilgamesh was denied immortality in the end by destiny. The *Epic of Gilgamesh* reflects an increased sense of activity by human beings. Gilgamesh is a powerful ruler who seeks his own salvation. He is able to kill a fire monster and a giant bull sent by the gods. But he cannot attain life eternal. The loss of afterlife represents a further distancing between god and humanity. In other words, the *Epic of Gilgamesh* reflects still another step in the development of urban life in Mesopotamia. It is significant that Utnapishtim was given the gift of immortality by the gods because he obeyed the gods. Gilgamesh, on the other hand, turned down the goddess Ishtar's proposal for marriage and then killed the bull that the god sent to destroy his city. Gilgamesh acted against the will of the gods and seeks his own immortality, a quest which, in the end, failed.

In the end, the story of Gilgamesh becomes exemplary for urban Mesopotamians. Man was created mortal and distant from the gods. Leo Oppenheim, a renowned expert in Mesopotamian religious studies, has argued that the *Epic of Creation* and the *Epic of Gilgamesh* were prepared by Sumerian court poets and later scribes, and were directed to a sophisticated public. While it may be true that only the educated elite in Mesopotamia actually read the *Epic of Creation* and the *Epic of Gilgamesh*, it does not necessarily follow that those myths were not known, or embodied by the general population. In other words, the absence of evidence does not prove evidence of absence. It may very well be the case that Mesopotamians inhabited the religious world articulated by the *Epic of Creation* and the *Epic of Gilgamesh*, even though most Mesopotamians never actually read those accounts. Just as most industrial capitalists have not read Adam Smith's *The Wealth of Nations*, they nevertheless embody its principles by and through their daily economic affairs; so too, it would seem, the Akkadians and Babylonians lived the meanings of the *Epic of Creation* and the *Epic of Gilgamesh*, respectively.

During the time of Hammurabi, about the same time as the *Epic of Gilgamesh*, there emerged a composition called "I will praise the Lord of Wisdom." It is similar in theme to the Book of Job in the Bible and was perhaps a precursor to Job. The story is about a very pious man who lived a good life, always acting correctly before the gods by regularly praying to the gods and sacrificing to them. He was also a man who praised the king and the king's palace. And yet, in spite of his righteousness, evils of the most serious kind occurred to him. He became diseased, blind, deaf and weak. Pain gripped him and he felt abandoned by the gods. At one point he was even given up for dead and funeral arrangements were made. This story is perhaps the first examination of what, in the West, is called the problem of theodicy, that is, the problem of righteous suffering. Here a pious, upright human being was stricken down by the gods and made to suffer greatly. In the end, the gods tell him that what seems praiseworthy to human beings may be contemptible before the gods, and what may seem before one's heart to be bad, may be good before god. "Who may comprehend the mind of gods in heaven's depth? The thoughts of a god are like deep waters, who could fathom them, how could mankind becloud and comprehend the ways of gods?" (Jacobsen "Mesopotamia" 215). In other words, god's will is unfathomable.

Skepticism, doubt and cynicism began to undermine religious orientation of Mesopotamians by the second millennium B.C.E. In the "Dialogue between Master and Slave," a master announces his intention to a slave to do a particular act. The slave agrees that he should do it. The master then immediately decides that he will not do the act described because of all of its negative consequences, to which the slave again agrees wholeheartedly. For example, the master says he will love a woman because such a man "forgets want and misery." Then he goes on to say to say that a woman is "a snare, a trap and a pitfall; woman is a sharpened iron sword which will cut a young man's neck." Similarly, the master talks about making a libation to the gods in order to put his heart at ease. Then he decides not to. Charity also is seen to be more negative than positive. In the end the master asks the slave to "mount thou upon the ruined mounds of ancient cities and walk around; behold the skulls of those of earlier and later times. Who is the evil doer, who is the benefactor?" (Eliade *A History* 81; Jacobsen "Mesopotamia" 216). In the end all people end up dead without the benefit of any ultimate significance or afterlife; therefore, human life is, in the end, meaningless.

Thus, by the first millennium in Babylon, the emphasis on human activity has begun to delimit the sphere of religious activity. But religion does not die in Mesopotamia. Humans still have a spirit, *ilu*, the spark of god which means, literally, "god." Cities are still modeled on the stars and Babylon was called Bab-il-ani, which means "Gate of the Gods." The city was seen as a link between heaven and earth, and each city was linked with a constellation — Sippar with Cancer, Niniveh with the Great Bear, and so forth. Indeed, observations of the stars proved so successful for later Mesopotamians in telling them when to plant their crops that it lead ultimately to a rather fatalistic world view in which it was felt that the stars controlled human destiny. Thus astrology was born of astronomy in Mesopotamia.

We discussed in the first chapter how, for many people and perhaps for humanity as a whole, the sky revealed itself at once as a majestic and powerful force. Humans realized their own insignificance and limits by simply seeing the sky. In Mesopotamia the father of the gods, Anu, was the power manifested in the sky. He was also the prototype of all fathers. Fathers on earth in Mesopotamia descended from the sky father, and he was also the prototype of the kings and rulers. It was Anu's command that issued through the king's mouth, and it was Anu's power that made the king effective. Anu was described as the "Sovereign of the gods, whose word prevails in the ordained assembly of the great gods" (Jacobsen "Mesopotamia" 140).

The god Enlil, or "Lord Storm," was, in a sense, the storm itself. He manifested himself and was the master of all space between sky and earth. Mesopotamians experienced Enlil as storm. Warfare was perceived to be the manifestation of Enlil as human storm. As Jacobson so rightly observed, Anu represents the passive authority of the sacred, and Enlil its active force. Thus Anu and Enlil embody, on a cosmic level, the two necessary ingredients for a state on the political level — authority and legitimate force ("Mesopotamia" 143).

Finally, the third great component of the visible cosmos was the Mesopotamian earth, denoted in a number of terms. The divine power of the earth was initially *Ki*, "earth," whose name eventually gave way to more anthropological forms. The earth became *Nintu*, "the lady who gives birth." She was also *nig-zi-gal-dim-me*, "the fashioner of everything wherein is the breath of life." Artwork depicts the earth as a woman suckling a child, and she is, as one inscription states, "the mother of all children." The earth was ultimately feminine, fertile and passive. The earth embodied the waters, Enki, which were perceived as male, "as lord of the earth." Water is not passive; it comes and goes, it floods and erodes, and it takes the shape of its container.

Each of the major Mesopotamian gods was associated with a particular city. Anu's center was at Erech, but like so many sky gods in other religions, Anu withdrew his influence and became a hidden god, or *deus otiosis*. Enlil gradually took over Anu's paramount position and came to be known as father of the gods and the king of heaven and earth. His temple was located at Nippur. Kramer, in his book *The Sumerians*, cites the following prayer which was recited at the temple in Nippur: "Without Enlil, the great mountain, no cities would be built, no settlements founded, no stalls would be built, no sheep fold established, no king would be raised, no high priest born.... the rivers dash, their floods waters would not bring overflow, the fish of the sea would lay no eggs in the cane brake, the birds of heavens would not build nests on the wide earth" (121).

Enki, the god of rivers, lakes and marshes, was the son of Enlil and was sometimes also known as the son or grandson of Anu. His main shrine was at Eridu and he was respected especially for his wisdom. Finally, the goddess Ninhursag, the earth, was revered as the mother of all creatures and was associated with the stony and rocky regions of the earth. Her main ceremonial centers were Adab and Kish.

Bibliography
Chapter 3 — Mesopotamia

Adams, Robert McCormick. *Heartland of Cities: Surveys of Ancient Settlement and Land Use on the Central Floodplain of the Euphrates.* Chicago, 1981.
Bottero, Jean. *Mesopotamia: Writing, Reasoning, and the Gods.* Chicago, 1992.
Childe, V. Gordon. *What Happened in History.* New York, 1946.
Cogan, M. "Omens and Ideology in the Babylon Inscriptions of Esarhaddon." *History, Historiography, and Interpretations: Studies in Biblical and Cuneiform Lituretures.* H. Tadmor and H. Weinfield. Editors. Jerusalem, 1983: 76–84.
Cunnison, Ian. "History and Genealogies in a Conquest State." *American Anthropologist* 57 (1957): 20–31.

Cunnison, Ian. *History on the Luapula: An Essay on the Historical Notions of a Central African Tribe.* Cape Town, London and New York, 1957.

Diakonoff, I.M. "A Babylonian Political Pamphlet From About 700 B.C." *Studies in Honor of Benno Landsberger.* Chicago, 1965: 343–349.

Eliade, Mircea. *A History of Religious Ideas.* Vol. 1 Trans. Willard R. Trask. Chicago, 1978.

_____. *The Myth of the Eternal Return, or Cosmos and History.* Trans. Willard R. Trask. Princeton, 1954.

Frame, Grant. *Rulers of Babylonia.* Toronto, 1995.

Garelli, P. "The Changing Facet of Conservative Mesopotamian Thought." *Wisdom, Revelation and Doubt: Perspective on the First Millennium B.C.* B.I. Schwartz. Editor. *Daedalus* (1975): 47–56.

Garraty, John, and Peter Gay. Editors. *The Columbia History of the World.* New York, 1972.

Gaster, Theodore H. *Thespis: Ritual, Myth, and Drama in the Ancient Near East.* New York, 1950.

Gordon, Edmund. *Sumerian Proverbs: Glimpses of Everyday Life in Ancient Mesopotamia.* With a chapter by Thorkild Jacobsen. Philadelphia, 1959.

Grayson, A.K. and W.G. Lambert. "Akkadian Prophecies." *Journal of Cuneiform Studies* 28 (1964): 7–30.

Hackman, George Gottlob. *Sumerian and Akkadian Administrative Texts.* New Haven, Connecticut, 1958.

Jacobsen, Thorkild. "Formative Tendencies and Sumerian Religion." *The Bible and the Ancient Near East.* N. Ernest Wright. Editor. New York, 1961: 267–268.

_____. *The Harab Myth.* Malibu, California, 1984.

_____. "Mesopotamia." *The Intellectual Adventure of Ancient Man: An Essay on Speculative Thought in the Ancient Near East.* Henri Frankfort, et al. Editors. Chicago, 1946.

_____. "Primitive Democracy in Ancient Mesopotamia." *Journal of Near Eastern Studies* II (1943): 159–172.

_____. *Salinity and Irrigation Agriculture in Antiquity.* Malibu. California, 1982.

_____. *The Sumerian King List.* Chicago, 1939.

_____. *The Sumerological Studies in Honor of Thorkild Jacobsen on His Seventieth Birthday, June 7, 1974.* Chicago, 1975.

_____. *Toward the Image of Tammuz and Other Essays on Mesopotamian History and Culture.* Cambridge, Massachusetts, 1970.

_____. "Toward the Image of Tammuz." *History of Religions* 1 (1961): 189–213.

_____. *Towards the Treasures of Darkness: A History of Mesopotamian Religion.* New Haven, Connecticut, 1976.

Kramer, S.N. *History Begins at Sumer.* New York, 1959.

_____. *The Sacred Marriage Rite: Aspects of Faith, Myth, and Ritual in Ancient Sumer.* 1969.

_____. *Sumerian Mythology.* Philadelphia, 1944.

_____. *The Sumerians: Their History, Culture and Character.* Chicago, 1963.

Lambert, W.G. *Babylonian Wisdom Literature.* Oxford, 1967.

_____. "Morals in Ancient Mesopotamia." *Jaarbericht van het Vooraziatisch—Egyptisch Genootschap.* 'Ex Oriente Lux.' Vol. XV (1957/8): 184–196.

Long, Charles H. Personal Communication.

McNeill, William. *The Rise of the West: A History of the Human Community*. Chicago and London, 1963.

Michalowski, Piotr. *Letters from Early Mesopotamia*. Atlanta, Georgia, 1993.

Oppenheim, A. Leo. "A Bird's Eye View of Mesopotamian Economic History." *Trade and Market in the Early Empires*. Karl Polanyi et al. Eds. Glencoe, Illinois, 1957: 27–37.

_____. *Ancient Mesopotamia: Portrait of a Dead Civilization*. Chicago, 1964.

_____. "The Intellectual in Mesopotamian Society." *Wisdom, Revelation and Doubt: Perspectives on the First Millennium B.C.* B.I. Schwartz. Editor. *Daedalus*. (1975): 37–46.

Pallis, Suend, A. *The Babylonian Akitu Festival*. Kobenhavn, 1926.

Parrot, A. *Sumer*. Paris, 1952.

Perdue, Theda. *The Cherokee*. New York, 1989.

Pritchard, J.B. Editor. *Ancient Near Eastern Texts Relating to the Old Testament*. Princeton, New Jersey, 1969.

Redman, Charles L. "Mesopotamia and the First Cities." *Old World Civilizations: The Rise of Cities and States*. Vol. 3. *The Illustrated History of Humankind*. Goran Burenhult. General Editor. New York, 1993: 17–20.

Roth, Martha T. *Law Collections from Mesopotamia and Asia Minor*. Atlanta, Georgia, 1997.

Rowley-Conwy, Peter. "Abu Hureya: The World's First Farmers." *People of the Stone Age: Hunter-Gatherers and Early Farmers*. Vol. 2. *The Illustrated History of Mankind*. Goran Burenhult. General Editor. New York, 1993: 27–29.

Schmandt-Besserat, Denise. Editor. *The Legacy of Sumer: Invited Lectures on the Middle East at the University of Texas at Austin*. Malibu, California, 1976.

Simmons, Stephen D. *Early Old Babylonian Documents*. New Haven, Connecticut, 1978.

Speiser, E.A. "Authority and Law in Mesopotamia." *Oriental and Biblical Studies, Collected Writings*. Philadelphia, 1967: 317.

Tadmor, H. "The Sin of Sargon." *Eretz Israel* 5 (1958): 93.

Toelken, Barre. "Seeing With a Native Eye: How Many Sheep Will it Hold?" *Seeing with a Native Eye: Essays on Native American Religion*. Walter H. Capps. Editor. New York, 1976: 1–24.

Vertovec, Steven. "Potlatching and the Mythic Past: A Re-Evaluation of the Traditional Northwest Coast Indian Complex." *Religion* 13 (1983): 323–344.

CHAPTER 4

Egypt — Land of the Nile

Egypt, like Mesopotamia, is perhaps best understood as a reflection of the river on which its peoples' lives depended. Egypt mirrors the rhythms of the Nile River and Valley. The Egyptian environment displayed a serenity and a symmetry which its people embodied in their orientation to the world. The Nile River is very different from the Tigris and Euphrates rivers. While the Tigris and Euphrates rivers were violent and unpredictable and had to be checked with a complex system of irrigation dikes and canals, the Nile River was very predictable, flooding each year at almost the same time. Except for the time of the flood, the Nile River was calm, predictable, peaceful and so too were the Egyptian people calm, predictable and peaceful.

The landscape was quite balanced. On each side of the Nile River there were five miles of black earth, renewed each year by annual floods. This soil was very fertile and capable of producing bountiful harvests which helped sustain the people of Egypt. The fertile ground of the Nile Valley ended so abruptly that it was possible to stand with one foot in rich soil and one foot in desert sand. Except for the silt that was deposited by the river on either side of its banks, Egypt was desert.

The symmetry of the Egyptian landscape is striking. Mountain ranges bordered the river on both the west and the east. Standing on either river bank in Egypt and looking east or west, one saw an oasis, then desert, then mountains. The desert and Nile River were quiet. Therefore, movements of living animals stood out starkly against the stillness of the Egyptian landscape. Thus alligators, falcons and cattle manifested themselves very powerfully in the perceptions of the Egyptian people. As the historian of religion John Wilson has shown us, the land of Egypt is essentially rainless ("Egypt" 35), and even today only 3.5 percent of Egypt is cultivable and habitable. The rest of the land is barren, desolate desert. Egypt's balance and order are furthermore revealed in the movements of the sun. Heat and light dominated the religious sensibilities of the Egyptian people. In the morning the sun rises in the east and crosses over the Nile River very slowly, setting in the evening in the west. The life and death of the sun, after the Nile River itself, became the primary religious symbol system of the Egyptian people. The sun was the source of light and "his" retreat into the underworld at night brought death and darkness to the world. The Nile, too, had its own cycle of birth, life and death, but one that manifested itself on an annual basis. In the summer, the river is restful, calm and slow. Greenery on either side dries up and the cattle grow thin. But just as the thought of famine begins to grip the people, sluggish waters begin to stir. The river swells and finally bursts its banks, rushing over miles of land on either side, renewing them with life giving silt. The Nile River played such a large part in the outlook of the Egyptian people that the Egyptian word "to go north" is the same word as "to go downstream," and the word "to go south" means "to go upstream." It is interesting to note that the sense of direction was so dominated by the directional flow of the Nile River that when the Egyptian people finally saw the Tigris for the first time, a river that flows north to south rather than south to north like the Nile, they described it as a river which "goes downstream in going upstream."

The Nile River was navigated. In going north one simply followed the current, but the Egyptians ingeniously developed the sailboat in order to capture the wind so that they could cruise south against the current. Egyptians are credited with having developed the sailboat, and its role in their lives was so great that two model sailboats were placed into some Egyptian tombs. One model had the sail down for sailing north with the current in the afterlife, while the other miniature had the sail up for sailing against the current to the south. The Nile was seen as the source of rain, and, indeed, rain for Egyptians was perceived to fall from a Nile in the sky.

The serenity of the Egyptian landscape was furthermore fostered by the fact that Egypt, unlike Mesopotamia, was not vulnerable to invasion from every direction. The Nile Valley was not only isolated, but it was also defended by the desert, the Red Sea and the Mediterranean. It is significant to note that until 1674 B.C.E. when the Hyksos (Syrians) invaded Egypt and ruled until about 1560 B.C.E., Egypt had no enemies. This lack of political turbulence from the outside also contributed significantly to the calm confidence which characterized Egyptian culture and religious life. Indeed, in contrast to Mesopotamian sculpture and artwork, which often depicts kings and priests with large, awestruck and sometimes terrified eyes, Egyptian pharaohs are generally depicted with subdued countenances. Geographically, the Egyptian world presented a very orderly and symmetrical cosmos, and politically there was no enemy from without. The Nile River flooded annually, and while the Egyptians practiced some irrigation, they did not have to intervene in nature the way that the Mesopotamians did.

There is a qualitative difference between the irrigation techniques of the Egyptians and those of the Mesopotamians. Egyptians did not construct canals until later times. Instead, they trapped the waters of the flooding Nile River behind solid dikes until the soil was thoroughly soaked. This basin-type irrigation involved much less digging than did the Mesopotamian type, and maintenance work was light because of the way the Nile River gradually swelled and overflowed its banks in contrast to the more violent flooding that characterized the Tigris and Euphrates rivers. Less manpower was required to maintain Egyptian irrigation so that there were several months before and after the annual flooding in which there was very little work to do on the land. This contrasts sharply with Mesopotamia where large amounts of manpower were constantly expended working to maintain the irrigation system.

We mentioned earlier that, in the Neolithic period, the development of agriculture and then cities saw life become more sedentary, contrasting clearly with the transhumant life of hunter-gatherers. The rhythms of city life also contrasted with the patterns of those people who live primarily by pastoralism. While cattle played an important part in the economic and religious life of Egyptians, the Egyptians could hardly be called pastoralists, and indeed they looked with disdain toward Asiatic Bedouins who did "not live in a single place" and whose "feet wander" (Wilson "Egypt" 39).

As we noted, the Nile and the sun were the two dominant features which oriented Egyptian life. While the sun comes to play the central part in Egyptian theology, the north-south orientation of the Nile River seems to have been older. Although the direction of east, the land of the rising sun, was called "God's Land," Egyptians seemed to look more fundamentally to the south, the source of the annual renewal of the lands, as the basis of the cosmos. As we shall see, throughout Egyptian history these complementary and sometimes conflicting, or at least competing, religious symbols reveal themselves.

The earth was conceived by the Egyptians as a platter which floated in water. The platter rested on the waters below, which the Egyptians called Nun. Nun was the underworld waters, the primordial waters out of which life first emerged. Life issued from these waters just as the sun each day emerged from the waters of Nun to renew life for another day. Above the earth was the vault of the sky, heaven, who was called Nut, supported by four posts representing the four cardinal directions. Also supporting the sky was Shu, the air god, who lived between the earth and the sky. The earth was Geb.

Cattle also played a prominent part in the religious life of Egyptians. We have discussed earlier the cattle complex which existed in East Africa and whose influence may have reached up into Egypt. We do know that the vault of heaven was sometimes represented as the underbelly of a celestial cow dotted with stars that produced the Milky Way. The moon did not seemingly play a central part in the religious life of Egyptians. The moon god was Thoth, who was also the god of wisdom and the god of writing. We shall return to Thoth later because he is linked with the ascension of male power in Egypt in an historically unprecedented manner that is very important religiously.

The historian Henry Frankfort has written that Egyptian religion is best understood in terms of three separate but interrelated spheres of the sacred. The three central foci of spirituality for Egyptians, according to Frankfort, are: the sun, which was linked with creation; the earth, which was associated with resurrection; and cattle, which were connected to procreation (*Ancient Egyptian Religion*). Frankfort also suggests that each of these spheres may possibly reflect the development and incorporation of three separate mythic traditions, a point that we shall return to later.

Sun

The sun god, Re, was seen as the supreme god in Egypt, and he was also a divine king. The most obvious and widely discussed aspect of Egyptian religion was the sun. The sun was of central importance to the Egyptians, and it was symbolized in many ways. Most commonly, the sun was depicted as moving by a sailboat across the sky. Each night, as the sun passed through the underworld, a giant serpent would battle with the sun in an attempt to swallow him and plunge the cosmos into darkness. The sun would then arise victorious each morning, having vanquished the great water serpent, who represented chaos, darkness and death. In connection with the conquest of death by the sun, we should mention the great Sphinx of Giza. The Sphinx is a monumental piece of architecture that was constructed during the Old Kingdom (2700–2200 B.C.E.). The Sphinx has the body of a lion and a human head and symbolizes the lionlike power of victory inherent in Re, the sun god, as he conquers death each morning at sunrise.

As we have seen, the link between serpent, water and the underworld is very old and probably dates back to the Paleolithic period. Mircea Eliade, a historian of religions, has shown how the sky god often withdraws into the background, giving rise to more active deities who then form the focus of religious worship. For some peoples the sky god becomes "solarized" and manifests certain aspects of himself through the sun. Egypt represents, perhaps, the classic example of the solarization of the Supreme Being. For example, in some ancient texts Horus is depicted as the ancient sky which the Egyptians originally perceived as the Supreme Being. Horus later becomes associated with the sun where he is sometimes called Harakhte which means "Horus on the horizon." As Harakhte, the sun god was perceived by the Egyptians as a falcon. The sun for many cultures is linked with men and war. We saw for example, that the Mbuti Pygmies likened the sun's rays to spears.

It is interesting to note that Horus is a bird of prey, a falcon. As such, he was associated with hunting and warfare. Thus the sun in Egypt embodied the sacrality of maleness, and this emphasis on the male sphere of sacrality is something that continues to crop up within the religious history of Egypt. It would seem that earlier Egyptian religion emphasized a more feminine structure of the sacred through the life giving powers of the underworld waters of Nun and through the powers of Osiris, who was the goddess of the underworld and of the earth. Indeed, Horus, in the oldest mythologies in Egypt, is seen as the son of Osiris, and only later is he fused with the sun.

The sun god was also represented as Khepri, or Kheprer, which means "the becoming one." One of the bases of Egyptian religious life was cattle. The raising of cattle provided a constant, dependable meat source for the Egyptians and perhaps was a carryover from an earlier Nilotic pastoral way of life. Egyptians perceived their world partially in terms of cattle. As noted earlier, Egyptians corralled their cattle in well-marked fenced areas and stables. Egyptians were a sedentary people whose orientation to space was to and from sacred centers and cities. Dung beetles lived in and among the cattle stables of Egypt and were often observed pushing balls of dung across the sand. Eventually the dung beetle, the scarab, came to symbolize Re, the sun god. The scarab in the sky rolled the sun disk across the sky. Eventually, in Egypt, creation myths arose in which god constructed the world from his own being. The dung beetle perhaps evoked the idea of god as self-created because the dung beetle rolled his own eggs up in dung balls and pushed them across the stable floor. Pushing the dung balls, the dung beetle created himself; thus Khepri is translated as the becoming one because god, as sun, is in a perpetual state of becoming. It is also easy to see how the sun became linked with the germ of life for Egyptians because the sun, as Khepri, contained its own future existence.

The sun was also known as Atum (Aton), which means "to be complete," "to be at an end." Atum represents the sun in the evening and just prior to sunrise when the sun resides in the primordial waters of Nun. The sun, as Atum, is also seen as self-created by the time of the *Book of the Dead*. The sun became by himself. The name Atum means everything and nothing. Atum represents the universality of the divine; he transcends all things. He is therefore nothing, which the Egyptians characterize as that which is finished, completed, perfected.

At Heliopolis we get a glimpse of the many sacred dimensions that are embodied in the passage of the sun in a single day. The sun is called Khepri in the morning, Re in the afternoon, and Atum in the evening.

Finally, the sun created *maat*, the cosmic world order, who was also anthropomorphized as a female goddess. The pharaoh's duty is to make the world prosper through the primeval plans of *maat*. *Maat* was especially emphasized in the Old Kingdom, where the emphasis was on this world rather than the next.

Earth

The earth for Egyptians was connected primarily with the rhythm of resurrection. The earth includes the underworld, and the underworld is the source of water. The mouth of the Nile River is in the south and is seen as the source of life itself. The Nile River floods annually and regenerates the vegetation that died during the hot summer. Osiris was considered the lord of the underworld, and Nun was the lord of the underground waters.

In the oldest Egyptian cosmogony Atum arises out of Nun and brings with it the primeval Hillock which becomes the land. The first piece of land was a triangular shaped structure that arose from the primordial waters of chaos. This primeval Hillock is symbolized by the great pyramids of Egypt, each of which represents the creation of the world itself. Pyramids were built on the west side of the Nile, facing the setting sun. Each side of the pyramid faced a cardinal direction and was linked with it. Pyramids were always built high above the river levels so that they would not be covered in the annual floods, and their shape symbolized the rays of the sun as they radiated to earth.

Pyramids therefore represent the center of the world. They link the three vertical regions — sky, earth and underworld — with the four cardinal directions. Thus, the pyramid is the spaceless space, the place where there is no place. By drawing together the four cardinal directions and the three vertical dimensions into a single point, the pyramid overcomes the separation of the world into various aspects. The pyramid unifies the cosmos into a single place. This helps explain why the kings of Egypt, the pharaohs, were buried in pyramids in the Old Kingdom. By placing the body of the pharaohs in the pyramid, the king's soul was reunited with the cosmic spiritual essence. Furthermore, by overcoming space at the pyramid, the pharoah overcame time, for space and time presuppose one another. By reunifying the pharaoh's body with the cosmos so that their separateness was overcome, the pharaohs were granted eternity and immortality. At the center the pharaoh was returned to the timeless time, or the time before there was time, when Atum, the sun god, arose out of the primeval waters of Nun and created the world. The cosmogony was ritually re-created on a microcosmic scale at the sun temple at Heliopolis in the Old Kingdom. Beside the sun temple is a pond and a mound of dirt. The pond represents the primordial waters of Nun, out of which arose the primeval Hillock. Within the sun temple at Heliopolis there is a succession of stairways which furthermore symbolize the primeval Hillock which was pulled out of the waters. The stairway also represents the ascension into the sky of Atum.

Pharaoh

In Mesopotamia the king represented the god Marduk on earth, and yet he was also considered to be very human. In Egypt there was no question about the divinity of the pharaoh. The pharaoh was the sun god incarnate. The spirit of the pharaoh at death returned to the sun, whose spirit then inhabited a successor to the dead pharaoh. Pharaoh, as sun god, also merged with qualities of other gods. Thus the king was said to be Horus, the falcon, and often wore a falcon headdress. The king was also called Khnum, the god who brings mankind into being on his potter's wheel. Ever since the Old Kingdom the Egyptian pharaoh was referred to as "the son of Re." The pharaoh was also referred to as the Lord of the Two Lands because he was the ruler of both Upper and Lower Egypt. In this capacity he wore the double crown which symbolized the union of the two regions. He was also known as the Two Ladies because he incorporated the two goddesses who represented the north and the south.

Kingship began in Egypt. While Mesopotamian culture was older, Egyptian kingship emerged first when Menes, about 3100 B.C.E., managed to unite Upper and Lower Egypt, something that Sargon did not do in

Mesopotamia for another 650 years. Yet interestingly, Egypt never developed great cities of the scale and grandeur in Mesopotamia. Egypt was divided into many centers which were ruled by representatives of the pharaoh, who himself was god incarnate. Because of his connection with the sun, the pharaoh was considered to be the creator, the first king, whose ruling was transmitted to his son and successor, the first pharaoh. The pharaoh went to the east bank of the Nile each day and faced the rising sun in order to recreate the world for another day. The pharaoh was also linked with the earth and was charged with regulating the flow of the Nile River and the growth of crops. He was also linked with cattle and was said to have been the chief herdsman of his land. The sun god "appointed him to be shepherd of this land, to keep alive the people and the folk" (Wilson "Egypt" 79). This is a very ancient concept as shown by the fact that one of the earliest signs of the pharaoh was the shepherd's crook.

The third great sphere of religiosity for the Egyptians was cattle, which were associated with procreation. The great symbol for Egypt was the bull, who symbolized fertility. The pharaoh was seen as the chief herdsman of Egypt who was concerned with cattle and with his people, who were likened to cattle. The sky itself was seen as the great underbelly of a cow. It is likely that the office of the pharaoh derived from an earlier Nilotic kingship structure in East Africa that was linked with pastoral peoples in the southern Nile.

History

It is fair to say that Egypt leaped into being. The emergence of the Egyptian Old Kingdom out of the small agricultural communities which preceded it is difficult to grasp. In Mesopotamia culture developed very slowly and steadily over several thousand years until it culminated in the great cities of Babylonia. Egypt, by contrast, seemed to arise out of nowhere. In one sense, Egypt ended when it began.

The early dynasties (3100–2700 B.C.E.) began when Upper and Lower Egypt were united. Menes traditionally gets credit for this, but a palette depicting King Narmer wearing the two crowns of Upper and Lower Egypt has prompted some scholars to credit King Narmer with the merger. It is from this early unification that we get the idea of the pharaoh as the Lord of the Two Lands. Many historians have argued that Menes did not really unite Egypt, but simply expressed the unification through division that was already there. It was then that Horus was established as the king. The first Egyptian site has been named Abados and has a temple constructed of sand and reed, representing the primeval mound of creation. It is said that the hawk was the first creature to find the Reed Island, and this discovery was always depicted in the temples of this period. During this period a system of pictorial writing called hieroglyphics was devised.

Next came the Old Kingdom (2700–2200 B.C.E.). This was the time when Egypt was characterized by great stability. Life was good in Egypt during the Old Kingdom, and the religious emphasis was on this world. Near the Step Pyramid at Saqqara, in the tomb of an official of the Old Kingdom dated about 2400 B.C.E., emphasis on the joys of this life are clearly depicted. The ruler is shown joyfully spearing fish while his servants bring in a hippopotamus. The roping and butchering of cattle is depicted, as is the plowing and harvesting of fields. Carpenters and metal workers are shown working in their shops. Children are shown playing while criminals are vigorously punished. At times of rest the official is portrayed listening while his wife plays the harp. During the Old Kingdom only the pharaoh and a few people buried with him were thought to achieve eternal life in the next world. But this life was sacred, it was good, and the people by and large seemed happy. The pharaoh during the Old Kingdom was likened more to Re, the sun god, rather than Osiris, and his afterlife was described as celestial, rather than chthonic.

Mention should be made of the Memphite theology which developed in the Old Kingdom. Ptah, a relatively new god, was equated with the primordial waters of Nun. Ptah begat the sun, Atum, and then rested after the creation. Interestingly, Ptah was said to create the world through an act of speech. This is one of the oldest myths of creation *ex nihilo* and demonstrates an understanding of the spiritual creation out of nothingness. Ptah says, "I the all god came into being and brought being into being, I am everything and I created things in perfect order." This mythology diverges noticeably with that in Mesopotamia, where the world was created out of the chaos represented by Tiamat, the primordial waters. Furthermore, the Memphite cosmogony represents an idea of perfect order and symmetry which never occurred in Mesopotamia. In Mesopotamia there always existed something wild and nonhuman which humans could never fully master or domesticate. There was no sense in Mesopotamia that the universe was created for human beings or that human beings had mastery over the world, as was the case particularly in the Old Kingdom of Egypt.

The period from 2200–2050 B.C.E. saw the decline of the Old Kingdom and the plunging of Egypt into spiritual chaos. Here texts were written on suicide and on the collapse of the pharaoh's sacred authority. Numerous writings state that the urban way of life is not the best. Still, despite questions concerning the urban way of life, the authority of the pharaohs was never truly questioned during this period.

From 2050 to 1670 B.C.E. Egypt enjoyed what is called the Middle Kingdom. Here Thebes became the great center and Egyptian religion became more a matter of individual concern. The distance between the pharaoh and the commoners was lessened during the Middle Kingdom because each individual gained access to the spiritual plenitude and afterlife which the pharaoh previously had enjoyed by himself. Near the very end of the Old Kingdom a new religious devotion sprang up which became popular with the masses, the cult of Osiris. The popularity of this cult increased dramatically during the Middle and New Kingdoms and offered to the common masses belief that they too would have a better afterlife than their ancestors had known. Osiris's son was Horus, who became identified with pharaoh, while Osiris came to represent the pharaoh's dead predecessor. All people came to be linked with Osiris by the end of the Middle Kingdom. In one coffin of a common man we read, "I live, I die, I am Osiris…. I grow up as grain…. The earth has concealed me. I live, I die, I am barley, I do not pass away" (quoted in Garraty 75).

Commoners became more involved in the priesthood, and, indeed, opportunities opened up for people to advance within Egyptian society. At the same time, the questioning of the urban way of life, which began in the previous transition period, further developed and the people became more and more concerned with human justice. It was during the Middle Kingdom that people began to question the pharaoh's authority, and he was often blamed for ruling without justice. Some scholars consider this time to have been the culmination of Egyptian society because commoners had more access to political power and the religious life. However, it should be noted that, throughout the Middle Kingdom, more emphasis was placed on reaching the life after death, a concern that paralleled the emergence of many urban problems.

Around 1785 B.C.E. rival governors began contending with one another for the throne, and this brought about a new time of trouble. In 1674 B.C.E., the Hyksos, a Semitic Syrian people, conquered the Egyptians and ruled them for a century until 1560 B.C.E. This was a difficult period for Egyptians to fathom because of the prior invulnerability that they had enjoyed with respect to outside invaders. The Hyksos were likened to Apophis, a primordial symbol of chaos. That is to say, the loss of self-determination by the Egyptian people was perceived in mythical terms as a return to the primordial chaos that existed prior to the establishment of the world.

Finally (1560–1080 B.C.E.) the New Kingdom emerged. Here the religious symbolisms of Re, the sun god, and Osiris, the god of the underworld, were synthesized. As the historian Rundle Clark observed, Re represented divine transcendence and Osiris stood for spiritual immanence. Both aspects come to be seen as complementary forms of the sacred. The realms of the sun and underworld were inseparably interrelated so that life and death were seen as complimentary parts in an eternal cycle of rhythm and movement. Re's descent into the underworld each night was both death and resurrection. About 1369–1355 B.C.E. a pharaoh ascended the throne as Amenhotep IV. He soon changed his name to Akhenaton, which means "glory to Aton," in order to announce his faith in Aton, who became a singular god that incorporated all aspects of the other gods. Akhenaton created a theology in which Aton was seen as the god who created all peoples and all places. This was the first known development of a religious system which was universal in scope and tried to account for the religions of all people. Akhenaton was very intolerant of the older religions and defaced a number of the older shrines. However, his excessive zeal was not very successful and the movement died soon after his death. Soon after the New Kingdom waned, the Hittites, the Libyans and the Assyrians swept into Egypt and forced its final decline. Egypt, like Mesopotamia, left very little influence on present day cultures in that area. Both Mesopotamia and Egypt were initially converted to Islam and the Muslim religion by and large supplanted the older forms and structures of the people. By the Late period of Egypt, around 600 B.C.E., tombs of officials show a very different world view than was the case during the Old Kingdom. There are no pictures of the joyfulness of life. Everyday life is not depicted; rather, the walls are covered with ritual and religious text which seem obsessed with obtaining life after death. Even the afterlife is not depicted in very much detail, and the life of this world seems completely lacking. Attainment of the afterlife seems to be the primary concern of these people by this period. In that sense, the Late period of Egypt corresponds to a degree with Mesopotamia during the time of Hammurabi when life in this world came to be so problematical that the primary concern shifted largely to the next world.

Anthropomorphism and the Problem of the Wild

Egypt, more than Mesopotamia, perceived the world in human terms. In Egypt there was a sense of self-sufficiency about the human way of life which was not the case in Mesopotamia. In Egypt the human way of life seemed to be particularly blessed and life seemed to be very good. It was almost as though the world was created just for the Egyptians. The independent self-reliance of Egyptians during the Pyramid Age stands apart from Mesopotamian religious life. In Mesopotamia humans were utterly dependent upon the will of the gods for survival. In Egypt, early on, the gods were very distant and humans worshipped primarily by paying homage to the pharaoh, who himself kept the world going through the primeval plans of *maat*. There seems to be very little question in the early periods of Egypt about whether or not the Egyptian way of life was good and whether it would survive.

This emphasis on humanity occasioned among Egyptians an anthropomorphic outlook which stands in naked contrast to the cosmomorphic view of Paleolithic humans. Whereas hunting-gathering peoples largely understood their own way of life in terms of the embodiment of the principles of the natural world, Egyptians projected the human principles and values onto the natural world. Unlike the Mesopotamians, for whom an element of wildness was always present, as, for example, was demonstrated by the wild man Enkidu, Egyptians attempted to humanize their world. The pharaoh was human and was also the embodiment of the sun god. The human way of life was exemplary for Egyptians. Perhaps this helps us to understand the widespread dissemination of creation myths in which an omniscient, omnipresent god created the world through speech and thought, distinctly human acts. In one Egyptian text it is stated that mankind was made in the image of god. "Well tended are men, the cattle of god. He made heaven and earth according to their desire.... they are his images that have issued from his body. He arises in heaven according to their desire" (quoted in Wilson "Egypt" 55).

The notion that the universe was made specifically to fulfill the desires of humans is not found in Mesopotamia. Still, Egyptians were religious. It is not that Egyptians were their own masters and lived in a world without gods; it is the case that the gods in Egypt made the world according to human beings.

Significantly, the culmination of the Middle Kingdom saw two important medical texts arise which are important religiously. Scholars have found small fragments of medical papyri, the oldest of which, *Kahun Papyrus*, dates from about 1900 B.C.E. The medical historian Ilza Veith has shown that this ancient text deals specifically with a female disorder, hysteria. Egyptian medicine linked most behavioral disorders with some bodily organ. Hysteria was caused by aberrations in the position of the womb. For Egyptians, the womb was considered to be an animal with a life of its own whose movements within the bodies of women could cause sickness. Treatment involved using sweet-smelling substances to attract the womb to its proper position, or foul-smelling materials to repel the womb from the upper part of the body to where it belonged.

The Egyptian concern for the hysteria phenomenon was furthermore expressed in a later text, *Papyrus Ebers*, which dates back to about 1600 B.C.E. In a chapter entitled "Diseases of Women" detailed treatments are outlined "to cause a woman's womb to go to its place" (Veith 5). Again, numerous fumigation treatments to lure the womb into place are mentioned. The most drastic treatment to realign the womb requires that an ibis of wax be melted so that the fumes enter the vulva. The god Thoth was symbolized by an ibis. Thoth personified the moon and was linked with the sun. He was the god of writing, medicine and wisdom. Thoth was a minor god until the Middle Kingdom, when he became more powerful. The rise of hysteria and the culmination of the Egyptian Middle Kingdom may be more than coincidental.

Egypt, as noted earlier, personified order. The sun was paramount and nothing was wild. Moreover, Egypt's solar religion emphasized male sacrality and concerns. It was within this anthropomorphic, male-dominated world that psychological female disorders like hysteria arose. The dominance of men over nature and women occasioned an eruption of female potency and power through hysteria. Egyptian religion became solarized and male such that the essential, life-giving, passive powers linked with women were eclipsed. The power of birth was linked with the womb and, therefore, the womb was the locus of hysterical phenomena. In the end, Egyptians recognized the "wildness" of the womb as a wandering animal. The anthropomorphic, male kingdom of Egypt tried to ignore the power of the female as manifested in a specifically female manner.

Interestingly, Thoth, the god of writing, was invoked to try and corral the migratory, animalistic forces that inhabited women. The god of writing exemplified the maleness of the kingdom, which is contrasted to a life of wandering. While the history of religions has many times shown the powerful connection between earth, agriculture and women, the feminine forces reach back into Paleolithic meandering. Agriculture, while initially viewed as female, often corresponds with the development of anthropomorphic world views and male political dominance. With that process may come a repression of the female structure of the sacred which is, arguably, what happened in Egypt during the Middle Kingdom. But the passivity of the sacred as revealed through women eventually expressed itself through hysterical phenomena.

With the stability and serenity of Egypt's kingdoms, humans became emphasized in a poignant way. Then, with male dominance, the receptivity of the sacred as expressed through birth was trivialized and overshadowed. But it could not be eliminated. Women inhabit a primordial spiritual plane that manifests itself in the most everyday and profane circumstances. It seems more than happenstance that Sigmund Freud, in the late nineteenth century, founded psychoanalysis through the rediscovery of hysteria in the rational, repressive, male-dominated world of Victorian Austria.

Bibliography
Chapter 4 — Egypt

Aldred, Cyril. *New Kingdom Art in Ancient Egypt during the Eighteenth Dynasty.* London, 1951.
Allen, T.C. *The Book of the Dead, or Going Forth by Day.* Chicago, 1974.
Armour, Robert A. *Gods and Myths of Ancient Egypt.* Cairo, Egypt, 1986.
Assmann, Jan. *English Egyptian Solar Religion in the New Kingdom: Re, Amun and the Crisis of Polytheism.* Trans. Anthony Alcock. London and New York, 1995.
_____. *Moses the Egyptian: The Memory of Egypt in Western Montheism.* Cambridge, Massachusetts, 1997.
Baumgartel, E.J. *The Cultures of Prehistoric Egypt.* London, 1955.
Bleeker, C.J. *Egyptian Festivals: Enactments of Religious Renewal.* Leiden, 1967.
_____. *Hathor and Thoth: Two Key Figures of the Ancient Egyptian Religion.* Leiden, 1973.
_____. "The Religion of Ancient Egypt." *Historia Religionum: Handbook for the History of Religions.* C.J. Bleeker and G. Widengren. Editors. Leiden, 1969.
Bolshakov, Andrey O. *Man and His Double in Egyptian Ideology of the Old Kingdom.* Wiesbaden, 1997.
Breasted, J.H. *Ancient Records of Egypt.* 5 Vols. Chicago, 1906–1907.
_____. *The Development of Religion and Thought in Ancient Egypt.* New York, 1912.
Bull, Ludlow. "Ancient Egypt." *The Idea of History in the Ancient Near East.* Robert C. Dentan. Editor. New Haven, Connecticut, 1955.
Cerny, Jaroslav. *Ancient Egyptian Religion.* London and New York, 1952.
Clark, R.T. Rundle. *Myth and Symbol in Ancient Egypt.* London, 1959.
Cleveland, Ingrid T. *The Egyptian Cults in Ancient Rome: A Study of the Diffusion and Popularity of the Cults in Roman Society.* M.A. Thesis. Central Missouri State University, 1987, 90 pp. typescript.
David, A. Rosalie. *The Ancient Egyptians: Religious Beliefs and Practices.* London, 1982.
_____. *Cult of the Sun: Myth and Magic in Ancient Egypt.* London, 1980.
Edwards, I.E.S. *The Pyramids of Egypt.* Harmondsworth, 1961.
Eliade, Mircea. *A History of Religious Ideas.* Vol. 1. Trans. Willard R. Trask. Chicago, 1978, pp. 85–113, 400–409.
_____. *Patterns in Comparative Religion.* Trans. Rosemary Sheed. New York, 1958.
Emery, W.B. *Archaic Egypt.* Harmondsworth, 1963.
Engberg, Robert M. *The Hyksos Reconsidered.* Chicago, 1939.
Faulkner, R.O. "The Dispute of a Man Weary of Life." *Journal of Egyptian Archeology* 42 (1956): 21–40.
Finnestad, R.B. "Ptah, Creator of the Gods." *Numen* 23 (1976): 81–113.

Foster, John L. *Hymns, Prayers and Songs: An Anthology of Ancient Egyptian Lyric Poetry.* Atlanta, Georgia, 1996.
Frankfort, Henri. *Ancient Egyptian Religion.* New York, 1948.
_____. *The Birth of Civilization in the Near East.* London, 1951.
_____. *Kingship and the Gods: A Study of Ancient Near Eastern Religion as the Integration of Society and Nature.* Chicago, 1948.
Garraty, John, and Peter Gay. "Egypt." *The Columbia History of the World.* New York, 1972: 67–81.
Harris, J.R. *The Legacy of Egypt.* Oxford, 1971.
Hayes, William C. *The Scepter of Egypt.* Vol. 1. *From the Earliest Times to the End of the Middle Kingdom.* New York, 1953.
Ions, Veronica. *Egyptian Mythology.* New York, 1983.
Johnson, Sally B. *The Cobra Goddess of Ancient Egypt: Predynastic, Early Dynastic, and Old Kingdom Periods.* London and New York, 1990.
Kristensen, William Brede. *Life Out of Death: Studies in the Religions of Egypt and of Ancient Greece.* Louvian, 1992.
Lesko, Barbara. "Egyptian Religion: An Overview." *Encyclopedia of Religion.* Mircea Eliade. Editor-in-Chief. New York, 1987: 37–54.
_____. *Women's Earliest Records: From Ancient Egypt and Western Asia.* Atlanta, 1989.
Lichteim, Miriam. *Maat in Egyptian Autobiographies and Related Studies.* Freiburg and Schweiz, 1992.
Meeks, Dimitri, and Christine Favard-Meeks. *Daily Life of the Egyptian Gods.* Ithaca, New York, 1996.
Morenz, Siegfried. *Egyptian Religion.* Trans. Ann Keep. Ithaca, New York, 1973.
Murray, Margaret. *The Splendour That Was Egypt.* London, 1949.
Raymond, E.A.E. *The Mythical Origin of the Egyptian Temple.* Manchester, England, 1969.
Sadek, Ashraf I. *Popular Religion in Egypt during the New Kingdom.* Hildesheim, 1987.
Saleh, A. "The So-Called 'Primeval Hill' and Other Related Elevations in Ancient Egyptian Mythology." *Mitteilungen des Deutschen Archaologischen Instituts* 25 (1969): 110–120.
Save-Soderbergh. "The Hyksos Rule in Egypt." *Journal of Egyptian Archeology* 37 (1951): 53–72.
Simpson, William Kelly. Editor. *The Literature of Ancient Egypt.* New Haven, Connecticut, 1973.
Veith, Ilza. *Hysteria: The History of a Disease.* Chicago and London, 1965.
Voss, M. Heerma van. Editor. *Studies in Egyptian Religion: Dedicated to Professor Jan Zandee.* Leiden, 1982.
Wilson, John A. *The Culture of Ancient Egypt.* Chicago, 1951.
_____. "Egypt." *Intellectual Adventure of Ancient Man: An Essay on Speculative Thought and Ancient Near East.* Henri Frankfort, et al. Editors. Chicago, 1946.
Winlock, H.E. *The Rise and Fall of the Middle Kingdom in Thebes.* New York, 1947.
Zabkar, Louis. *A Study of the Ba Concept in Ancient Egyptian Texts.* Chicago, 1968.
Zandee, J. *Death as an Enemy According to Ancient Egyptian Conceptions.* Leiden, 1960.

CHAPTER 5

India and Hinduism

Unlike Mesopotamia and Egypt, India possesses a great sense of cultural and religious continuity from the Neolithic to the present. The *enuma elish* is no longer recited and ritually reenacted in Mesopotamia, and there are no more pharaohs in Egypt; but in India, Vedas are still chanted, and religious symbols and meanings which arose in the earliest Neolithic continue to influence the religious lives of the people. Perhaps because of the profound link with the past, Indians demonstrate little concern about their history. It has been said that Indians live their history; they do not write about it. Until recently there were very few Indian scholars who chronicled the unique events that make up their history. Indians have truly changed little since the Neolithic, and the transformations that did occur have been engulfed in mythology. This perhaps helps us to understand India's lack of social reform prior to Mohandas Gandhi. India has seen very few political revolts to change history because, in India, there is no history to change.

The Vedic Indians practiced agriculture, but their economy was primarily pastoral. Cattle performed the function of money. Milk and its products were eaten, as was the meat of cattle. Horses were highly esteemed but were used only for raiding and for the royal rituals. The Neolithic Revolution occurred in Northwest India in what is today Pakistan. Between 2500 and 1500 B.C. over sixty towns were constructed portraying a kingdom twice the size of Egypt. Two cities, Harappa and Mohenjo-daro, brought to light the existence of a mercantile and theocratic urban community. Harappa, in particular, is most notable for its almost total lack of change or innovation for over a thousand years. While Harappan technology equaled that in Egypt and Mesopotamia, the majority of its products lack creativity, which professors Allchin interpret as suggesting that the Harrapan people focused their attention on another world. The incredible sense of continuity and uniformity in the city of Harappa seems best explained by the presence of a strong religious leadership.

One important find, excavated near the Porali River and called the "Edith Shahr Complex," has a mound seven to twelve meters high together with a number of walled structures. The mound rose at its summit in the form of a ziggurat, and several stairways led to a platform. This complex seems to have been very rarely inhabited, and all indications are that it was used for ceremonial purposes primarily. The historian Walter Fairservis argues that both Mohenjo-daro and Harappa were originally ceremonial centers, a point some scholars dispute, but certainly the sites were important religiously for these people.

Harappa was located on the Ravi River and Mohenjo-daro on the Indus River. These cities were about 400 miles apart and yet quite similar. Each was built upon successive layers and had a well-structured monotonous gridding, which seems to indicate that both cities were planned. At Mohenjo-daro there was a great water tank, probably used for ritual purification, but that is difficult to say since their written scripture remains untranslated. The language of these people has more than 250 characters.

While we cannot yet translate the language, we have uncovered numerous symbols of fertility. Scholars have found a number of female figurines, and also male symbols such as the bull, unicorn and water buffalo. Interestingly, the female figurines are reminiscent of the Venus statuettes of the Paleolithic period. Sir John Marshall uncovered a three-faced deity with horns and an erect penis who sat in a yogic position. He was surrounded by wild animals and probably represented the prototype of the Hindu god Shiva. Various tree spirits are depicted on a number of seals. A number of artworks show the use of the turban, nasal ornaments and the ivory comb, all of which were unknown in Vedic texts. Interestingly, the proto-Shiva is sitting in a lotus position with an ascetic hairstyle. Often depicted in the artwork of Indus Valley cities is the fig tree which later symbolizes Buddhism. Also uncovered at Harappa was an image of a "speaking tree." Legend has it that a speaking tree told Alexander the Great that India could not be conquered because its cyclical rhythms ultimately engulf everything.

The Indus Valley peoples traded with Mesopotamia by land and sea. The empire of these peoples seems to have been more priestly than warlike. In other words, the Indus Valley was more like Egypt than Mesopotamia. Very few walls and weapons have been uncovered at Mohenjo-daro and Harappa. This is a bit surprising since the Ravi and Indus rivers are quite violent and unpredictable like the Tigris and Euphrates rivers of Mesopotamia. We do not know what led to the decline of the Indus Valley civilization, but between 1750 and 1500 B.C.E. a combination of floods, internal problems and invasion from the Indo-European speaking Aryans from the north (Iran?) resulted in the fall of these cities. The light-skinned Aryans ("noble folk") who invaded from the north conquered the cities of the Indus Valley, but the cadence and vacillations of the cities, in turn, assimilated them. The mingling of these two peoples is reflected historically in the Vedic literature which followed. The Aryans called the original inhabitants *dasa* or *dasyu* ("Dravidians"), who were a dark-skinned people. The Aryans wrote of the widespread fertility rites of the native peoples which the Aryans found disgusting. Aryans spoke Sanskrit, an Indo-European language related to Persian, Latin, Celtic, German and Greek.

The historian of religions George Dumezil notes that Indo-European peoples tended to structure society according to a tripartite division — priest, warriors and merchants. Or it may be more accurate to say that Indo-Europeans at least talked about society as though it were divided into three parts. The famous caste system, or *varna* ("color"), seems to be of Indo-European origin. It was not until after the coming of the Aryans that society in India is divided into four basic castes: Brahmin — priest; Ksatriya — warrior; Vaisya — merchant; and Sudra — servant. The varna is further subdivided into thousands of *jati* which represent the many occupations of the India subcontinent.

Indian religious literature is so vast that one cannot read it all. In a sense, Indian religious writings destroy the significance of the written word through its overwhelming volume. Unlike Christianity, Indian religion does not have a closed canon. Indeed, religious literature is still being written in India to this very day.

Vedas

The oldest written religious literature that has been deciphered in India are the Vedas (1200–800 B.C.E.). Veda means "knowledge." Vedas are meant to be chanted and are part of the *Sruti* ("hearing") tradition along with the Brahmanas and Upanishads. They are collections of hymns and formulae called Samhitas. There are four Vedas — *Rig*, *Sama*, *Yajur* and *Atharva*. The *Rig Veda* is the most revered, and its tenth chapter is considered the most philosophical, although it is primarily a supplement to the horse sacrifice (Asvamedha).

The horse sacrifice is clearly Indo-European in origin. A new year festival, the horse sacrifice linked a horse with the cosmos ("Prajapati"). The horse's sacrifice reproduced the creation of the world. Only the king performed the horse sacrifice, and he did so for the good of the entire world. At the moment of sacrifice a priest asked that all people within the kingdom do their social duties and that rain fall, cows give milk, and crops ripen. The horse sacrifice regenerated the cosmos and reestablished all social classes and vocations. In Vedic India cosmic order was denoted by the term *rta* and the horse sacrifice resuscitated *rta* to ensure the existence of the world for another year. But the horse also represented royal power, *ksatra*, and hence, the king. The rite was also symbolic of Yama, the creator god, and Aditya, the sun.

This connection between the king and the sun in India parallels the solar symbolism of Egypt. The sacrifice of the horse represented the destruction of the old year so that the world could be recreated anew. With time the ceremony got very complex; eventually priests recognized more than 240,000 parts of the horse, each of which corresponded to a particular part of the kingdom. The horse was allowed to roam for one year and the land circled by the horse became the cosmos and kingdom. In traversing the boundaries of the world the horse symbolically created the world. During the course of the year the world lost its energy and vitality. Then, at the end of the year, the horse, which represented the entire cosmos, was suffocated, cut up and burned, thus representing the reversion of the world into the primordial waters of chaos, so that the world could be regenerated.

Eventually, human sacrifice ("Purusamedha") replaced the horse sacrifice. In Purusamedha, the sacrificial victim represented the god Purusa-Prajapati. Purusa was a cosmic giant who was sacrificed in the beginning of time to create the world. This theme of creation-by-sacrifice was encountered earlier in Mesopotamia and shall be seen again in the Chinese myth of Pan'ku. In the Purusamedha a Brahmin priest or a Ksatriya warrior was purchased for one thousand cows and one hundred horses. It seems questionable as to whether a human was ever actually sacrificed, and we do know that a horse was often substituted at the last moment in this ritual.

In the Vedas, *maya* is also mentioned alongside *rta*. Maya comes from the root *may*, which means "to change." In the *Rig Veda*, *maya* designates good and evil alterations of the world. *Maya* may impair cosmic order, or it may sustain cosmic order. *Maya* is both creation and destruction, but in either case it can be seen how the later concept of *maya* as cosmic illusion or non-being was foreshadowed by the earlier Vedic notion of *maya* as change, or transformation.

Vedic Cosmogony

Four types of creation mythologies are outlined in Vedic literature. In the first type the world is created by the fertilization of the original primeval waters. In *Rig Veda* 10.121, Hiranyagarbha ("Golden Embryo") enters the primeval waters and fertilizes them. The primeval waters then give birth to Agni, the god of fire. In a second creation myth found in *Rig Veda* 10.90, a primeval giant (Purusa) exists in the beginning. He represents the cosmic totality. The other gods sacrifice him and create the world from his dismembered parts — the sky comes from his head, the earth from his feet, the moon from his consciousness, the sun from his gaze, and the wind from his breath. In a third Vedic cosmogony, 10.129, the world is created out of a unity-totality. In the beginning there exists the One, which is simultaneously being and non-being. The One creates the world from himself and generates heat ("tapas") from his ascetic meditation. From this heat develops an embryo which represents cosmic potentiality. Potentiality creates kama, or desire, which is the first seed of consciousness. With the first seed of consciousness comes the creation of the world. Finally, *Rig Veda* 1.32 states that, in the beginning, there was a cosmic serpent named Vrtra. Indra kills Vrtra with a thunderbolt and dissects her, thus separating heaven and earth and creating the world. This myth also parallels the Mesopotamian myth, the *enuma elish,* in which Marduk severed Tiamat to create heaven and earth.

Vedic Deities

A number of scholars have described the Vedic worship of gods as Cathenotheism, which means the worship of many gods, one at a time. There were many gods in Vedic India.

As in many Neolithic civilizations, Dyaus Pitar, the sovereign, celestial god, recedes into the background where his name becomes Sky or Day. He becomes a hidden god and is supplanted by Varuna, who becomes the sovereign god. Varuna reigns over the world, the gods, Devas and human beings. He sees everything, knows everything and is infallible. As *Rig Veda* 15.85.1–2 states, Varuna put "milk in cows, intelligence in hearts, fire in the waters, and the sky the sun, *soma* on the mountain." Varuna is intimately linked with two religious concepts that are very important in Indian religion, *rta* and *maya*. His ascendancy to the top of the Vedic pantheon seems to parallel the Aryan conquest of India.

Indra is the most popular god in the *Rig Veda*. Some 250 hymns are addressed to him. He is clearly the hero without rival. The most important myth in the *Rig Veda* is the myth in which Indra slays the giant dragon, Vrtra, who held back the waters in the "hollow of the mountains." Strengthened by soma, Indra slays the serpent Vrtra with his thunderbolt, splits open his head and frees the waters.

Mention should also be made of two gods who played a small role in the Vedas, but who assumed great importance in classical Hinduism, Rudra-Shiva and Vishnu. In *Rig Veda* 1.186.10 Vishnu appears as a divinity who is friendly towards human beings by helping Indra in his battle against Vrtra. Vishnu is later identified with sacrifice in the *Satapatha Brahmana* 14.1.1.6. Vishnu is linked with Prajapati later in the Brahmanas, but it is not until the Upanishads, about the fourth century B.C., that Vishnu is exalted as a supreme god.

Rudra-Shiva is a god with no friends who is armed with bows and arrows and dressed in animal skins. He is associated with a number of demonic beings. Rudra-Shiva lives in the forests and jungles and is called lord of the wild beasts (Satapatha Brahmana 12.7.3.20). He appears to represent the demonic, or perhaps more accurately, the wild and undomesticated. It is interesting that not only is he linked with wild animals and uninhabited places, his mysterious powers can be directed towards good since he is also called physician of physicians. Later in the Upanishads he also becomes a supreme being and one of the prominent gods of classical Hinduism. The sun god is Mitri, who is linked with Varuna and is also seen as a sovereign god. It is said that the sun is the eye of Varuna.

Finally, there are the earthly gods. Here Agni was seen as a messenger between the sky and earth. He was eternally young and was reborn with each and every fire. Agni dispelled darkness, disease and sorcery. Agni, as fire, was also associated with lightening and the sun. In one myth it was said that he came from the waters. According to another myth, Agni penetrated the waters and fertilized them. He is very intelligent and is linked with the sun and indirectly with the tapas or heat of yoga.

Mention should also be made of Soma, the drink of non-death. Soma is a plant which grows at the center of the world according to *Rig Veda* 10.82.3 and he is a friend especially of Indra who gives courage and immortality to those who drink of his essence.

The Brahmanas

The Brahmanas were written from 1000 to 700 B.C.E. in India. Concerned with the creation of the world by the god Purusa, the *Purusasukta* represents the point of departure for this phase of Indian religious literature. Purusa gave himself for the creation of the world. Prajapati, the created world, suffers exhaustion after his formation and must be regenerated. In the Brahmanas, Purusa represents chaos while Prajapati represents order. Purusa-Prajapati thus represents the two aspects of Brahman, the unity-totality. Desire (*kama*) prompted the unity and totality to multiply and reproduce himself (Satapatha Brahmana 6.1.1). He heated himself by asceticism and emanated the Vedas by sweat or seminal emission. The word of the Vedas created the waters and penetrated them to give birth to the egg, or earth.

Prajapati represents the universe, the year and the fire altar. Sacrifice in the Brahmanas comes to be seen as the sacrifice of chaos, Purusa, in order to create the world of order, Prajapati. The horse sacrifice symbolizes both acts simultaneously. Prajapati exhausts himself each year. His joints, which represent day and night, full and new moon, become dislocated. Through the fire sacrifice, Prajapati is reconstituted for another year (Satapatha Brahmana 1.6.3; 10.4.2.2). The fire sacrifice is done daily to the rising sun in order to reconstitute the world for another day (Satapatha Brahmana 2.3.1.5).

Soon a new meaning emerges. The sacrifice of the horse not only restores Prajapati, but also creates a spiritual being, *atman*. In rejoining Prajapati, the sacrificer performs the same act on himself. This makes possible a new mode of being in Indian religious life. The sacrificer now identifies himself with Prajapati and ascends to heaven where he himself attains immortality (Satapatha Brahmana 10.2.6.8). By sacrificing a horse, the priest gets *atman* just as the gods get *brahman* (Satapatha Brahmana 11.2.3.6) Through sacrifice, which itself is based ultimately on the cosmongonic myth, both humans and the gods receive immortality. Prajapati is likened to *brahman*, and *brahman* and *atman* are the same. Through the repetition of the creation myth the universe is sustained through *brahman*. In the Brahmanas cosmic order now is adumbrated by the notion of *brahman* rather than *rta*, as it was in the Vedas, and *brahman* comes to be seen as *prana*, or breath.

The Vedas were concerned primarily with the maintenance of the cosmic rhythms upon which Indian lives depended. In the Brahmanas, Indian religious literature develops its first notion of life after death through the Doctrine of the Five Fires. The Brahmanas are concerned very much with the fundamental basis of cosmic order. Throughout the Brahmanas the writers seek, within the rhythms of life and death, chaos and order, that which is eternal and unchanging. The Brahmanas conclude that the structure of the cosmos, which is shared by the gods and humans alike, is breath, or *prana*. The central rituals in India at this time are various fire rituals which are performed daily, annually and at major transition points of life, such as birth, marriage and death.

The Brahmanas developed the Doctrine of the Five Fires, which foreshadowed the later doctrine of reincarnation. The first fire is the fire ritual which may be performed at a number of occasions. The fire ritual was performed daily in Indian households, and at other auspicious times such as birth, marriage, death and the New Year. The fire rite represents the first fire. The smoke which rises from the fire and ascends into the sky to the clouds is the second fire. The third fire represents the clouds which are formed from the rising smoke and which drop rain to the earth. Fourth, crops drink rain, then grow, and then are harvested and eaten by human beings. Finally, there is the fifth fire. Men, who are sustained by the crops, plant their seed in women. Women give birth to babies, some of whom are boys who become priests that conduct the fire rituals, or heads of households who offer the daily fire rites to the gods (*Agnihotta*). Finally, all people die and are burned on the funeral pyre, which itself is a first fire.

That which is eternal and constant throughout the Doctrine of the Five Fires is *prana*, or breath. Breath is eternal, everlasting and omnipresent and embodies the spiritual foundation of Indian religion during the period of the Brahmanas. Breath is moist, and thus babies who are created from the fluids of human beings are moist, while elderly people who are nearing the end of their lives are dry and brittle.

The Aranyakas

Between 700 and 300 B.C.E. Indian religious literature became quite sophisticated. In the Brahmanas the multiplicity of Vedic gods was ultimately subsumed under the umbrella of the god Prajapati, who became the primary god of the horse sacrifice. The Aranyakas culminated in the Upanishads in which the horse sacrifice became spiritualized further. The priests of the Aranyakas are *rishis*. They are religious zealots who withdraw from society. *Rishis* ask each other profound riddles, the purpose of which is to uncover the deepest meanings of the horse sacrifice. The emergence of *Rishis* parallels the development of urbanity in India. The Indian cities, like others, were initially grounded upon ceremonial centers. But Indian cities at this point in history were experiencing the same problems that eventually arose in Mesopotamia and Egypt. In India, the religious significance of the ceremonial center declined and worldly problems emerged.

It was during this period of time in India that Indian religion underwent a fundamental shift. The primary religious emphasis became the quest for religious meaning, values and purposes that are not of this world. Indeed, concentration on transcending the values and meaning of the city is denoted in the very term of the Aranyakas, which means "of the forest." The Aranyakas begin the Indian process of critiquing spiritual paths that find satisfaction from the things of this world. As the *Katha Upanishad* states, the self is not to be sought through the senses.

Religious leaders of the Upanishads internalized the meaning of the horse sacrifice. Each individual body becomes linked with the cosmos. A horse is described no longer as marking the geographical boundaries of the world in external space, but as running within each person's own body. Every individual comes to be seen as Purusa so that there is a unity between each person and the world. Because it is a knowledge that would destroy the city, the profound spiritual meanings of the horse sacrifice can only be discussed in the woods. The way of wisdom now replaces the way of sacrifice. *Jnana kanda*, the way of wisdom, now replaces *karman kanda*, sacrificial acts, as the primary path to divinity. The Upanishads state that the gods are hidden inside human beings. Through what has been called the "interiorization of sacrifice" there emerges a desire to know the sacred by knowing one's own person. Therefore the true sacred center is no longer found at the ceremonial center, but within each person.

The Aranyakas culminate in the Upanishads, which means "secret teachings." The world of sacrificial acts perishes. *Rishis* now seek immortality through wisdom. As the *Brhadaranyaka Upanishad* 1.3.28 states, "From non-being lead me to being; from darkness lead me to light; from death lead me to immortality." However, the change of emphasis from sacrifice to meditation is not abrupt or complete during the Upanishads. The Upanishads still very much talk about the horse sacrifice in cosmic terms. For example, in the *Brhadaranyaka Upanishad* dawn is likened to the head of the sacrificial horse — the sun is its eyes, the wind is its breath, the sky is its back, and the year is the horse itself. Thus the old cosmic symbolism of the horse sacrifice is still discussed alongside this new emphasis on the spiritualization of ritual activity.

The horse sacrifice is said to yield the eternal *atman*. Furthermore, at this time in Indian religious history a new concept develops called *karma*. All acts are said to have consequences. Because all acts have consequences, a blissful afterlife is not eternal because the *atman* must continue. Because the effects of one's life must continue into a new existence, the soul, *atman*, becomes reincarnated in a new life. *Samsara*, or the doctrine of reincarnation, first appears in the Upanishads in connection with a new goal, *moksha*, which is the release from *karma* and *samsara*. Since every act perpetuates *samsara*, sacrifice cannot fully release one from the cosmic cycles of life, death and rebirth. The only way to be released from this eternal cycle of rebirths is through the destruction of ignorance, *avidya*. Through wisdom one can overcome one's attachment to the world and find final spiritual release of the *atman*.

It is interesting that this emphasis on seeking liberation from rebirth parallels the development of urban life in India. It appears that the combination of urban problems and the increased sophistication of religious thought prompted Indians to seek disengagement from this world into a purely spiritual plane. Aside from the historical problems of the city, all humans suffer disease and death. Indian religious understanding takes for granted that death is followed by a rebirth into a new life. But for Indians this comes to be seen negatively as a spiritual trap from which each person ultimately seeks escape into spiritual bliss.

The name for the One of the beginning is *brahman*. *Brahman* is described in the *Chandogya Upanishad* 3.14.2–4 as "the whole world," which is nonetheless "spiritual in nature." *Brahman* dwells in the earth, yet the earth knows him not, according to the *Brhadaranyaka Upanishad* 3.7.3. *Brahman* is greater than these worlds, yet is also *atman*, smaller than a barley grain or a mustard seed (*Chandogya Upanishad* 3.14.2–4). Thus, Brahman is immanent, yet transcendent, distinct from the cosmos, yet omnipresent in the world. Brahman inhabits the heart of humans, yet transcends the entire universe.

It is important to keep in mind that, for Indians, the Upanishads are a spiritual exercise, not a chain of reasoning. The Upanishads offered to Indians a way of touching the sacred. This was done by yoga, a technique credited to Pantanjali, who may have lived some time in the second century B.C.E. Pantanjali outlined an eight-fold path of yoga which constitutes the basis of Indian meditation techniques. The first path contains the five yamas, which concern moral behavior. These are non injury, truthfulness, honesty, chastity and no greed. The second step contains the niyamas, or mental virtues: purity and cleanliness of body and diet, contentment, austerity, study and meditation. The third stage in yoga is asana, or seat. In asana the yogic learns to sit still, stopping all bodily fluctuations. Then comes the fourth step, prana yama, or breath control. Pantanjali discovered that psychic states correspond to breath rates. Thus, by controlling one's breath, one controls one's state of mind. The fifth step is pratyahara, which means "to free the senses from the domination of external objects." Sixth is dharana, which is the steady power of concentration. The seventh step is dhyana, which means meditation on symbols. Some of the most popular symbols of meditation for yogas are "thou art that," "I am *brahman*" and "om," the significance of which we will discuss shortly. Finally, the eighth step of yoga is samadhi, which means concentration. By concentrating on a single point, one gains access to unlimited reality. Those who attain liberation from the world while living are called *jivanmukta*.

Indians discovered that there were several states of consciousness: waking, dreaming, deep sleep and the fourth state. Each of these were related to breathing rates. The slower one breathes, the less awake one is. Dreams are important, but they come from the gross external body and cannot be understood until one awakes, at which point the dream ends. Since one does not control the gross body, one does not control dreams and other states. Through yoga, Indians attempted to penetrate all states of consciousness in order to achieve a fluidity of consciousness that transcended all senses and matter. To be autonomous, to be free of the world, is the goal. Then one can see the spiritual essence, "the horse inside one's self." Through yoga one seeks the true self through self exploration and control, but what one finds is that the authentic self is not the personal ego. The real self transcends all things, even breath (*prana*). In the Upanishads, Indians discovered that the true self is absolutely free of all matter; it is *atman*, which is the same as *brahman*. Yoga helps one realize that one's eternal self is *brahman*. Thus, the yogic exclaims *tat tvam asi*—"thou art that," or "I am *brahman*." With the realization of one's spiritual goal, subject becomes object, knower becomes known. One attains unity with the world, but it is a unity of which one is aware. Thus, as Mircea Eliade noted, yogic bliss is transconsciousness, not unconsciousness. By recognizing that reality is spirit, the yoga is freed from sticky *karma* and attains release, *moksha*.

Ultimately, the unity between self and world cannot be described except negatively through three predicates that are outlined for teaching purposes to differentiate transconsciousness from animality, death or the simple extinction of consciousness. The unity between *atman* and *brahman* is not *sat* (existence), it is not *chit* (consciousness), and it is not *ananda* or bliss. In discussing this non-differentiation between person and world, Upanishadic writers also use the terms *kam* (bliss) and *kham* (space). Whereas bliss is normally seen as temporary and internal, space is seen as eternal and universal, and *samadhi* is eternal bliss.

The doctrine of cosmic consequences, *karma*, leads to the doctrine of *samsara*, or reincarnation. Reincarnation becomes problematic because the world is profane due to urban development and also because there is always suffering and death. The specifically human vicissitudes of city life overshadow the sacrality of the center which created the city, and thus people look elsewhere for divinity. It is within this context that yoga arises. To find the god within, one must first stop bodily fluctuations. One must learn to sit still. Next, one must control psychic fluctuations by controlling one's breath. When one can achieve this freedom over body and mind, one discovers one's true self, *atman*. Indeed, it is *atman* that allows one to gain such discovery of one's true self through body and mind control.

There are a number of interesting stories in the Upanishads which outline the spiritual essence of ultimate reality. In the *Brhadaranyaka Upanishad* 3.6, Gargi, a female student, goes through a series of questions with her teacher, Yajnavlkya.

> Then Gargi Vacaknavi questioned him, saying: "Yajnavlkya, since this whole universe is woven, warp and woof, on water, what is it on which water is woven, warp and woof?" "On the wind, Gargi," said he. "What is it, then, on which the wind is woven, warp and woof?" "On the worlds of the atmosphere, Gargi." "What is it, then, on which the worlds of the atmosphere are woven, warp and woof?" "On the worlds of the Gandharvas, Gargi." "What is it, then, on which the worlds of the Gandharvas are woven, warp and woof?" "On the worlds of the sun, Gargi." "What is it, then, on which the worlds of the sun are woven, warp and woof?" "On the worlds of the moon, Gargi." "What is it, then, on which the worlds of the moon are woven, warp and woof?" "On the worlds of the stars, Gargi." "What is it, then, on which the worlds of the stars are woven, warp and woof?" "On the worlds of the gods, Gargi." "What is it, then, on which the worlds of the gods are woven, warp and woof?" "On the worlds of Indra, Gargi." "What is it, then, on which the worlds of Indra are woven, warp and woof?" "On the worlds of Prajapati, Gargi." "What is it, then, on which the worlds of Prajapati are woven, warp and woof?" "On the worlds of Brahman, Gargi." "What is it, then, on which the worlds of Brahman are woven, warp and woof?" "Gargi," he said, "do not question overmuch lest your head should fall off. You are asking too many questions about a deity about which too many questions should not be asked. Do not question overmuch." Then Gargi Vacaknavi held her peace.

Next, Yajnavalkya uses another higher method of teaching Gargi, describing *brahman* being "not this," *neti*.

> It is not coarse nor fine; not short nor long; not red (like fire) nor adhesive (like water). It casts no shadow, is not darkness. It is not wind nor is it space. It is not attached to anything. It is not taste or smell; it

is not eye or ear; it is not voice or mind; it is not light (tejas) or life
(prana); it has no face or measure; it has no within, no without. Nothing does It consume nor is It consumed by anyone at all (3.8).

The *Chandogya Upanishads* tell the story of Svetaketu and Uddalaka. Svetaketu was the son of the Brahmin Uddalaka and was sent off by Uddalaka to study the Vedas. After twelve years of study, Uddalaka teaches his son a new lesson. He tells his son to put salt in the water and to taste it, exclaiming that one could not perceive the salt, although it was there. "This finest essence," Uddalaka says, "the whole universe has it as itself; that is the real; that is the self. That you are Svetaketu." Uddalaka then goes on to show that not only is Brahman present, but it is also the source of life. Svetaketu did not understand, at which point Uddalaka pointed to the banyan tree whose seeds are not visible to the naked eye, but which grow the mighty banyan tree. All comes from nothing.

In the Upanishads, *maya* is called creative power, nature, or *prakriti*. A famous yogi who developed Upanishadic thought was Samkhya, who wrote the *Karika*, the oldest writing from this school, about 200 C.E. Samkhya said that he came from a long line of teachers whose founder was Kapila, who lived in the seventh century B.C.E.

For Samkhya the universe was divided into two parts, spirit, or *purusa*, and matter, *prakriti*. This is a position outlined in the later Upanishads. *Prakriti* is divided into three gunas: 1) *sattva*, which is associated with heaven, the color white, and the human attribute of altruism; 2) *rajas*, which is associated with the earth, the color gray, and with human passion; and 3) *tamas*, which is linked with the underworld, the color black and dull wit. According to Samkhya and the later Upanishads, all matter is composed of all three gunas, but one or the other gunas may predominate. *Purusa* has four attributes. It is isolated, indifferent, consciousness and inactive. According to Samkhya's philosophy, one rises or falls in the caste system through reincarnation, according to which guna most characterized one's previous life. Ultimate enlightenment comes when one meditates backwards through one's life to the moment of conception. At the very moment of conception one is able to experience the initial attachment of spirit to matter. At that moment, one realizes that *purusa* is separate from *prakriti*, thereby reaching *kaivalya*, or absolute isolation of spirit from matter.

The more traditional Vedic priests in the sixth century B.C.E. were somewhat upset by the "other worldly" character of the Upanishads and put together a synthesis of religious ideas that maintained the legitimacy of the caste system and the traditional social structure. This Brahminical synthesis is called the *varnasrama dharma*. Each caste, or *varna*, goes through four stages (*asrama*) of life. The four stages are loosely linked with the four goals (*purusarthas*). The four stages of life are student, house holder, forest dweller and *samnyasin*. The four goals of life are *dharma* (law), *arta* (success), *kama* (love) and *moksha* (release).

One should live within the boundaries of one's own caste system until the end of life. First, one lives the life of a student, studying the ways of one's caste. Then one marries and becomes a house holder and parent. In older age, after one's children have left home, one goes with one's spouse, if he or she is still living, into the forest, where meditation upon the Upanishads begins to take place. And finally, one develops into a *samnyasin*, a wandering monk who, unattached to any place or person, travels across the world seeking perfect unity with the sacred. Of the four goals of life, the first three — law, success and love — are worldly. One must follow the law of one's caste, seek success within one's own *jati* ("occupation") and enjoy the fruits of family love. Then, in the last stage of life, when one becomes a *samnyasin*, one seeks *moksha*, or release from the entanglements of this world. Thus, the fourth stage and fourth goal correspond. The *samnyasin* embodies *moksha*. Within the Brahminical synthesis, there is no pressure to reach *moksha*. Because the dead are reincarnated, one may always try to seek *moksha* in the next life. Most Hindus simply stay house holders, although the ultimate goal is to seek transcendence from this world.

The Upanishads furthermore discussed the concept of *maya*, which means creative power, or nature. This concept is further elaborated in the ninth century C.E. by Sankara, a famous yogi who walked by foot over all of India debating with other religious thinkers. For Sankara only the spiritual essence of the universe is real and therefore *maya*, as nature, is illusory. Sankara founded the Advaita Vedanta School, which means "all is one." More specifically, Advaita Vedanta means "non-dual" because the word "one" is too specific. Vedanta means "end of the Vedas" because he considered his philosophy to culminate Vedic thought. Influenced by the triple canon of the Upanishads, *Bhagavad Gita* and Brahma Sutras, Advaita Vedanta thought also drew upon certain Mahayana Buddhist concepts.

Sankara rejected all attempted compromises of his thought, and his primary adversary was a yogi by the name of Bhaskara. Bhaskara taught that one should follow the caste system until the end of life, and that one should study the Vedas first and then the Upanishads. Bhaskara also taught that reality is different and yet non-different from the spiritual essence. Just as the spider spins the web, the one makes the many, says Bhaskara. Sankara argued that the caste stages are not necessary to spiritual development and that one should simply study the Upanishads and not the Vedas. Sankara also argued that Bhaskara's theory that the many come from the one is partially correct, for practical purposes, but it is ignorant to think that the world really exists. The world is *maya*, illusion. Only Brahman is real. *Maya* conceals the unity of Brahman and evokes *moha*, or delusion. Still, Sankara makes it clear that the world of *maya* must be dealt with practically.

In one famous example a king put Sankara to the test. Sankara was visiting the king when an elephant was let loose at Sankara, who in fear ran up a tree. The king asked Sankara why he ran up a tree if an elephant is illusory? Sankara, regaining his composure, replied that the king saw an illusory me run up an illusory tree. In a second story an elephant approaches a master and a student in the road. The student stands firm in front of the elephant saying that everything is *brahman* and *brahman* should not fear *brahman*. The elephant tramples the student and runs on, after which the guru tells the student that both the elephant and the student were *brahman*, but so was the teacher saying clear the way. Thus, the material world is illusory in Upanishadic thought, but no more than an elephant bearing down on one.

Finally, there is the story of Narada and Vishnu. Narada was a famous yogi who was struggling to understand the essence of *maya*. Vishnu is one of the three primary gods of classical Hinduism and *maya* is understood to be primarily the work of Vishnu. Narada asks Vishnu if he will explain his *maya*, to which Vishnu says that he will if Narada will fetch him a glass of water from the house down in the valley below. Narada goes to a farmhouse, knocks on the door and meets a very beautiful woman. He falls in love with her, marries her and she bears him several children. Once there is a terrible flood and Narada tries to escape across a raging river with his wife and three children. He loses all of them to the waters and finally he too becomes unconscious and is swept away by the water to a little cliff. When Narada awakes he is lying at the foot of Vishnu. Looking down at him, a smiling Vishnu asks if he has brought a glass of water since he has been waiting for over thirty minutes. Vishnu then looks at Narada and asks, "Do you comprehend now the secret of my Maya?" (Zimmer 34).

Bhagavad-Gita

Containing 90,000 verses, the *Mahabharata* is the longest written epic in the world. Most scholars believe the epic poem was essentially finished between the seventh and sixth centuries B.C.E. and that it assumed its present form between 200 B.C.E. and 200 C.E.

The sixth book is the most famous chapter in the epic. It addresses a critical social problem in India, the widespread abandonment of social duties by young men who were disillusioned with the world.

The first scene finds Arjuna, a Pandava warrior, depressed over the prospect of fighting a war. By duty he is bound to fight against the Kauravas. As he looks across the battlefield, he sees relatives and respected teachers among the Kauravas, and he shudders at the horror of war. He throws down his weapons and asks his charioteer for advice; Krsna, the incarnation of Vishnu, is the chariot driver.

Krsna delivers a profound message to Arjuna. First, he took up the traditional teaching of *karma* yoga. All must perform well their caste duty because Vishnu himself is tirelessly engaged in the activity of creating and sustaining the world. At the same time, one should not feel attachment to the world in which one lives. In so doing Krsna reveals to Arjuna the meaning of duty as warrior (*Ksatriya*) without being bound by *karma*.

Next Krsna instructs Arjuna about the way of knowledge (*jnana*) as outlined in the Upanishads. Krsna articulates the equivalence of Vedanta, Samkhya and Yoga and reminds Arjuna that ultimate reality — the *atman-brahman* of the Upanishads — transcends all pairs of contraries (Eliade vol. 2 *A History of Religious Ideas* 237).

In the final message of the *Gita*, Krsna introduces a new way of salvation — love (*bhakti*). Krsna implores Arjuna to love him with all his heart in order to reach salvation:

> And now again give ear to this my all-highest word,
> Of all the most mysterious:
> "I love thee well."
> Therefore will I tell thee thy salvation.
> Bear in mind, love Me and Worship Me.
> (quoted in Zaehner XX)

Thus Krsna tells Arjuna that liberation is not the highest goal of the religious life. One must surrender oneself in love in order to attain a personal relationship with God. This is the most widespread religious belief in India today.

Bibliography
Chapter 5 — India and Hinduism

Adams, Charles J. Editor. "Hinduism." *Reader's Guide to the Great Religions*. 2nd Ed. New York, 1977: 106–155.

Allchin, Bridget, and Raymond Allchin. *The Birth of Indian Civilization*. Baltimore, 1968.

Basham, A.L. *The Wonder that was India.* New York, 1955.
Bhandarkar, R.G. *Vaisnavism, Saivism, and Minor Religious Systems.* Reprint. Varanasi, 1965.
Bharati, Agehananda. *The Tantric Tradition.* London, 1965.
Bolle, Kees. *The Bhagavadgita.* Berkeley, California, 1979.
Brockington, J.L. *The Sacred Thread: Hinduism in Its Continuity and Diversity.* New York, 1981.
Buhler, Georg. Trans. *The Laws of Manu.* Mystic, Connecticut, 1965.
Dasgupta, Surendranath. *A History of Indian Philosophy.* 5 Vols. Cambridge, Massachusetts, 1922–1955.
Deussen, Paul. *The Philosophy of the Upanishads.* Trans. A.S. Gelden. N.Y., 1966.
Deutsch, Eliot. *Adviata Vedanta: A Philosophical Reconstruction.* Honolulu, 1969.
Dimmitt, Cornelia, and J.A.B. Van Buitenen. Trans. and Editors. *Classical Hindu Mythology: A Reader in the Sanskrit Puranas.* Philadelphia, 1978.
Dumezil, Georges. *Archaic Roman Religion.* Trans. Phillip Krapp. Foreword. Mircea Eliade. Chicago, 1970.
Eliade, Mircea. *A History of Religious Ideas.* Vol. 2. Trans. W. R. Trask. Chicago, 1982.
_____. *Yoga: Immortality and Freedom.* Trans. W.R. Trask. New York, 1958.
Embree, Ainslee T. Editor. *The Hindu Tradition.* Westminster, Maryland, 1972.
Fairservis, Walter A. *The Roots of Ancient India: The Archaeology of Early Indian Civilization.* New York, 1971.
Flood, Gavin. *An Introduction to Hinduism.* New York, 1996.
Gonda, Jan. *Ancient Indian Kingship from the Religious Point of View.* Leiden, 1966.
_____. *Change and Continuity in Indian Religion.* The Hague, 1965.
_____. *Vedic Literature: Samhitas and Brahmanas.* Wiesbaden, 1975.
_____. *The Vision of the Vedic Poets.* The Hague, 1965
_____. *Visnuism and Sivaism.* New York, 1976.
Griffith, Ralph T.H. Trans. *The Hymns of the Rigveda.* Rev. Ed. Livingston, New Jersey, 1976.
Grousett, Rene. *India.* Vol. 2. *The Civilizations of the East.* London, 1931.
Heine-Geldern, R. "The Coming of the Aryans and the End of the Harappa Culture." *Man* 56 (1956): 136–140.
Hiltebeitel, Alf. "Hinduism." *Encyclopedia of Religion.* Vol. 6. Mircea Eliade. Editor-in-Chief. Chicago, 1987: 336–360.
Hopkins, E. Washburn. *Epic Mythology.* Reprint, New York, 1969.
Hopkins, Thomas. *The Hindu Religious Tradition.* Encino, California, 1971.
Hume, Robert E. Trans. and Editor. *The Thirteen Principal Upanishads.* New York, 1962.
Keith, A.B. *The Religion and Philosophy of the Veda and Upanishads.* 2 Vols. Cambridge, Massachusetts, 1925.
King, Richard. *Early Advaita Vedanta and Buddhism: The Mahayana Context of the Guadapadiya-karika.* Albany, New York, 1995.
Kramrisch, Stella. "The Triple Structure of Creation in the Rig Veda." *History of Religions* 2 (1962–63): 140–175, 256–291.

Lal, B.B., and S.P. Gupta. Editors. *Frontiers of the Indus Civilization: Sir Mortimer Wheeler Commemoration Volume*. New Delhi, 1984.
Lannoy, Richard. *The Speaking Tree: A Study of Indian Culture and Society*. Oxford, 1971.
MacDonell, Arthur Anthony. Trans. *Hymns From the Rig Vedas*. Vol. 1. Calcutta, n.d.
_____. *Vedic Mythology*. Reprint. New York, 1974.
Majumdar, R.C. *The Vedic Age*. Vol. 1 *History and Culture of the Indian People*. London, 1951.
Marshall, Sir John. *Mohenjo-Daro and the Indist Culture*. London, 1931.
Penner, Hans. "Cosmogony as Myth in the Vishnu Purana." *History of Religions* 5 (1966): 283–299.
Puhvel, Jaan. "Aspects of Equine Functionality." *Myth and Law Among the Indo-Europeans*. Berkeley, California, 1970.
Radhakrishnan, S. *The Principal Upanishads*. New York, 1953.
Ranade, R.D. *A Constructive Survey of Upanishadic Philosophy*. Poona, 1926.
Renou, Louis. *Religions of Ancient India*. London, 1953.
Reynolds, Frank E., and Charles Hallesey. "Buddhism: An Overview." *Encyclopedia of Religion*. Vol. 2. Mircea Eliade. Editor-in-Chief. Chicago, 1987: 334–351.
Sauve, James L. "The Divine Victim: Aspects of Human Sacrifice in Viking Scandinavia and Vedic India." *Myth and Law among the Indo-Europeans*. J. Puhvel. Editor. Berkeley, California, 1970: 173–191.
Singh, Gurdip. "The Indus Valley Culture." *Ancient Cities of the Indus*. G.L. Possehl. Editor. New Dehli, 1979: 234–249.
Thapai, B.K. "Climate during the Period of the Indus Civilization: Evidence from Kalibangan." *Ecology and Archeology of Western India*. D.P. Agrawal and B.M. Pande. Editors. New Dehli, 1977: 67–73.
Valmiki. *Ramayana*. 3 Vols. Trans. H.P. Sastri. Livingston, New Jersey, 1976.
Wheeler, R.E. Mortimer. *Early India and Pakistan: To Asoka*. New York, 1959.
_____. *The Indus Civilization*. Cambridge, Massachusetts, 1968.
_____. *Mohenjo-Daro*. Karachi, Pakistan, n.d.
Zaehner, R.C. *Hindu Scriptures*. London and Toronto, 1966.
Zimmer, Heinrich. *Myths and Symbols in Indian Art and Civilization*. Joseph Campbell. Editor. Princeton, New Jersey, 1946.
_____. *Philosophies of India*. New York, 1951.

CHAPTER 6

Ancient China

China, unlike India, has kept good chronological records of its historical affairs. While India has sabotaged history, China has preserved it better than any other civilization on earth. China has the oldest continuous kingdom in human history. By 6000 B.C.E. rice cultivation existed in the Yangtze Valley and millet was grown in the Yellow River Valley. Beginning sometime before 5000 B.C.E. around the big bend of the Yellow River, including the lower Fen and Wei River valleys, an early Neolithic community called Yang Shao thrived from about 4365 B.C.E. to 2500 B.C.E.

These people practiced slash-and-burn agriculture and lived in small and temporary villages. As they exhausted the soil in a particular region, they would pack up and move to another. Attracted to the turns and bends of the river, the Yang Shao people would periodically return to the area once the soil had recovered. The Yang Shao's most important crops were millet and wheat, and they kept dogs, pigs, sheep, and perhaps goats and cattle as well. Significantly, they supplemented their agricultural and pastoral way of life with some hunting, gathering and fishing. They also learned to make silk.

The Yang Shao also produced pottery painted in red and black which was quite complex in design. These vessels, filled with food, were often found in grave sites. At Pan Po in the Shensi Providence, Yang Shao occupied a site for some 600 years. Ping-ti Ho theorizes that the Yang Shao culture was not the earliest Neolithic community in China and pushes back the discovery of agriculture to the sixth millennium. Ping-ti Ho is also firmly of the opinion that the Chinese discovery of agriculture, as well as the domestication of certain animals, the development of pottery, and even the metallurgy of bronze were all local developments and were not the result of dissemination from several centers in the ancient Near East.

Beginning about 2500 B.C.E., the Yang Shao evolved into the Lung Shan culture which got its name from a principal archeological site in Shantung. The Lung Shan show cultural enhancement in all areas. Their pottery was predominantly gray and black and varied in design and structure. Towards the end of the period decorative geometric patterns became popular. Furthermore, the pottery wheel was developed in the Lung Shan period. Rice was added to the staple crops and chickens and horses were domesticated at this time. Hunting continued to supplement food supplies. Not only were the Lung Shan more developed than the Yang Shao, they also covered a much greater area in northern and southeastern China.

Religiously, the Yang Shao proved to be a typical Neolithic agricultural community primarily concerned with birth, death and fertility. Villages were oriented around a ceremonial center. Small houses were half underground or entered through a central smoke hole by ladder. Interestingly, this type of house was found on the west coast of North America dating back to the Upper Paleolithic period (12,000–8000 B.C.E.). In North America the prehistoric record shows that these half-underground houses later became the underground ceremonial centers (kivas) of the Pueblo Indians of the Southwest whose creation mythology speaks of the emergence of human beings from the underworld. In the Yang Shao period children were buried close to the houses in large urns, having an opening at the top to permit the soul to go out. In the Southwestern United States, during prehistoric times, children were buried in underground pits inside, and later, around houses. On Yang Shao funerary vessels three motifs are found: triangle, chess board and cowrie. These symbols are associated with sexual union, birth, death and rebirth, and are probably prayers for life in another world. Ping-ti Ho states that the societies of the Yan-Shao period were matrilineal.

Kinship became patrilineal in the Lung Shan period of Chinese prehistory. Ping-ti Ho, along with several other scholars, interprets certain stone objects and paintings on vessels as phallic symbols which are tied up with ancestor worship. Indeed, Bernard Karlgren argues that the Chou pictogram designating "ancestor" was derived from the drawing of a phallus, but Carl Hentze thinks that the so-called phallic symbols are really designs representing burial urns which he says are the forerunners to the later "ancestor tablets" of historical times (Eliade 9).

The Hsia (Xia)

Although the archaeological record has not confirmed it, the Chinese say that their high culture was created by three wise rulers of remote antiquity. One, Fu Hsi, was a serpent-bodied emperor who taught the early people of China how to use iron to make hunting and fishing tools, fish with nets, domesticate animals, forecast the future and play upon musical instruments that he invented. Shen Nung, the ox-headed divine farmer, taught the Chinese the arts of agriculture and medicine and invented ox drawn carts. The yellow emperor, Huang Ti, the most famous of all in later times, invented bricks, pottery, a calendar based on astronomical observations and money. His principal wife taught the people how to manufacture silk. According to Chinese mythology, the first of the three great kings was preceded by other emperors who were half-human and half-animal and whose reign lasted over two million years.

Modern archaeology locates the Hsia at about the end of the third millennium B.C.E. The Hsia people probably lived along the middle and lower reaches of the Yellow River, especially on the lower bank. Hundreds of sites have been excavated there, unearthing pottery, stone artifacts, house remains and burials.

The Shang

The Chinese Bronze Age begins with the Shang dynasty which emerged a little before the Lung Shan age had come to an end. Stone continued to be used for tools in the rural areas, but bronze increasingly replaced stone in the urban areas during the Shang period. The orthodox Chinese chronology dates the Shang Dynasty 1766 to 1122 B.C.E., but the Bamboo Annals date the Shang somewhat later (1523–1027 B.C.E.). The Shang is characterized by the production of bronze, the appearance of urban centers and capital cities, the presence of a permanent military, the institution of the emperor and the beginnings of writings.

Documentation for the religious life is plentiful in this period and is best revealed on the discovery of the numerous oracle bones. The Shang Dynasty continued and refined the technique of divination by heating bones which had begun earlier in the Lung Shan period. Bronze vessels of unprecedented beauty and sophistication were produced during the Shang Dynasty. Containing a rich iconography, these bronze containers reflect religious continuity in Neolithic China. Some motifs, such as the salamander, the tiger and the dragon were carried over from the painted pottery of Yang Shao and the following periods. Also widespread are symbols of the cicada and the *t'ao-t'ieh* mask which represent cycles of birth, death and rebirth. Equally significant in this period are the images involving bi-polar opposites such as the feathered snake or the snake and eagle. These symbols point to the unity of sky and earth and show the early Chinese concern with cosmic unity and totality.

By 1300 B.C.E. writing appears on deer and oxen shoulder blades as well as turtle shells. Shang bronze vessels are unsurpassed in beauty and craftsmanship in the Neolithic period. From these oracular inscriptions we learn that a supreme celestial god, Ti, "Lord," or Shang Ti, "Lord on High," comes into view. Ti directs the great cosmic rhythms and produces the changing of the seasons, rain, wind and drought. The emperor is dependent upon Ti for victory in war and a successful harvest, and all disasters are blamed on him. But Ti is not the primary god of the Shang Dynasty, for like sky gods in other Neolithic communities, he is somewhat remote. Religion is centered in the Shang primarily around worship of the ancestors of royal family. Interestingly, the Chinese prayed to Ti for rain and fertility and success in warfare.

A Shang king was called the Sun of Heaven, and he was the only person in Chinese society who could supplicate Ti directly. The emperor performed regular and complicated sacrifices to his ancestors and to various nature gods. The most common sacrificial animals were cattle, sheep, pigs and dogs. Sets of animals were often found buried together, such as two pigs, three sheep and five oxen. Human sacrifices were common, both at burials and at the consecration of buildings and could involve over 100 victims at a single time. But while Ti was the supreme god, religious life centered around the veneration of the ancestors which itself was linked closely to the typical Neolithic concerns of fertility, life and rebirth.

The exact size of the Shang state is unknown. It was not large, and it centered on the Honan plain on both sides of the Yellow River. The Shang people considered the neighbors on either side as barbarians as long as they did not recognize the legitimacy of the Sun of Heaven, although the neighbors were neither ethnically nor linguistically different. Bronze forging and casting produced not only some of the world's most beautiful vessels, but also helmets, body armor, shields and dagger-axes. While the horse was not ridden, war chariots on two wheels drawn by two horses were known. It was the king who made fruitful harvest and victories possible by the sacrifices he offered and the divinations he made. The king depended heavily upon his own ancestors, but, in turn, the ancestors depended for their strength upon the offerings of grain, flesh and blood of animals and humans, and the wine libations that were offered to them by the king. Royal sacrifices could involve several hundred head of cattle at a time. Shang religious practice rested upon the belief that correct religious procedure by the Shang emperor would result in favors conferred by Ti. A rigid and routine sacrificial schedule emerged in the Shang period which became orderly and even predictable. As David Keightley argues, "the success of the offering depended upon the correct fulfillment of 'defined duties,' that is 'the right number of cattle to the right ancestor on the right date'" (215). It may be, as Keightley says, that the concern with ritual number in sacrificial divinations brought about the Chinese commitment to numbers and quantification. Sacrifice was viewed as a contractual matter for the Shang, and the Shang felt quite optimistic in the effectiveness of their ritual procedures. Concern for the ancestors eventually became not only systematic, but almost mathematical in its precision and specificity.

Ancestors were ranked by generation and this involved both the living and the dead. It was frequently the case that the older the ancestor, the more powerful he was, and those ancestors who were most ancient lost their individual personalities and came to represent abstract impersonal powers. Their strength lay in their rank, not their personality. Still, it seemed that ancestors were bound to honor their sacred contractual obligations in a way that was never the case for Ti. Rain, warfare, draught, harvest, epidemics and the king's person were all under the dominion of Ti while the ancestors had jurisdiction over harvests, rain, livestock and child birth. Ancestors were ranked in a way homologous to the social system of Shang China, and the ancestors had their own hierarchical obligations, attitudes and duties.

Thus, in the Shang period the religious concern with hierarchy and relationship affected Chinese social structure, which in turn furthered the bureaucratic nature of ancestor worship. While ancestor worship was practiced at some level among all people, it culminated in the ritual acts of the emperor. The emperor, assisted by diviners, would put questions to the ancestors. Heat was then applied to bones of either the shoulder blades of pig, sheep or cattle, and later, mainly tortoise shells. Cracks would appear from the heat and from these answers to the questions were received. Sometimes the question, as well as the answer, was incised on the bone. More than a hundred inscribed bones have been found, and on these appear not only the traditional name of most of the Shang kings, but also the names of some kings whose existence had not previously been known.

The Chou

In 1122 B.C.E. or 1027 B.C.E. the last Shang Dynasty was overthrown by neighbors to the west, a people who called themselves the Chou. Having settled in the High Valley of the Wei River, about 300 miles southwest of the Shang Kingdom, the Chou were a non-literate farming people who assimilated many Shang ideas and customs. The first emperor of the Chou stated that he received a mandate from heaven ordering him to put an end to the corrupt Shang Kingdom, but connections with the Shang remained strong, and the Chou rulers continued to make sacrifices to the ancestors of former Shang rulers for some 800 years.

Farming techniques were further developed in the Chou, and increased food production brought about a large population increase. For example, the chest harness was developed for a plow horse which allowed a single horse to plow as much as four horses. The development of the Chou is further demonstrated by the metallurgy of iron, which was forged and cast by 513 B.C.E. With the development of a highly sophisticated bellows, steel was smelted by the second century B.C.E.

Scores of new cities were built in Chou times, usually rectangular and square and on a north-south axis. The cities had double walls and occasionally a moat. The residences of the nobles and administrative buildings were placed within the inner wall, while craftsmen lived and worked between the inner and outer walls, clustering in particular corners according to their trade. Warfare was further developed; the infantry now added the sword and the cross-bow to its arsenal.

Among the gods that the Chou brought with them were T'ien (heaven) and Hou Ji (god of millet). Hou Ji was an agricultural god who controlled the fortunes of the primary staple, and the ruling family considered themselves descendants of this deity. T'ien was a high god who was very similar to Ti of the Shang people. Indeed, the two gods were so closely identified that they were finally brought together under the title Huang-tian Shang-Ti (sovereign, heaven/supreme deity). Interestingly, T'ien was never viewed as an ancestor of the rulers and was much more abstract than was Shang Ti. The emperor's title, Son of Heaven, became a term of relationship rather than descent — the emperor reigned only because he had the "mandate of heaven." The doctrine of the mandate of heaven became the principle of Chinese political authority until the overthrow of the Manchu dynasty in 1911 during the Communist Revolution.

As in other urban civilizations, Chinese cities also spread out from a ceremonial center. A city is above all the center of the world and the center makes possible communications between heaven, earth and the underworld. The ultimate city for China was the capital of the kingdom. The capital was placed at the center of the universe, which is the site of a sacred tree called upright wood, "Chien-Mu." Because it is in the center of the world, it cast no shadow at noon. Furthermore, every capital according to Chinese tradition must possess a Ming t'ang, a ritual place that transcends both space and time. The Ming t'ang is built on a square base which represents the earth and is covered by a round thatched roof symbolizing heaven. The emperor lives in different quarters of the palace according to the seasons and by so moving he inaugurates the annual cycle.

At the popular level of society, each village contained a mound of earth symbolizing the fertility of the soil called *she*, which was generally placed in a sacred grove. Rites were performed at this mound of earth in honor of the local gods of the soil in order to increase the fertility of the ground to insure a good harvest. Dancing and ceremonial songs were performed around this mound of dirt in the springtime and other festivals were performed in the fall during the harvest. During the Chou period, the land was dotted with larger mounds, one of which was put in each provincial capital to symbolize the territory of the feudal lord, while one was situated at the imperial capital.

The ancient calendar began in February, which was the month which heralded the beginning of spring time. The emperor purified himself ritually and joined with many high officials to "meet the spring in the eastern suburb" of the capital. The emperor then prayed for a good year and plowed a furrow in the sacred mound with his own hand in order to insure a bountiful agricultural season. Because this ritual was a prayer for the renewal of life during the upcoming season, all Chinese at this time were prohibited from cutting down trees, destroying bird nests or animal young and preparing for war. Those actions embodied destructive and negative spirituality and were considered counterproductive to the beginning of a new agricultural year.

Ancestor worship continued throughout the Chou period. The Shang funeral urn house was replaced by a tablet which a son deposited in the temple of the ancestors. Four times a year complex ceremonies took place in which cooked foods, cereals and various drinks were offered to the ancestors. The spirit of the venerated ancestor was thought to inhabit one of the family members, usually a grandson, and this person prepared the offerings he received. It should be noted that the highly developed bronze art work of the Shang period became more simplified and uniform during the Chou dynasty. After 771 B.C.E. Chou political power shifted from the west to the east and it was during this time that the famous philosophers Confucius and Lao-Tzu emerged.

Divination

Divination is a persistent theme in traditional Chinese religion. During the Shang dynasty a favorite method was to scrape thin some spot on a tortoise shell or piece of bone, heat it by a flame and have the diviners read the cracks that appeared. During the Chou dynasty these cracks were seen to conform to yin and yang lines found in the Pa Kua, or eight trigrams. As the Chou period developed, royal religion seemed to emphasize more and more the relationship between the emperor and the celestial sphere. Still, ancestor worship and agricultural rituals played a prominent part in Chinese religion. The sun, for example, does not become an important god until near the end of the Chou dynasty. Sometime around 1000 B.C.E. the Chinese, drawing upon earlier and less well defined religious principles, classified the cosmos in terms of opposite forces which complemented one another—yin-yang. Carl Hentze writes that the polar symbolism of yin-yang found its roots in the Shang in such conjunctive symbols as the owl with solar eyes, feathered snake, and the snake and eagle (Eliade). Later, in the Chou, the symbolism of polar opposition was articulated as the doctrine of yin-yang.

The formal doctrine seems to have been occasioned by the Chou's concern with the agricultural cycle and fertility, for yin originally meant "covered by the clouds." Yin, according to Marcel Granet, referred to dark, hidden, secret and cold, while yang suggested the idea of sunny weather, heat, light and warmth (Eliade). One divination text speaks of a "time of light" and a "time of darkness," indicating that yin-yang were originally terms designating the agricultural seasons, which seasons were seen as cyclical. Laurence Thompson therefore defines yin-yang as "definable phases in a ceaseless flow of change." (*Chinese Religion* 3)

Yin-yang are not abstract principles which are applied in a singular manner to all objects and processes of the cosmos. The principles of yin-yang inhabit and embody the world in a concrete way, and thus an object that is yin at one moment or in one context may be yang in another. A feminine nature is attributed to everything that is yin, and a masculine nature to that which is yang. Underlying these two antagonistic complements is a cosmic unity that is defined as Tao. Indeed, the earliest scholarly definition of Tao mentions yin-yang: "a yin, a yang—that is the Tao." (Eliade 19).

The eternal movement of yin-yang was underscored in Chinese religion by a perceived unity and symmetry. Tao literally means "a way," or "a road." It is sometimes denoted as "the channel of a river" and ultimately connotes the underlying principle of the universe. The way of the world is ultimately harmonious, integrated and symmetrical. The Tao is the principle of order that is immanent in all of the world's rhythms.

Tao is well articulated later by a number of Chinese thinkers such as Lao Tzu. In the *Tao Te Ching* it is written, "The Tao gave birth to one.

One gave birth to two. Two gave birth to Three. Three gave birth to the ten thousand beings, the ten thousand beings carried the yin on their back and encircled the yang" (quoted in Eliade 20). For Lao Tzu, the One already represents a stage of creation underlying it is a mysterious and incomprehensible creative potency called the Tao. Lao Tzu also called the Tao "an undifferentiated and perfect being, born before heaven and earth.... We can consider it the mother of this world, but I do not know its name; I will call it Tao; and, if it must be named, its name will be: the Immense [*ta*]" (quoted in Eliade 21).

We shall return later to discuss the thought of Lao Tzu, but note now only that Tao is ultimately seen as a feminine principle of sacrality that is ultimately ineffable and unknowable. In other words, to quote the historian of religions Mircea Eliade, "The Tao is a primordial totality, living and creative but formless and nameless" (21).

In the Chou period divination was interpreted according to the Pa Kua, or eight trigrams. Each trigram consisted of three lines which were either broken or unbroken. The unbroken line was called the yang-yao because it was held to represent the male or the male principle, while the broken line was called the yin-yao and represented the female principle. The eight trigrams were arranged within an octagon with the yin-yang symbol in the center to represent creation. The trigrams, beginning at the top and proceeding clockwise, represent the following: 1) moving water as rain or streams and moon, Kan; 2) thunder, Chen; 3) earth, Kun; 4) mountain, Ken; 5) fire, sun and lightning, Li; 6) wind and wood, Sun; 7) heaven or sky, Ch'ien; 8) collected water as in a marsh or lake, Tui. These trigrams, when combined in all possible pairs, compose 64 hexagrams which represent every aspect of the universe.

Broken and unbroken stalks of the milfoil or yarrow plant, when dropped to the ground, produced designs which conformed to one or the other of the eight trigrams or 64 hexagrams. The diviners could read them, uncover the present state of things and predict the future. These interpretations became standard and found their way into the famous classic, *I Ching*, or *Book of Changes*. The *Book of Changes* outlines the waxing and waning of yin-yang, which has regulated the history of the universe and of human time. In the second and third centuries B.C.E. a less complicated method of predicting the future was distilled from the interactions of yin-yang and the five elements, water, fire, wood, metal and earth. For example, water was connected especially with rain, north, kidney, salt and black, while fire was linked with warm air, south, red, eyesight and lungs.

Subsequently, and continuing into the present time, other methods of divination were utilized. The most common divination method is called *feng-shui*, which means literally "wind and water." In this method of divination a geomancer was able to uncover the yin and yang principles in a given spot of land in order to see how to properly situate a dwelling on it. *Feng-shui* was part and parcel of the Chinese religious effort to improve one's destiny by aligning oneself with the patterns of the cosmos in a balanced way. In feng-shui the east was associated with yang and the blue dragon, while the west was linked with yin and the white tiger. Whenever a dwelling was built, the east must be to one's left and the west to one's right. The geomancer looked for the dragon and the tiger within the topography of the building site and then found the auspicious place which was "U-shaped" where their powers complimented each other in perfect harmony. That was the place where their breaths, *ch'i*, met. The ying-yang diagram is called the *t'ai-chi tu* which means "diagram of extreme limits."

Spirit Worship

For the ancient Chinese a large number of spirits inhabited the natural world. There were numerous spirits of the sky, including the sun, the moon, the five planets, the seven stars of the great bear and the 28 principal constellations, as well as the stars, the winds, the clouds, the rain and the thunder. Of course, not all spirits were in the sky. Spirits lived in the hills and streams and cultivated fields; the Yellow River and the principal mountains of China were always considered residences of spiritual presence. For the Chinese, not all spirits were considered helpful. There were demons and devilish spirits that haunted human dwellings, lonely spots and all roads especially at night fall. Other evil spirits inhabited the shadows of the forests and the mountains.

It seems there was a negative spirit to almost every aspect of the cosmos, and a list would be long indeed. Spirits inhabited the water, the soil, the air and all varieties of animals, including birds, fish and snakes. Even plants and inanimate objects were considered to have demons present. Eventually, about 200 B.C.E., during the first Han dynasty, all of these were categorized into two classes, *shen*, which were yang in character, and *quei*, which were yin. Both kinds of spirits were considered to be almost infinite in number. No one has gone through more trouble than the Chinese to keep the good spirits on their side. The sun came to be seen as the chief opponent of the *quei*. Earthenware roosters were thought to have special power over demons and were often placed on the house tops of Chinese peasants. Spring itself was seen as a good power and was symbolized primarily by the peach blossom. Therefore, since ancient times, the peach tree has symbolized the good spirits of life. Because of their association with good spirits and life, peach blossoms are often nailed to doors and gates on New Year's Day. Bonfires, torches, candles, lanterns and firecrackers scared off the *quei* and were used during a number of popular festivals and especially on New Year's Day.

Creation Mythology

Fragments of a number of creation stories have made their way to us through more philosophical writings of Chinese historians. This is not the place to take up the controversy over whether the Chinese are unique among all peoples in the world in not having a creation mythology. Professor Girardot has shown that there is evidence of a very old stratum of creation mythologies in Chinese religious imagination which, in part, was overlooked by western scholars early on because Chinese mythology did not correspond to Judeo-Christian mythology. Girardot goes on to show that there are some important cosmogonic themes sprinkled throughout China, although, with the exception of P'an Ku, there does not seem to be a complete cosmogonic narrative ("The Problem of Creation Mythology").

The most complete cosmogonic myth in China is not articulated until the Three Kingdoms period (220–280 C.E.), in a text called *Wu-yun-li-nien-chi*. According to that myth, "in the time when heaven and earth were a chaos resembling an egg" there was born P'an Ku, a primordial cosmic giant. P'an Ku's death finalized the creation: "From his skull was shaped the dome of the sky, and from his flesh was formed the soil of the fields; from his bones came the rocks, from his blood the rivers and seas; from his hair came all vegetation. His breath was the wind; his voice made thunder; his right eye became the moon, his left eye, the sun. From his saliva or sweat came rain" (quoted in Sproul 202).

This myth seems structurally similar to the creation by sacrifice of a primordial being that we saw both in Mesopotamia and India. The Chinese call the primordial totality-unity out of which P'an Ku was born *hun-tun*. The precept of *hun-tun* seems to be part and parcel of a much earlier cosmogonic tradition which emphasized a feminine potency out of which all of life emerged, a theme that the Taoists later take up and elaborate. It is too simple to say that the Chinese had little interest in cosmic origins. As we shall see later, Taoists reflect a great deal on world beginnings. The perception of cosmic chaos as reflected in P'an Ku seems to hark back to a very ancient mythological tradition that is still embodied in Taoist Chinese religious thought and ritual. It may be fairly said that, at least for that strand of Chinese religion that is best articulated by the Taoists, the Chinese do not articulate their mythology verbally because they still embody it. If Taoism's religious thought is seen as the natural development of an old strand of Neolithic religion in China, then it may be that Chinese cosmogonic myths are scarce because the Chinese continue to inhabit that early mythical world to an unprecedented degree. In that sense the lack of articulated creation mythology with respect to the establishment of the natural world does not reflect a lack of concern with that aspect of the world, but rather with the maintenance of a close relationship such that mythology is embodied at almost an unconscious level in their lives.

In another old myth the world was seen as a square from whose corners rose four pillars that supported the vault of heaven, which was shaped like a bowl. One of these pillars was knocked out of position by the black dragon Kong-kong so that the bowl of the heavens tipped to one side. A dragon goddess, Nu-kua, came to the rescue and fashioned four pillars out of the legs of a tortoise and lifted the heavens back to where they belonged. In another story she formed royalty from the yellow earth, and from the mud, the poor and the wretched. This mythology was articulated by the third century B.C.E. and became the myth upon which the emperor's palace was later modeled.

We discussed earlier the three mythical kings who were attributed historical dates and existence by Chinese historians. Myths of the three great emperors are concerned with more existential and day to day activities and concerns for the Chinese, such as agriculture, architecture, warfare, metallurgy, silk and medicine. The mythical heroes of those stories, Fu Hsi, Shen Nung, Huang Ti, and later Yu the Great, established the basis of the Chinese human order which was carried down until the Communist Revolution of 1911. While Taoists are interested and concerned with the primordial foundations of the Chinese cosmos, it is fair to say that Chinese creation mythology is concerned more with the establishment of the human world than with the natural forms and rhythms of the universe. Chinese mythology is more concerned with the establishment of architecture, the calendar, money, dikes and canals and music than it is with the origin of the world itself. Thus it is simply incorrect to say that the Chinese were not concerned with creation mythology. At the same time, it is fair to say that Chinese mythology is somewhat unique in the way and to the degree it emphasizes specifically human aspects of the world.

The Chinese emphasis on the creation and maintenance of human relationships with other humans and with the world reaches its pinnacle in the thought of Confucius (K'ung Fu-tzu). It is difficult to understand the thought of Confucius apart from the Chinese mythology of everyday concerns. What is unique about Chinese mythology is not, as some scholars say, that they have no interest in their beginnings, but rather that they have elevated the mythology of human origins to an unprecedented degree. Therefore, it should be noted that their earliest mythological story represents the primordial principle of chaos as anthropomorphic (P'an Ku). Of all the Neolithic religions, China's is perhaps the most anthropomorphic. Interestingly, it was in China that human beings first discovered fire, the definitive act which separates Homo sapiens from their zoological relatives.

In China the specifically human dimension seems to be most elevated and emphasized. And yet, China never developed an elaborate solar mythology as did Egypt, which may be understood in part by the fact that the Chinese, while elevating specifically human concerns to an unequaled level, embodied at an almost mute level of their existence the more archaic, passive, feminine religious principles which were later emphasized by the Taoists. This may help explain why humans were said to originate from the vermin on P'an Ku's body (Sproul 202).

China is indeed a country of religious extremes, for it seems that Chinese religion silently embodies cosmic-mythic themes while simultaneously emphasizing the specifically human aspect of their religious orientation. As we shall see, both of these themes are carried on by the Taoists, who continue to maintain the earlier cosmic tradition, and the Confucians, who expand the specifically human aspect of Chinese religion.

Bibliography
Chapter 6 — Ancient China

Ahern, Emily M. *The Cult of the Dead in a Chinese Village.* Stanford, California, 1973.
Allan, Sarah. *The Heir and the Sage: Dynastic Legend in Early China.* San Francisco, 1981.
_____. "Sons of Suns: Myth and Totemism in Early China." *Bulletin of the School of Oriental and African Studies* 44 (1981): 290–326.
Anderson, A.G. *Children of the Yellow Earth.* London, 1934.
Barnes, Gina, and Peter Bellwood. "Stone Age Farmers in Southern and Eastern Asia." *People of the Stone Age: Hunter-gatherers and Early Farmers.* Vol. 3. *The Illustrated History of Humankind.* Goran Burenhult. General Editor. New York, 1993: 123–27.
Bilsky, Lester James. *The State Religion of Ancient China.* 2 Vols. Taipei, 1975.
Bishop, C.W. "Origin and Early Diffusion of the Traction Plow." *Smithsonian Institution Annual Report of the Board of Regents* (1937): 531–547.
Bodde, Derk. "Myths of Ancient China." *Mythologies of the Ancient World.* S.N. Kramer. Editor. New York, 1961: 369–408.

_____. *Festivals in Classical China: New Year and other Annual Observances during the Han Dynasty, 206 B.C.–A.D. 220.* Princeton, 1975.

Boo, Mu-chou. "Popular Religion in Pre-Imperial China: Observation on the Almanacs of Shui-hu-ti." *Journal T'Oung Pao* 79 (1993): 225–48.

Chang, Kwang-chih. *Art, Myth and Ritual: The Path to Political Authority in Ancient China.* Cambridge, Massachusetts, 1983.

_____. *Early Chinese Civilization: Anthropological Perspectives.* Cambridge, Massachusetts, 1976.

_____. *Shang Civilization.* New Haven, Connecticut, 1980.

_____. *Sources of Shang History.* Berkeley, California, 1978.

Chi, Li. *The Beginning of Chinese Civilization.* Seattle and London, 1957.

Ching, Julia. *Mysticism and Kingship in China: The Heart of Chinese Wisdom.* Cambridge, 1997.

Cohen, Alvin P. "Chinese Religion: Popular Religion." *Encyclopedia of Religion.* Vol. 3. Mircea Eliade. Editor-in-Chief. Chicago, 1987: 289–296.

Creel, H.G. *The Birth of China: A Study of the Formative Period of Chinese Civilization.* New York, 1957.

Eberhard, Wolfram. *Chinese Festivals.* Rev. Ed. Taipei, 1972.

Eliade, Mircea. *A History of Religious Ideas.* Vol. 2. Trans. W. R. Trask. Chicago and London, 1982.

Eno, Robert. "Deities and Ancestors in Early Oracle Inscriptions." *Religions of China in Practice.* Donald S. Lopez, Jr. Editor. Princeton, 1996: 41–51.

Girardot, N.J. "Chinese Religion: Mythic Themes." *Encyclopedia of Religion.* Vol. 3. Mircea Eliade. Editor-in-Chief. Chicago, 1987: 296–305.

_____. "The Problem of Creation Mythology and the Study of Chinese Religion." *History of Religions* 15 (1976): 289–318.

Henderson, John B. *Development and Decline of Chinese Cosmology.* New York, 1984.

Ho, Ping-Ti. *The Cradle of the East: An Inquiry into the Indigenous Origins and Techniques and Ideas of Neolithic and Early China. 5000–1000 B.C.* Hong Kong and Chicago, 1975.

Hsu, Cho-Yun. "Dynasties in China: From Early States to Nationhood." *Old World Civilizations: The Rise of Cities and States.* Vol. 3 *The Illustrated History of Humankind.* Goran Burenhult. General Editor. New York, 1994: 101–109.

Hsu, Francis L.K. *Under the Ancestors' Shadow: Chinese Culture and Personality.* New York, 1948.

Johnson, David. "The City-God Cults of T'ang and Sung China." *Harvard Journal of Asiatic Studies* 45 (1985).

Karlgren, Bernhard. "Legends and Cults of Ancient China." *Bulletin of the Far Eastern Antiquities* 18 (1946): 199–365.

Keightley, David. "The Religious Commitment: Shang Theology and the Genesis of Chinese Political Culture." *History of Religions* 17 (1978): 211–225.

Major, John S. "Cosmology, and the Origins of Chinese Science." *Journal of Chinese Philosophy* (1978).

Maspero, Henri. *China in Antiquity.* Trans. Frank A. Kieman, Jr. Amherst, Massachusetts, 1979.

Meyer, Jeffrey F. "Feng-shui of the Chinese City." *History of Religions* 18 (1978): 138–155.
Overmyer, Daniel L. "Chinese Religion: An Overview." *Encyclopedia of Religion*. Mircea Eliade. Editor-in-Chief. New York, 1987: 257–289.
Shia, Joseph. "The Notion of God in the Ancient Chinese Religion." *Numen* 16 (1969): 99–138.
Sommer, Deborah. *Chinese Religion: An Anthology of Sources*. New York, 1995.
Sproul Barbara. *Primal Myths: Creation Myths around the World*. San Francisco, 1979.
T'ang, Chun-i. "Cosmologies in Ancient Chinese Philosophy." *Chinese Studies in Philosophy* 5 (1973): 4–47.
Te-K'un, Ch'en. *Archeology in China*. Vol. 1. *Prehistoric China*. Cambridge, 1959.
Thompson, Laurence G. *Chinese Religion: An Introduction*. Encino, California, 1969.
_____. *The Chinese Way in Religion*. Belmont, California, 1973.
Watson, William. *Early Civilization in China*. London 1966.
Wheatley, Paul. *The Pivot of the Four Quarters: A Preliminary Inquiry into the Origins and Characters of the Ancient Chinese City*. Chicago, 1971.
Wolf, Arthur P. *Religion and Ritual in Chinese Society*. Stanford, California, 1974.
_____. *Cultural Frontiers in Ancient East Asia*. Edinburgh, 1971.
Yang, C.K. *Religion in Chinese Society*. Berkeley, 1967.

CHAPTER 7

Judaism

The religion of the Hebrews in the Neolithic period presents a special case for the historian of religions. Arising about the second millennium B.C.E. around the great urban civilizations of Mesopotamia and Egypt, the Jews were a relatively small pastoral community. Jewish influence on the ancient Near East was marginal in its beginnings but later made a lasting and prominent influence on the entire Western world. The historical records of the beginnings of the Hebrew religion are unparalleled anywhere. While the history of the Jews embodies religious and sacred meanings, it is nevertheless the most accurate and complete chronology of Neolithic beginnings.

Archeological and linguistic records and discoveries have made it clear that the Bible contains the basic story of the Jewish people. The Jews appeared to have been very closely related to the nomadic and semi-nomadic pastoral peoples who roamed over North Arabia and contiguous lands in the second millennium B.C.E. According to Genesis 11:31, Terah, father of Abraham, migrated from Ur-Kasdim, in the region of the Babylonian city of Ur, to the region of Huran, which lies near the Euphrates River northeast of Syria. From there Abraham migrated to Canaan. In Canaan the Hebrew tribes continued moving south and occupied the land of Goshen on the eastern side of the Nile delta.

The first five books of the Bible are called the Pentateuch, considered to be the most sacred and important of Jewish writings. The first eleven chapters of Genesis recount the creation of the world itself, while the remainder of the Pentateuch is concerned with the sacred history of the Jewish people following Abraham, who was called the "Father of Faith." Old Testament scholars, by employing complex methods of textual analysis and criticism, have determined that the Pentateuch consists of four different literary sources, none of which were written earlier than the tenth or ninth century B.C.E.

The oldest tradition is called Yahwistic because it calls God "Yahweh." The Elohistic tradition arises a little later and uses the name Elohim for God. The book of Deuteronomy seems to have been written from a single source, and the latest work is called the Sacerdotal, which seems to have been the work of priests concerned primarily with Jewish ritual practice and law.

Significantly, in the story of the creation of the world there is both a Yahwistic and Elohistic tradition. Genesis 1:2–4 begins with the famous passage: "In the beginning God [Elohim] created the heaven and the earth. Now the earth was a formless void, there was darkness over the deep, and God's spirit ["wind"] hovered over the water." The archaic structure of the Jewish cosmogony is clearly present in the opening lines of the Bible. God's spirit is likened to the wind which exists in the beginning with the primordial waters of chaos. However, the character of the Hebrew creation story changes very quickly, because God then begins creating the world through acts of speech. Thus the word of God becomes foundational for Hebrews because the world itself was brought into being through God's speech. Many authors have stated that Genesis represents an example of creation *ex nihilo,* that is, creation from nothing.

But it would be more accurate to say that the creation in Genesis represents the organization of chaos (*tohu wa bohu*), which is brought about by the word of God. "And God said, 'Let there be light,' and there was light" (Genesis 1:3). God's divine word completes the successive stages of creation. While Elohim does seem to be an all powerful being who creates the world consciously and deliberately, a more archaic notion of creation from chaos is still retained in Jewish scripture (Torah). Thus in Psalms 24:1–2 it is stated that, "The earth is the Lord's, and the fullness thereof, the world and those who dwell therein; for he hath founded it upon the seas, and established it upon the rivers."

It seems that writers of Genesis were aware of ancient Near Eastern mythical traditions in which the world was brought forth by the sacrifice of a primordial god or goddess. It may even be the case that the *enuma elish* of Mesopotamia was familiar to the author of the biblical text. Interestingly, the primordial ocean in Hebrew is called *tehom,* a word related to the Babylonian Tiamat. And even though neither Genesis creation narrative mentions the sacrifice of a primordial serpent, Isaiah 51:9 begins, "Awake, awake, put on strength, O arm of the Lord; awake, as in days of old, the generations of long ago. Was it not thou that didst cut Rahab in pieces, that didst pierce the dragon?" Therefore Jewish tradition retains the notion of creation from chaos and even references a cosmogonic combat as was the case in Mesopotamia.

Still there is another element present in the Jewish creation myth which is nowhere found in Mesopotamian texts. It is possible and perhaps even likely that the creation of the world through conscious acts of speech in Genesis was borrowed by the short-lived monotheistic tradition of Akhenaton. Indeed it is interesting that Psalms 104 has been compared to certain Egyptian hymns written during the time of Akhenaton.

Be that as it may, the Yahwistic tradition in Genesis makes it clear that the world created by Elohim is good and culminates with the creation of human beings in the image of God. Genesis 2:4–3:24 recites the Yahwistic cosmogonic tradition. The chronology of events in this tradition is a bit different because Yahweh creates Adam and Eve, the first humans, immediately upon making the earth and the heaven. Then, after creating Adam and Eve, "the Lord God planted a Garden in Eden, in the east; and there he put the man whom he had formed. And out of the ground the Lord God made to grow every tree that is pleasant to the sight and good for food, the tree of life also in the midst of the garden, and the tree of the knowledge of good and evil." The link between the Garden of Eden and the Yahwistic Genesis account and Mesopotamia is made clear because the Garden of Eden is bounded on one side by the Euphrates River. Life was paradisal for Adam and Eve in the Garden of Eden. All types of food were readily available; there was no death, no sickness and no work in the Garden of Eden. But God tells Adam and Eve not to eat from the Tree of the Knowledge of Good and Evil. The serpent tempts Eve to taste of the fruit from the Tree of the Knowledge of Good and Evil, and Eve, in turn, tempts Adam who also breaks this prohibition. By eating of the fruit of the Tree of the Knowledge of Good and Evil, Adam and Eve are expelled from their perfect life in Eden into a fully human existence. From that point forward humans are condemned to hard work and pain in childbirth. Furthermore, by being driven from the Garden of Eden, humans no longer had access to the Tree of Life and thus were the Jews introduced to death.

The knowledge of good and evil is consciousness. In other words, the story of Adam and Eve in Genesis is the Jewish myth of the origin of the human mode of being. When Jewish people became human, they acquired consciousness of good and evil and awareness of their own mortality. Life in the Garden of Eden was perfect. Adam and Eve lived in perfect unity and harmony with God. There was no distance between humans and God, therefore there was no knowledge of God. Paradoxically, the expulsion of Adam and Eve from the Garden of Eden paralleled human awareness of the divine, for it was only by maintaining distance from the sacred that one could know it in any sense. Thus the story of Adam and Eve for Jews is not simply a negative story about the fall of the Jewish people from paradise; it is simultaneously the story of the creation of the human mode of being by God. Adam and Eve did not decide to transgress God's law and commit a wrong by disobeying God's command and eating from the Tree of the Knowledge of Good and Evil. Rather, the story of their eating from the Tree of the Knowledge of Good and Evil is the Jewish mythic expression of the origin of the human way of life. Adam and Eve could not have knowingly committed a wrong by eating from the Tree of the Knowledge of Good and Evil for they had no consciousness until they had eaten from the tree.

Cain and Abel

Adam and Eve had two sons, Cain and Abel. Cain was a farmer and Abel was a shepherd. Both Cain and Abel made offerings to the Lord. Cain offered the fruits of the ground, and Abel the first born of his flock. The Lord cherished the gifts of the shepherd Abel but had no regard for the agricultural produce of Cain. Cain became jealous and murdered his brother (Genesis 4:8). Then Cain, traveling east, left the land of Eden and became the founder of cities (Genesis 4:16–17). Cain was also the ancestor of Tu'bal-cain, who was "the forger of all instruments of bronze and iron" (Genesis 4:22). Cain, whose name means "smith," is linked with the origins of agriculture, cities, metallurgy and murder. Jewish tradition also maintains that Cain became the ancestor of the Kenites. Kenites, because they smithed metals and played metal instruments, were viewed very suspiciously by their Hebrew relatives.

The haughtiness of mining is further adumbrated in Job 28 where mining is described as a supremely human triumph over nature. Mining requires very sophisticated thinking and technology which no animal possesses and which represents one of the highest orders of human intellect. At the same time, mining represents human arrogance and ultimately human ignorance of the truth that is knowledge of God. While mining yields gold, silver and gems, it does not yield wisdom, which is hidden from the eyes of all living beings.

> Surely there is a mine for silver, and a place for gold which they refine. Iron is taken out of the earth, and copper is smelted from the ore. Men put an end to darkness, and search out to the farthest bound the ore in gloom and deep darkness. They open shafts in a valley away from where men live; they are forgotten by travelers, they hang afar from

men, they swing to and fro. As for the earth, out of it comes bread; but underneath it is turned up as by fire. Its stones are the place of sapphires, and it has dust of gold. That path no bird of prey knows, and the falcon's eye has not seen it. The proud beasts have not trodden it; the lion has not passed over it. Man puts his hand to the flinty rock, and overturns mountains by the roots. He cuts out channels in the rocks, and his eye sees every precious thing. He binds up the streams so that they do not trickle, and the thing that is hid he brings forth to light. But where shall wisdom be found? And where is the place of understanding? Man does not know the way to it, and it is not found in the land of the living. The deep says, "It is not in me," and the sea says, "It is not with me." It cannot be gotten for gold, and silver cannot be weighed as its price. It cannot be valued in the gold of Ophir, in precious onyx or sapphire. Gold and glass cannot equal it, nor can it be exchanged for jewels of fine gold. No mention shall be made of coral or of crystal; the price of wisdom is above pearls. The topaz of Ethiopia cannot compare with it, nor can it be valued in pure gold. Whence then comes wisdom? And where is the place of understanding? It is hid from the eyes of all living, and concealed from the birds of the air. Abaddon and Death say, "We have heard a rumor of it with our ears. God understands the way to it, and he knows its place. For he looks to the ends of the earth, and sees everything under the heavens. When he gave to the wind its weight, and meted out the waters by measure; when he made a decree for the rain, and a way for the lightning of the thunder; then he saw it and declared it; he established it, and searched it out." And he said to man, "Behold, the fear of the Lord, that is wisdom; and to depart from evil is understanding" (Job 28).

We have already touched on the religious dimensions of farming, urban development and metallurgy, all of which parallel the potential eclipse of the passivity of religious experience. Those developments are all present in early Genesis. By contrast, Abel, the ancestor of shepherds, is involved in a subsistence modality which God himself favors.

Noah and the Tower of Babel

Genesis next chronicles the multiplication of people on the face of the earth. Genealogies are kept, but they are of a mythical or at least legendary character as humans are said to live for hundreds of years at a time. People become wicked, and a righteous man, Noah, is selected by God to build a large ark on which he is to put two of each kind of animal species. Noah does as he is told, and the Lord God makes it rain for 40 days upon the earth, destroying all life. The Lord establishes a covenant with Noah and his descendants to never again destroy life by flood or to ever destroy the earth again by flood. Within this new world, "Noah was the first tiller of the soil" (Genesis 9:9–20).

The Bible next lists numerous genealogies. The population grew and everyone spoke the same language (Genesis 11:1). After settling in the land of Shinär, the people decided to build a great city whose tower would touch the heavens. This was perceived as an arrogant act and an expression of human will that would result in the elevation of human power over the sacred (Genesis 11:6). The Lord God gave different languages to the people and thus they were scattered over the earth.

Abraham

Next the Lord called Abram to leave his homeland and travel to another area (Genesis 12:1–5). The story of Abram, later Abraham, has been dated to about 2000 B.C.E. Abram departed from Haran and set forth to the land of Canaan. From there he journeyed on and went up from Egypt. Abram was a cattleherder. At some point there was a dispute between the herdsmen of Abram's cattle and the herdsmen of Lot's cattle (Genesis 13:7). Eventually God renames Abram "Abraham" and establishes a covenant making Abraham the father of nations, "Behold my covenant is with you, and you shall be the father of a multitude of nations" (Genesis 17:4).God then promises that Abraham's people shall receive the land of Canaan and that there shall be an everlasting covenant between God and Abraham's descendants (Genesis 17:7–8). Here, in contrast to the covenant with Noah, a condition is placed upon the Jews. Each Jewish male is to be circumcised as a sign of the covenant between God and Abraham's people.

But the definitive story of Abraham for the Jewish people is found in Genesis 22:1–19. Abraham and his wife, Sarah, who are both quite old, were miraculously blessed with the birth of a son, Isaac. Abraham, on the basis of faith in God, left his homeland and set up a new way of life in a foreign country. Having shown his obedience to God, he was blessed, as were all subsequent generations.

Now, however, God tests Abraham's faith: "He said, 'take your son, your only son Isaac, whom you love, and go to the land of Mori'ah, and offer him there as a burnt offering upon one of the mountains of which I shall tell you'" (Genesis 22:2). Abraham takes his son to the place that God shows him, builds an altar, binds his son and lays him on the altar. Then Abraham takes the knife and prepares to slay his son. At that very moment God, through an angel, spares Isaac and substitutes a ram in his place.

This is a simple story which has far reaching and profound meanings in religious history, especially for the Jewish people. While it is true that the Jews knew of human sacrifice, sacrifice was always performed for some particular reason which was understood. Thus, for example, Mes'ha, king of the Mo'abites, sacrificed his oldest son in order to secure victory in war from Israel (2 Kings 3:2–7). Jeph'thah promised Yahweh that he would sacrifice the first person he met after victory in battle in honor of him. He encountered his own son and sacrificed him (Judges 11:30 ff.).

Some scholars have argued that child sacrifice was practiced by various ancient Near Eastern peoples, but there is no evidence that the Jewish people ever participated in such a ritual. There seems to be no precedent or tradition for killing one's first born, and no reason is given for this act except that "God tested Abraham" (Genesis 22:1). Abraham did not understand why he was being asked to perform this horrific act, and yet he obeyed God's command to do so. Until this time all sacrifices and indeed all ritual acts had purposes and meanings that were understood. Ritual participants inhabited a world of religious significance which made sense to them and had a purpose that was comprehensible. Not so with Abraham. There existed no traditional basis in Judaism for such an act; Abraham complied with God's command on the basis of "faith" alone. Thus Abraham came to be called the "Father of Faith" because of his willingness to blindly obey the unfathomable dictates of God.

Now, for the first time in human history, God is understood to manifest himself in unique, novel and unprecedented historical events rather than through the timeless vicissitudes, rhythms and forms of the cosmos (Eliade). With Abraham, faith replaced perception and understanding as the primary modality of religious apprehension. Prior to Abraham, singular and unique events carried no sacred significance; indeed, they were meaningless because they were not performed first in mythic times.

We have already discussed how the New Year ritual reenacted the creation of the world for ancient Neolithic peoples. Indeed everywhere in the world it was felt that the world was recreated during the new year. In that sense each year was a repetition of the first year, and life acquired religious significance through its cyclical, repetitious nature. For all ancient peoples the patterns of human existence were laid down in the beginning by the gods, and humans reestablished those primordial times through the embodiment of those ways of life. People hunted, farmed, built houses, cooked food and raised children the way they did because the ancestors did so in mythical time. The Jews were no different in that respect, until Abraham. With the story of Abraham and Isaac, Jewish religion embarks on unparalleled transformation in religious history. Historical events, which prior to Abraham had been profane, now are seen as sacred insofar as they are willed by God. God, who traditionally was understood to manifest himself by and through the natural rhythms of the world, is now understood to manifest himself in specifically human events. The Jews did not discover chronology, for all Neolithic kingdoms kept genealogies of the royal family. However, Mesopotamians, Egyptians, Indians and Chinese inhabited a world in which religious meaning was perceived and understood, whereas the faith of Abraham was incomprehensible.

Just as traditional societies saw time as cyclical, they also perceived space as centered. We have already seen how Paleolithic and Neolithic communities experienced certain places as particularly auspicious and significant. The sacred center was the spaceless space, the place where heaven, earth, the underworld and four cardinal directions intersected. The center allowed one to experience unity with the world. Space for the Jews was not centered. Abraham, when his name was still Abram, was uprooted from his traditional homeland and told to go to a new place because God willed it. God, for the Hebrews, did not manifest himself through the cosmos but rather through the history of the Jewish people. The Hebrew God was a transcendent God whose will was unknowable, and the Jews obeyed his will through the practice of faith. The God of history manifests himself directly through the lives of his people in a manner that is not connected to any particular sacred center. This was unique in world history and raised significant questions for the Jewish people as we shall see.

The Exodus

Hebrews emphasize that the beginnings of the religion of Israel are outlined in Genesis chapters 46 through 50, in Exodus and in the book of Numbers. These books show in a very powerful way how events in Jewish history were directly willed by God. The first significant example of God's will was Moses' encounter with the burning bush, which represented his first encounter with Yahweh. At that time God relayed to Moses his mission — to lead the Jewish people out of bondage in Egypt. God later sent ten plagues upon the Egyptians to force the Pharaoh to consent to let the Jewish people leave Egypt. As the Israelites left Egypt, the Sea of Reeds (not the Red Sea) parted in order to let the Jewish people cross. When the Egyptians attempted to pursue the Jews in order to slaughter them, the Sea of Reeds collapsed upon them, destroying them (Exodus 1–15:21). This event is called the Exodus and is relived each year in the Jewish Passover ritual. The Exodus, the escape from Egypt by the Jews, was and is seen as divinely inspired. The God of history directly intervened in the lives of the Israelites in order to free them from their subordinate condition in Egypt.

Following the Exodus, the Israelites wandered through the desert for a number of years seeking the promised land. When they reached Sinai, the people of Israel and Yahweh entered into a solemn pact, or covenant. Yahweh delivered to Moses the "Ten Commandments," which became the basis of Jewish religious ethics. God, who confronted Moses, stated that he is the God of Abraham and the other patriarchs (Exodus 20:3–17). According to the *Bible*, Moses received the tablets containing the Ten Commandments about three months after the Exodus from Egypt.

The Jews then spent 40 years in the desert practicing a cult established by Yahweh. Little is known about their religion at this period although Exodus 26 and 38:8–38 give fairly detailed descriptions of the desert sanctuary, a tent which held the Ark of the Covenant. After forty years Moses dies in the Plain of Moab, opposite Jericho. Moses is shown the promised land of Canaan, but he is not allowed to cross into it because he failed to keep the faith at certain critical junctures during the desert years. In Deuteronomy 32:48–52 it is said,

> And the Lord said to Moses that very day, "Ascend this mountain of the Ab'arim, Mount Nebo, which is in the land of Moab, opposite Jericho; and view the land of Canaan, which I give to the people of Israel for a possession; and die on the mountain which you ascend, and be gathered to your people, as Aaron your brother died in Mount Hor, and was gathered to his people; because you broke faith with me in the midst of the people of Israel at the waters of Meri-bah-Ka'-desh, in the wilderness of Zin; because you did not revere me as holy in the midst of the people of Israel. For you shall see the land before you; but you shall not go there, into the land which I give to the people of Israel."

During the desert years the people were thirsty, and the Lord told Moses at Zin to assemble the people and, before their eyes, tell the rock to yield its water in order that they might drink (Numbers 20:8). Instead, Moses took his rod and struck the rock twice and brought forth abundant water (Numbers 20:10–11). Then the Lord said to Moses, "Because you did not believe in me, to sanctify me in the eyes of the people of Israel, therefore you shall not bring this assembly into the land which I have given them" (Numbers 20:12; 27:12–14).

Thus faith is such a central part of Jewish religion that even Moses, who was selected by Yahweh to lead the people out of Egypt and who received the "Ten Commandments," was not allowed to go into Canaan, the land promised to Abraham, because he did not keep the faith. The God of Moses is a god of history who directs the unique and irreversible events of the Jewish people:

> And because he loved your fathers and chose their descendants after them, and brought you out of Egypt with his own presence, by his great power, driving out before you nations greater and mightier than yourselves, to bring you in to give you their land for an inheritance, as at this day; know therefore this day, and lay it to your heart, that the Lord is God in heaven above and on earth beneath, there is no other (Deuteronomy 4:37–40).

In the above passage the God of the Jews is seen as both the director of historical events and as the only God. This is not the place to enter into discussion about the monotheistic aspect of the Jewish God. At this stage Yahweh was perhaps not a fully articulated monotheistic divinity but the outlines of such a supreme being are arguably in place.

Joshua, not Moses, led the people over the Jordan River into the promised land of Canaan. This conquest period has been dated about 1250 B.C.E. and shows that the establishment of Israel was very slow and difficult. When the nomadic pastoral tribes of Israel settled in Canaan, they confronted an urban agricultural community grounded in fertility rights and connected with numerous gods. The period between 1250 B.C.E. until 1020 B.C.E., when Saul was proclaimed king, is called the Age of Judges. During this period Yahweh directly intervened in battles to assure the Israelites victory over the Canaanites. He assured Joshua that an enemy had been delivered into his power (Joshua 10:8), and Yahweh even caused large hail stones to fall from heaven killing the enemy by the thousands (Joshua 10:11).

The cult of Yahweh begins to spread over the land. At the same time confrontation with the Canaanite religion has marked consequences for the cult of Yahweh. Yahweh is linked with Baal during the Age of Judges, and it seems that Yahweh and Baal are venerated side by side. Only later in the period is the worship of Baal condemned. Much of the Canaanite sacrificial system was adopted by the Hebrews, and sanctuaries are modeled on Canaanite examples. Most significantly, later Israelite prophecy has deep roots in Canaanite religion. Throughout the books of Joshua, Judges, Samuel and Kings the conflict and interrelationship between Baal and Yahweh is discussed. In the end Yahweh, who guided the Hebrews into the desert and into Canaan, assumes the aspects of the Canaanite gods. Yahweh becomes a monotheistic divinity who both directs history and is also the giver of fertility and rain.

Age of Kings

As the Hebrews became more and more settled, problems of political organization emerged. The people petitioned Samuel for a king to govern them (I Samuel 8:5–6). Yahweh instructed Samuel to warn the people of the ways of a king and he did so. Samuel told the people that a king would draft some of their sons into the army and others to tend his farms, and he would force daughters to cook and bake for him. Confiscating the best fields and flocks for himself, a king would also exact tribute from his subjects. Still the people clamored for a king, and Yahweh instructed Samuel to give them what they wanted.

Saul thus became the first king of Israel. David succeeded Saul as king of Israel and ruled from 1011 to 971 B.C.E. Interestingly, through this transformation, the Jews reinstated the structure of kingship from which they escaped with Moses during the Exodus from Egypt. However, the king of Israel is not divine initially. The book of Judges states that the only king of Israel is God himself. For the Jews the king organizes the people into a community that functions politically. But with the passage of time the population put more emphasis on the king rather than God, and Jerusalem came to be seen as a ceremonial city, as the city of God. Whereas in the beginning the entire land of Canaan was seen as the land of God, eventually Jerusalem itself began to emerge as a typical Neolithic center.

Solomon (971–932 B.C.E.) continued the Davidic kingdom. Solomon put the Ark of the Covenant in his temple, which came to be seen as sacred (Jeremiah 7). During the rule of Solomon, the ark itself is almost completely forgotten, as it is mentioned only once in the book of Psalms. The sacrality of the Davidic city of Jerusalem comes to be seen as almost independent of the ark. Mount Zion becomes a towering mountain shrine, an *axis mundi*, which links heaven and earth and replaces Mount Sinai as the locus of revelation.

The original covenant established between Yahweh and Moses was conditional (Deuteronomy 30:15–18). Yahweh told Moses that his people shall be blessed if they obeyed God. During the period of the monarchy when Jerusalem was heralded as an impregnable city ruled by a king who mediates God and the people, the conditional covenant of Moses became unconditional. The Jewish dynasty was seen as everlasting. For example, in Psalms 72, David and Solomon are both described as intermediaries and priests, and the king is characterized as divine in Psalms 89:26. In Isaiah 9:6 the king was called the Son of God at his coronation. Thus the Davidic covenant is substituted for Moses' covenant.

Jewish Prophets

It is in this context that the Jewish prophets emerged. Yahweh expressed his anger over the building of the temple adjoining the palace of the king. Outraged that the divine realm of the temple is separated from the palace by "only a wall," Yahweh decried this juxtaposition of sacred and secular realms as "idolatry" (Ezekiel 43:6–9). After the death of Solomon the northern and southern portions of the kingdom split. The north became Israel and existed from 922 to 722 B.C.E. when it was sacked by Syria. The southern kingdom, Judah, was sacked by Nebuchadnezzar and the Babylonians in 586 B.C.E. In short, the rhythms of urbanity, which were always rejected and criticized by the Hebrew people since their pastoral beginnings, eventually engulfed the Jewish people and lead to a decline of the Jewish religion and eventually the conquest of the kingdoms of Israel and Judah.

Jewish concerns with the evils of city life are nowhere better expressed than in Leviticus 26:25–26 which links city life with famine, disease and violence. Epidemic disease was clearly rampant during the Age of Judges (Numbers 21:6, 11:1.3, 14:11; Exodus 32). These epidemics seemed to be related to the urbanized life of Hebrew kingdoms and these plagues severely reduced the population of the common folk at a time when the Israelite community was trying to build its numbers. During this period women were highly valued in Israel because of their childbearing capacities. Then, with the establishment of the monarchy, the priesthood became male-dominated and women were viewed in a more negative light (Meyers). Women were needed more and more to propagate the species, and yet, because their childbearing capacities were emphasized in purely utilitarian terms, they became less and less involved in religious affairs. With urbanization and male agricultural production, women became minimally involved in the economic sphere, which again led to their diminished significance. As we shall see, the mistreatment of women, along with elderly and sick people, gave rise to a very powerful prophetic movement within the Hebrew tradition.

Bibliography
Chapter 7 — Judaism

Albrecht, Alt. *Essays on Old Testament History and Religion*. Trans. R.A. Wilson. New York, 1968.

Albright, W.F. *Archeology and the Religion of Israel*. 2nd Ed. Baltimore, 1946.

_____. *The Archaeology of Palestine.* Harmondsworth and Middlesex, 1960.
_____. *The Biblical Period From Abraham to Ezra.* New York, 1963.
_____. *From the Stone Age to Christianity.* 2nd Ed. Baltimore, 1957.
Altmann, Alexander. *The Meaning of Jewish Existence: Theological Essays, 1930–1939.* Alfred L. Ivry. Editor. Hanover, 1991.
Anderson, Bernhard W. *Understanding the Old Testament.* Englewood Cliffs, New Jersey, 1957.
Ashton, Dianne, and Allen M. Umansky. *Four Centuries of Jewish Women's Spirituality: A Sourcebook.* Boston, 1992.
Baron, Salo W. *Social and Religious History of the Jews.* 16 Vols. New York, 1952 *et seq.*
Bickerman, E. *From Ezra to the Last of the Maccabees: Foundations of Post-Biblical Judaism.* New York, 1962.
Borowitz, Eugene B. "Judaism: An Overview." *Encyclopedia of Religion.* Vol. 8. Mircea Eliade. Editor-in-Chief. New York, 1987: 127–149.
Bright, J. *A History of Israel.* Philadelphia, 1959.
Charles, R.H. *Apocrypha and Pseudepigrapha of the Old Testament.* Oxford, 1913.
Cornfield, Gaalyahu. Editor. *Adam to Daniel.* New York, 1961.
De Lange, N.R.M. *Judaism.* Oxford and New York, 1986.
Eissfeldt, Otto. *The Old Testament: An Introduction.* New York, 1965.
Eliade, Mircea. *The Myth of the Eternal Return, or Cosmos and History.* Trans. W. R. Trask. Princeton, 1954.
The Encyclopedia Judaica. 16 Vols. Jerusalem, 1971.
Finklestein, L. Editor. *The Jews: Their History, Culture and Religion.* New York, 1960.
Flavius, Josephus. *The Jewish War.* Trans. G.A. Williamson. London and Baltimore, 1970.
Fohrer, G. *History of Israelite Religion.* Nashville and New York, 1972.
Goldstein, J.A. "The Tales of the Tobiads." *Christianity, Judaism, and other Greco-Roman Cults: Studies for Morton Smith.* Vol. 3. Leiden, 1975: 85–123.
Gordis, R. *Koheleth: The Man and His World.* New York, 1951.
Grant, F.C. *Hellenistic Religion: The Age of Syncretism.* New York, 1953.
Grazel, Solomon. *A History of the Jews.* New York, 1968.
Hadas, M. *Aristeas to Philocrates: Jewish Apocryphal Literature.* New York, 1951.
Heschel, Abraham Joshua. *The Prophets.* New York, 1962.
Irwin, William. "The Hebrews." *The Intellectual Adventure of Ancient Man: An Essay on Speculative Thought in the Ancient Near East.* H. Frankfort et al. Editors. Chicago, 1946.
_____. *The Old Testament: Keystone of Human Culture.* New York, 1952.
Janowsky, Oscar I. *The American Jew: A Composite Portrait.* New York, 1932.
Kaufmann, Yehezkel. *The Religion of Israel: From Its Beginnings to the Babylonian Exile.* Trans. and Abridged M. Greenburg. Chicago, 1966.
Kittel, Rudolph. *The Religion of the People of Israel.* New York, 1925.
Klausner, Joseph. *The Messianic Idea in Israel from Its Beginning to the Completion of the Mishnah.* New York, 1955.
Lieberman, S. *Greeks in Jewish Palestine.* New York, 1942.
_____. *Hellenism in Jewish Palestine.* New York, 1950.
Lindhagen, C. *The Servant Motif in the Old Testament.* Uppsala, 1950.

Loehr, Max. *A History of Religion in the Old Testament*. New York, 1936.
Margolis, Max, and Alexander Marx. *History of the Jewish People*. Philadelphia, 1953.
Markus, Jacob R. Editor. *The Jew and the Medieval World: A Source Book: The Years 351–1791*. New York, 1965.
Mason, T.W. *The Servant-Messiah*. Cambridge, 1952.
Mendenhall, C.E. *Law and Covenant in Israel and the Ancient Near East*. Pittsburgh, 1955.
Meyers, Carol. "The Roots of Restriction: Women in Early Israel." *Biblical Archeologist* 41 (1978): 91–103.
Moore, G.F. *Judaism in the First Centuries of the Christian Era*. Cambridge, Massachusetts, 1927.
Muilenburg, James. "The History of the Religion of Israel." *The Interpreter's Bible*. Vol. 1. New York and Nashville, 1952: 292–348.
Myres, I.L. "Persia, Greece and Israel." *Palestine Exploration Quarterly* 85 (1953): 8–22.
Neusner, Jacob. *Lectures on Judaism in the History of Religions*. Atlanta, Georgia, 1990.
_____. *The Way of Torah: An Introduction to Judaism*. 3rd Ed. Belmont, California, 1979.
North, C.R. *The Suffering Servant in Deutero-Isaiah*. 2nd Ed. London, 1956.
Noth, M. *The History of Israel*. Trans. S. Godman. London, 1958.
Oesterley, W.O.E., and T.H. Robinson. *A History of Israel*. 2 Vols. Oxford, 1932.
Pendersen, J. *Israel, Its Life and Culture*. 4 Vols. Oxford, 1926–46.
Pfeiffer, Robert H. *The Apocrypha*. New York, 1953.
Philipson, David. *The Reform Movement in Judaism*. New York, 1931.
Rad, G. von. *Old Testament Theology*, Vol. 1. New York, 1962.
Rojtman, Betty. *Black Fire on White: An Essay on Jewish Hermeneutics, from Midrash to Kabbalah*. Trans. Steven Rendall. Berkeley, California, 1998.
Roth, Cecil. *Short History of the Jewish People*. London, 1953.
Sachar, Abram Leon. *A History of the Jews*. New York, 1930.
Seltzer, Robert M. *Jewish People, Jewish Thought: The Jewish Experience in History*. New York, 1980.
Silver, Daniel Jeremy, and Bernard Martin. *A History of Judaism*. 2 Vols. N.Y., 1974.
Smith, Jonathan Z. *Imagining Religion: From Babylon to Jonestown*. Chicago: University of Chicago Press, 1982.
Smith, Morton. *Palestinian Parties and Politics that Shaped the Old Testament*. New York and London, 1971.
Solomon, Norman. *Judaism: A Very Short Introduction*. Oxford and New York, 1996.
Steinberg, Milton. *Basic Judaism*. Northvale, New Jersey, 1987.
Vaux, R. de. *Ancient Israel: Its Life and Institutions*. Trans. John McHugh. New York, 1961.
Wiesel, Elie. *Souls on Fire: Portraits and Legends of Hasidic Leaders*. Trans. Marian Wiesel. New York, 1972.
Winston, David. "The Book of Wisdom's Theory of Cosmogony." *History of Religions* 11 (1971): 185–202.
Wright, G.E. *The Old Testament Against Its Environment*. Chicago, 1951.
The Encyclopedia Judaica. 16 vols. Jerusalem, 1971.

Chapter 8

The Axial Age

The philosopher Karl Jaspers described the period in world history from 800 B.C.E. to 200 B.C.E. as "The Axial period," so called because a number of pivotal religious and philosophical figures emerged during that time. Similarly, the historian Arnold Toynbee once asked, "Who are ... the greatest benefactors of the living generation of mankind? I should say: 'Confucius and Laotze, the Buddha, the Prophets of Israel and Judah, Zoroaster, Jesus, Muhammad and Socrates.'" (Toynbee 156).

Around 900 B.C.E. nomads of the west-central Asian steppe had learned how to control their horses with their legs so that they could free their arms for shooting bows and arrows. With this mastery of horse and weapon Assyria founded the cavalry and created an empire that spread from the Mediterranean through Central Asia. Communications between previously isolated areas increased dramatically and a sort of cultural unification was achieved. However, because Assyrians slaughtered their enemies and extracted huge tribute, their subjects rose up and attacked the great city of Nineveh, sacking it.

Still alliances were sprouted. All countries in the Ancient Near East participated in trade. Agriculture, mining and manufacturing all increased supplies of goods. Luxury items included Phoenician glass, dyed fabrics, ivory, perfume, Egyptian linens, amulets and papyrus scrolls. Wine and oil were perhaps the most widely traded goods, but metals and slaves were also important. A new wealthy class emerged and so did money. With coinage came lending and usury, which resulted in default, loss of land and enslavement. Cities began to fill with dispossessed and bitter men. Still urbanity grew.

Cyrus the Great began his career as a ruler in southwestern Persia in

559 B.C.E. He successfully conquered Medes, Lydia, Asia Minor, Babylon, northeastern Persia and Egypt. His successor, Darius, took over in 522 B.C.E. and organized what Cyrus conquered. The largest the world had ever seen, Darius' empire included Asia Minor, Armenia, Azerbaijan, Syria, Palestine, Egypt, northern Arabia, Mesopotamia, Persia, Afghanistan, Turkestan, Uzbekistan, the Tadzhik and part of the Kirgiz republics, western Pakistan, Indus Valley, Thrace, Macedon and Cyrenaica (Garraty and Gay). A network of urban societies extended continuously from the Atlantic coast of Spain to the Jaxartes River in Central Asia and the Ganges River in India, and from southern Arabia to the north coasts of the Black Sea and the Mediterranean (Childe). Especially Persians and Greeks felt at home in a world at least four times as large as Babylonians and Egyptians could have imagined. Furthermore, Darius united his vast territory with a sophisticated web of roads. Using fast horses and relay stations like the Pony Express of the American West, messengers could travel the almost 1,700 mile route from Susa to Sardis in nine days, ten days to the port cities of Ephesus or Smyrna. In the fourth century B.C.E. Herodotus spoke highly of the efficiency of this system.

During this period the camel caravans of the western leg of the Silk Road headed toward Babylon and from there to Aleppo or Damascus through the Great Desert Route (Franck and Brownstone). In Assyrian times travelers generally crossed the Tigris River near the old capital of Nineveh (today Mosul) and the Euphrates River at Zeugma. But the Persian Royal Road took a more northwest orientation toward Anatolia and the Greek cities on the Aegean and Black Seas. Though the land trip was arduous and took about 90 days, it was considered preferable to sea travel because of pirates on the Mediterranean.

It was in this period that the great caravan cities of Syria, especially Damascus, became economic and cultural crossroads. The Persians encouraged trade furthermore by minting coins and introducing standard weights and measures. Eventually, the Silk Road became relatively secure and carried everyday household wares, cheap clothing and grain, in addition to luxury items and vital metals.

The international nature of trade during the time of Darius is nowhere better shown than by his own palace inscription about 521 B.C.E.:

> This is the palace which I built at Susa. From afar its ornamentation was brought ... the earth was dug downward, and ... the rubble was packed down, and ... the sun dried brick was molded, [by] the Babylonian people.... The cedar timber ... [is] from a mountain named [Lebanon] ... the Assyrian people brought it to Babylon; from Babylon the Carians and the Ionians brought it to Susa. The yaku timber was

brought from Gandara [in India] and from Carmania. The gold was brought from Sardis and from Bactria, which here was wrought. The precious stone lapis-lazuli and carnelian, which was wrought here, was brought from Sogdiana. The precious stone turquoise was brought from Chorasmia, which was wrought here. The silver and the ebony were brought from Egypt. The ornamentation with which the wall was adorned was brought from Ionia. The ivory, which was wrought here, was brought from Ethiopia and from Sind and from Arachosia. The stone columns, which here were wrought, were brought from Elam. The stone-cutters who wrought the stone were Ionians and Sardians. The goldsmiths who wrought the gold were Medes and Egyptians. The men who wrought the baked brick were Babylonians. The men who adorned the well were Medes and Egyptians (Franck and Brownstone 65–66).

In trade the camel was unsurpassed. While the horse was the vehicle of the messenger, the camel carried the caravan. Professional camel drivers became an integral part of the Silk Road. Indeed Zarathustra, the founder of Zoroastrianism, means "camel-driver," and Muhammad sold camels to caravans crossing the Sahara. The development of shoes made of horsehair, copper and leather for horses, donkeys and camels in the fourth century B.C.E. made travel over rough roads easier.

If the Persians brought the Silk Road under one ruler, it was the Greeks who unified it culturally, if only for a short time. Responsible for this development was the Macedonian general Alexander the Great. His empire reached halfway across Asia. Furthermore, non-Greeks composed half of his army. Thracians, Illyrians, Iranians, Anatolians, Semites, Indians and others were incorporated into his ranks, and at each new city that fell many of the vanquished would join him. Not only that, but his army included engineers and mechanics, guides and interpreters, physicians and veterinarians, merchants, artists, bankers and wives, children, slaves and prostitutes. As historian Mikhail Rostovtzev put it, Alexander's army was a moving capital that was larger than many Hellenistic cities. He established Alexandria as a trade capital in the west, and in the east he tapped Bactra (formerly Zariaspa) as his eastern capital.

It is not clear if Alexander knew about China, but certainly the Greeks were familiar with silk. Small amounts of this precious fabric reached Eastern Europe by the fifth century B.C.E., but it is not clear if silk was known in the Mediterranean. Some silk may have found its way into Europe by way of India. Some scholars say that silk did not reach the West until nearly 100 B.C.E. when the first Chinese envoys reached Iran, but that indirect contact was probably made sooner.

Following Alexander, the western portion of the Silk Road was roughly divided by two rivals. By 300 B.C.E. Seleucus Nicator controlled the western and larger part: Afghanistan, Bactria, Persia, Mesopotamia, Armenia, Syria and parts of Anatolia. Seleucus built Antioch in 300 B.C.E. and thereby established the end of the transcontinental highway for centuries to come. His chief rival was Ptolemy, who controlled Alexandria, the coastal cities and the Spice Route from India.

The Seleucid Empire did not long control northern India. In 321 B.C.E. Indians under the Mauryan leader Chandragupta regained their lands. Seleucus did not try to reconquer India but preferred to maintain peaceful and profitable commercial relations with India. India under the Mauryan empire managed their 2,600 mile Grand Road that formed parts of the Silk Road. Road crews worked full-time to keep the highway clear and shelters were strategically positioned along the way for travelers, traders and pilgrims. Asoka, grandson of Chandragupta and the last of the Mauryans, converted to Buddhism shortly after 261 B.C.E. He sent missionaries along the Grand Road and Silk Road all the way to Syria, Egypt, Macedonia, Crete and Tibet. The influence of Hellenistic culture was substantial. A form of common Greek became the international language of the time and no doubt resulted in a Greek coloring of Judaism and Christianity. Greek art became widespread and the conventional representation of the Buddha was a creation of Hellenism. The Hellenistic age gave science and technology a boost. Geography, botany, astronomy and mathematics all benefited. A number of inventions appeared, including the bill of exchange in banking, the water lifting screw, the threshing drag in agriculture, the sternpost rudder in shipping and the most famous of all, the lighthouse.

China remained a somewhat feudal society in the eighth through the third centuries. Called the period of the Warring States, China was only peripherally connected to the West. Still, warfare was widespread and existed not only among the Chinese but between the Chinese and the Hsiung-nu to the north. Finally, in 246 B.C.E. King Cheng emerged as ruler of the northern state of Ch'in. Over the next 25 years he unified all kingdoms along the Wei and Huang Rivers and in 221 B.C.E. took the name Ch'in Shih Huang Ti (first emperor of the Ch'in dynasty). He joined the several defensive walls into the Great Wall to protect China to the north and west. Roads were improved and standard weights and measures were introduced. He unified China and expanded China's boundaries into the desert land of Central Asia. But in 202 B.C.E. the Ch'in dynasty was succeeded by the Han, who were to rule for the next four centuries. In 115 B.C.E. China, under the Han dynasty, made direct contact with the Near East and launched trade caravans along the eastern end of the Silk Road.

A dozen times a year camels loaded mostly with silks but also ivory, precious stones, furs, ceramics and spices crossed the Central Asian deserts from China to Turkestan by two principle routes (Shafi). The great caravan route started from Chang-an (Xian), capital of China during the Chin, Han, Sui and Tang dynasties. After passing through Kansu, the road split at Anxi. The northern route ran along oases like Hami (Kumul, Yiwen), Turfan (Gaocheng and Jiahoe), and Urmuqu (Tihua, Baishbalik) and either continued west to Ili to the Caspian Sea or dipped south to Korla Kucha, Asku and Kashgar. It then went around the edge of the Taklamakan Desert (Tarim Basin). The southern route passed through Dun Huang, Niya, Keria, Khotan (He Tian), Karghalik, Yarkland (Shache) and joined the northern route at Kashgar.

At Kashgar the road again split. The western route continued over the Roof of the World (Pamirs) towards Samarkand, Balkh, Bukhara, Meru, Nissa, through Parthia to Antioch. There, across the Mediterranean, the route continued by ship to Rome and Alexandria. The southern route dropped to Tashkurghan and across the Karakorams and then to the great Buddhist school at Taxila or to Peshawar, the center of the Gandhara empire. Other routes went to Srinagar in Kashmir and Afghanistan and Persia (Iran). Citizens of the major cities of the Silk Road saw elephants, tigers, monkeys, cotton, silk, furs, myrrh, pepper, olives, ebony, coral, lapis lazuli, amber, songbirds, honey and slaves.

Back in the West, Hellenism survived somewhat transformed through the Romans. Ascending to power after defeating Philip V of Macedon in 197 B.C.E. and Antiochus III, a Seleucid, in 190 B.C.E., Rome dominated the Western world through a powerful empire until the Muslims sacked Alexandria in 640 C.E.

The Romans spent great effort in developing and maintaining a vast road system that linked cities within the empire and accessed the East. Two of the most important highway systems were the "common route" and the Via Egnatia. The former spread across Asia Minor from Ephesus, Tralles, Laodicea, Apameia, Antioch by Pisidia, Philomelium, Iconium, Laranda, Tarsus and then either to Antioch in Syria or to the Euphrates River at Zeugma (Friedlander 268–322). As the *New Testament* scholar Wayne Meeks has shown, the "common route," in reverse order, is a virtual map of early Pauline Christian movement from Antioch to the Aegean (17). Farther west, Rome was connected to the East through the Via Egnatia. It began in the Greek Adriatic coast in two places, Dyrrhachium (Durres, Albania) and Apollonia (Pojan), joining in Clodiana. From there it ran to Candavia, Lychnidos, Herclea, Edessa, Thesselonica and on to Phillipi. From Phillipi one could continue by land to Byzantium or travel by sea to Byzantium (Charlesworth 115f).

Confessional Religions

It was along the Silk Road that the world's great religions emerged. From about 600 B.C.E. to 622 C.E. several great religious figures emerged — the Buddha, Lao Tzu, Jewish prophets such as Jeremiah, Amos and Hosea, Kung Fu-tzu (Confucius), Socrates, Jesus and Muhammad. The world which these individuals inhabited gave rise to religions which have been classified as Confessional or Soteriological.

At the same time it is important to note that the Axial Age did not cause new religions to arise. In some places along the Silk Road there was much trade but no new religious development. It would be overstated to say that the economy of the Silk Road gave birth to the Confessional religions; rather global trade and religious change presupposed one another. The historian of religions Joseph Kitagawa wrote a fine article some years back in which he noted that there were three fundamental features of the great world religions. First, religion is addressed to each individual rather than the community as was the case in the Paleolithic and Neolithic periods. Put differently, religion in the Axial Age is addressed to a global community rather than to a particular tribal, ethnic or geographical community. For example, early Christian communities most often referred to themselves by the term *ekklesia*, the Greek word for the assembly of all free citizens (Koester 17). The cities along the Silk Road did not integrate people into a unified community or kingdom. During this period, people traveled all over the world and the cities of the *oikoumene* were ethnic and cultural melting pots. Secondly, the Axial period religions view the world as inadequate for spiritual fulfillment and therefore looked to other worlds or another world of meaning (Kitagawa). Glimpses of this trend were seen towards the end of the Neolithic with the decline of the great kingdoms, but it is in the Axial Age that religion becomes focused on transcending the problematic nature of this world.

Third, according to Kitagawa, the religious and mythic dimensions of human existence become differentiated from the other aspects of life. Religion becomes something apart from subsistence, modalities, architecture, knowledge and social structure, although still loosely related. In the Paleolithic period hunting, gathering, tool-making and fire building were all seen as religious activities. Similarly, in the Neolithic period farming, herding, and city workers such as artists, soldiers, lawyers and merchants were all first understood in religious terms. Shamanic knowledge in the Paleolithic period was directly related to religious concerns and the same was true for Neolithic priests. The mathematicians and scientists of Mesopotamia and Egypt understood their work to be divinely inspired and the ultimate goal of their investigations was religious awareness and a proper relationship with the gods.

The religious message of the Axial period is very paradoxical. Religion becomes very moral and ethical, yet not moral and ethical. By separating religion from the other aspects of human existence the Axial Age religions reveal quite profoundly the *sui generis* character of religion. Religion cannot be reduced to economic, political or social concerns.

Nonetheless, ethical concerns enter the picture in all Confessional religions, for during the Axial period the biggest problem is no longer the cosmos but people. Until the code of Hammurabi there was no systematic written law in the Neolithic period, and behavior was regulated by tribal or royal custom. But custom was no longer able to regulate the actions of people in the Axial Age cities for a number of reasons.

First, in the Axial period cities became quite large with qualitatively denser human populations. One scholar estimated that the average population density of Roman Empire cities was about 200 per acre, equaled only by the crowding found in Western industrial slums (Meeks 28). Second, inhabitants of the Axial Age urban centers were racially, culturally and geographically international. Therefore there was no one tribal or royal custom which could hold them all together into a unified community. Within this type of teeming metropolitan environment the need arose for an explicit written ethical code which superseded the diversity of underlying cultural traditions. All of the Axial Age religions criticized the givenness of community which typified the Paleolithic and Neolithic periods. Each of the religious leaders addressed specifically human problems in a fundamental way. The primary religious problem was no longer time and space but people in time and space. The question was not how can humans survive in the cosmos but rather how they might live in the midst of humanity.

The demographic structure of the Silk Road parallels exchanges that are best understood religiously, not economically. The word "economics" is related to "ecumenical," which is also derived from the Greek word *oikoumene*. The economy is first discussed in terms of the distribution of the sacred among people. In the Axial Age peoples from all over the world meet and interact. Through these international meetings and through the increase and the density of populations and cities, people bring about the conflicts that they tried to resolve. Although the messages of the various religious leaders of the period differ, they are all addressed to each person in the world. Tribal religions do not do this. Tribes and kingdoms have their own gods. With the exception of Akenahton's unsuccessful attempt to develop a universal monotheism in Egypt, there was no sense of a single god for everyone in the Neolithic. Akenahton failed miserably because his theology did not speak to the condition of the Egyptian people at that time.

With the development of full blown international cities a new valuation of the human emerges which can be exchanged throughout the Silk Road. This was perhaps less true of Confucius, who spoke mainly to China rather than to the entire world. China was a large area, more separated from the other major urban areas although clearly connected to the Mediterranean indirectly by way of trade. Still, China remained culturally closed to the rest of the world until 115 B.C.E. Confucius was primarily trying to unite a number of dynasties within China, and that was the focus of his thought. However, during Chou times Chinese religion did become somewhat universal, at least in theory. Holding that everyone, including the barbarians, were to submit to the rule of the emperor, "Son of Heaven," the Chinese clearly had stepped into the Axial Age.

Cities afforded no cosmic orientation. The archetypes of birth, life, death and rebirth could not account for the many vicissitudes of urban existence. The existential situation of individuals became the major focus of religion and community was discussed in global rather than regional terms. Human rhythms rather than cosmic rhythms formed the focus of everyday life. Furthermore, the sacred was not found in the cities except among people because they alone were created by God. The city is a human creation whose vicissitudes eventually overshadow the great cosmic rhythms of sky, earth, water and stone. As we shall see, all of the Axial Age religions function in part as a critique of urban life and existence.

Christianity held that there is a God who created the world and sent his son to save the world which is in need of redemption because of the sinful character of human relations. All human acts have negative consequences and are sins. Christianity's message is directed especially to the poor and the down-trodden urban communities. Christ sets the example for a new form of human relationship. For Christianity, action is sin except for the ahistorical acts of Jesus. There is an action that can stop the evil consequences of human behavior. Human behavior within the city creates all types of problems and tensions, the most severe of which is warfare. Warfare and police oppression make up what Mircea Eliade has called the "terror of history" (Eliade). In James 4:1–2 it is written that desire causes war and fighting: "What causes wars, and what causes fightings among you? Is it not your passions that are at war with your members? You desire and do not have; so you kill. You covet and cannot obtain; so you fight and wage war." Christ showed how the terror of history can be stopped. Through forgiveness human transgressions are not escalated into conflict and war.

Christians may be dominated and even killed, as was Jesus, but Christianity, through resurrection, overcomes the ability of death to make life meaningless. By attaining an eternal life through the second coming of Christ, Christians transcend the ability of death to make life meaningless (I Peter 1:3). Indeed, as Paul wrote, without the resurrection of the dead, Christian faith would be futile (I Corinthians 15: 12–20).

Certain themes expounded in Buddhism actually began in the Upanishads and the Varnasrama Dharma. Unlike Christianity, Buddhism does not emphasize the issues of the poor and the oppressed but rather desire, birth, life, suffering, death and reincarnation. Through karma and samsara, actions bring about consequences and ultimately another life. Rebirth is problematical because of urbanity. The Buddhist message is directed at stopping action altogether in order to stop rebirth (Hinayana) or critique city life (Mahayana). In one sense, according to Buddhism, the desire to be is the most basic action which must be overcome in order to attain the salvific state, nirvana. Yet Buddhism presupposes a world to escape and therefore must include a way to keep the world going. For Buddhism, mendicancy is the answer. Buddhist monks in the early schools of Buddhism possessed virtually nothing and asked the laity, those who have something, to feed them. In one sense Buddhism is about the economics of begging and it is through that process that the exchange of Buddhist values took place. By giving food to a monk through filling his empty bowl, the laity created a world. A monk must eat to live. The emptiness of a Buddhist bowl represents the nothingness of nirvana and the action of feeding the monks is an actionless action that keeps the world in place. Through the Christian doctrine of forgiveness and the Buddhist doctrine of overcoming desire both Christ and the Buddha deliver the message that urban populations must stop creating the problems that they have to solve.

Islam sanctioned urban life more than the other Confessional religions but nevertheless directed its message to the immorality, poverty and injustice of the city. Islam thus differs from the other Confessional religions by directing proper urban relations rather than critiquing cities fundamentally. Indeed, the spread of Islam across the Middle East was initially concentrated on major urban areas.

Therefore, in the Axial Age something about the vicissitudes of the human condition become essential to their message. The city now makes certain claims on human fulfillment that are no longer encompassed within the archetypes of nature. A mercantile world with diverse peoples brings about new problems of human orientation that were not present before. Specifically human traits now form the locus of religious concern rather than the human embodiment of cosmic rhythms. As humans lose their relationship with nature in the city, they distance themselves from the sacred and they need salvation.

Paradoxically, humans also become the locus of the sacred in the city because they are the only thing there which God created. In the Axial Age the center is no longer located within the city but is found inside each individual person. The sacred inhabits human beings individually, and it is through the messages of the new religious leaders that God is found again. The Confessional religions are universal in scope and address everyone. One may belong to any ethnic, geographical or cultural group and be a Buddhist. Christians can live anywhere, and anyone can become a Muslim. Again the exception seems to be Confucius, who was primarily trying to create a united China out of feudal division.

In the Axial Age cities rise which, in turn, overtake the religious significance of the ceremonial center which occasioned them. With the loss of cosmic orientation the archetypes of soteriology emerge and the ceremonial center is now located in each individual person. In turn each person is part of one world or one city, if you will. Thus the Axial Age religions depict a change from the ceremonial center to internal human space. With this transition comes a need for salvation or fulfillment that exists apart from being a member of a particular society or community.

Interestingly, the personal lives of the Axial Age religious founders were involved in the problems that they addressed. They underwent the very existential turmoil that they addressed. Their humanity was stressed over their divinity. This was true even of Jesus, who was considered to be the incarnation of God. We hear very little of Jesus in heaven, in contrast to Marduk of Mesopotamia, again showing how the human was the new locus of religion. Religious orientation in the Axial Age takes into account the bizarre urban phenomena. Prior to this time period there were no existential questions with respect to salvation. Paleolithic hunters did not inhabit a religious world which emphasized another life or another world of meaning. The same was true in Egypt.

The Silk Road arose within a mercantile structure that defines human relationships more fundamentally than kinship. As a result, religion is no longer tied simply to the family or even the kingdom but is directed at everyone. Thus Jesus exhorts his followers to love everyone and the Buddha asks that his faithful have compassion for all. Socrates looks for a polis order that is universal and exclaims, "I am a citizen of the world." The extra-local belonging of human beings rests on the giveness of human beings, and this emerges within cities while simultaneously criticizing them. All of the Axial Age leaders are linked with cities — Jesus with Jerusalem, Buddha with Benaras, Socrates with Athens, the Jewish prophets with

Jerusalem, Muhammad with Mecca and Confucius with Chu Fu. All of the religions have a simple message: everybody can be saved. The thrust of each of these religions is applicable to everyone, and each has a message that is easily remembered.

Interestingly, the Axial Age religions also influenced one another. For example, Christian missionaries traveling to India heard the story of the Buddha and a certain Cardinal Baronius added him (under the name of Josaphat) to the Roman Martyrology and gave him a feast day (Hand). Ellen Goldberg has written a book detailing the life of a Jewish community in southwestern India (presently Kerala State). Sprouting in the second century, this community thrived until recently. While retaining most of the basics of Judaism, this group adopted a number of important Hindu rituals and customs. A fascinating and compassionate study, Goldberg's book convincingly shows that Jewish and Indian identities are not mutually exclusive.

Jewish Prophets

No one critiques the problems of the city more than the Jewish prophets of the Davidic kingdom prior to the Babylonian exile. The second great division of the Bible is called "The Prophets." The prophets, or *nabi*, communicated God's will to the Jewish people. Perhaps the greatest of the prophets was Elijah. His career centered around two distinctively Jewish religious concerns: the faith in one God and the passion for righteousness. As he contests with the priests of Baal on Mt. Carmel, he battled against the worship of many gods in Israel. Furthermore, in his encounter with the weak-willed king Ahab, whose greed had led him to commit murder, Elijah stood forth as a courageous champion of social justice. Unfortunately he left no writings behind.

The high water mark of the kingdoms of Israel and Judah was in the 8th century. There the prophets rose up as opponents of the *status quo*. Jeroboam II ruled the northern kingdom and Uzziah, king of Judah, successfully restored the boundaries of the Solomonic kingdom. Jerusalem's fortifications were strengthened, and the country became rich because of the spoils of victory. A growing international trade brought heavy tolls along the great trade routes which linked Israel and Judah with Egypt and Mesopotamia. Architecture and exquisite clothing flourished. A strong sense of national confidence developed. However, despite these great advances, there was ever-growing insecurity and outright need for the masses. Independent farmers were crowded out, their land was foreclosed and their children were sold into slavery to pay debts. Many farmers found themselves working as tenants on fields that they once had called their own. The moral stamina of the people was being sapped. It was in this decline of political, social and religious rights that the prophets arose.

The prophets attacked the evils of a complex and decadent urban kingdom. The prophets said that they were trying to restore the Jewish people to their pristine traditions. In criticizing Jewish urbanity the prophets recited the ideals of the nomadic, pastoral way of life. Nomadic society is fiercely egalitarian and the establishment of a monarchy undercut the democratic institutions of the old assembly. Furthermore, in the Jewish pastoralism there was virtually no private ownership of wealth. The flocks were owned in common and rights to wells and pasture grounds were vested in the tribe as a whole. Even after this nomadic pastoral way of life gave way to agriculture and urbanity the ideals associated with common ownership were still very important to the Hebrew people. Furthermore, the pastoral way of life was marked by a strong sense of mutual responsibility and help.

As the monarchs thrived, the poor, the weak and the women were exploited or forgotten about. A number of nostalgic groups arose within the Jewish society at this time. One group called the Rechabites sought to revert to a simpler culture by living only in tents and abstaining from wine. Similarly, the Nazirites took a vow not to cut their hair and to abstain from wine.

The prophets did not urge a return to nomadic conditions, nor did they forbid the drinking of wine or the practice of agriculture. A settled life was accepted by them as inevitable. Still, they did seek to restore the sense of mutual responsibility and the concern for human equality. As Hosea said, "Sow to yourselves according to righteousness, reap according to mercy, break up your fallow ground. For it is time to seek the Lord, till he come and cause righteousness to rain upon you" (10:12). Moreover, the prophets heralded the arrival of Axial Age concerns by enunciating a message that transcended tribal concerns. For nomads, morality and custom do not reach beyond the tribe. The prophets broke these tribal barriers that hemmed Israel in and became the fathers of not only a Jewish nationalism but of a united universal humanity.

The first three prophetic books follow a broad chronological order. Isaiah belongs to the late 8th century, Jeremiah to the late 7th century, while Ezekiel was a somewhat younger contemporary of Jeremiah. Twelve minor prophets, including Amos and Hosea, come after Isaiah, Jeremiah and Ezekiel in the middle of the 8th century. Micah was a younger contemporary of Isaiah. These prophets played an important part of Jewish religion during this critical period prior to the fall of the monarchy and the beginning of the Diaspora.

While Judaism as such is not considered a Confessional or Axial Age religion, there was a Confessional dimension to the religious message of the Jewish prophets. Jewish prophets such as Amos, Hosea, Jeremiah, Ezekiel and Micah all speak powerfully against the evil of human life in the city. For example, Micah states that Jerusalem is a wicked place which must be destroyed (6:9–16). Jeremiah also rails against the corruption of Jerusalem (5:1–6:30), and Ezekiel warns of the fall of Jerusalem because it has become such a wicked place (1:21). This message is furthermore carried on in Hosea 12:1–14:9 and Amos 3:1–6:14.

The message of the prophets is addressed to each individual rather than to whole families. Each person is responsible for establishing and maintaining a proper relationship with Yahweh, and he or she will be judged accordingly (Ezekiel 18:1–35). Not only do the prophets speak to every person individually, but God rules over all people, not just the Jews. In Isaiah it is announced that Yahweh is not just a God to the Jewish people but of all nations (45:14–25). The idea that Yahweh is the Lord of all people is furthermore depicted in Amos 9:7–10.

Political Order

Socrates was not a leader of the polis and he asked different questions from the political leaders. He put forth questions which showed language's ability to radically critique the rhetoric of leadership. In exploring the foundations of what it means to have a human order he looked for a universal community and was ultimately assassinated by the local leaders. In *Laches* Socrates examined courage. A couple of fathers asked two generals and Socrates to come and teach young soldiers at the academy the meaning of courage. Socrates agreed to do so but first told the generals that he wished to make sure that they all agreed as to what courage is. Through a series of questions, Socrates brings the generals to the realization that they do not know what courage is. Socrates then breaks off the conversation by saying they need to go study the idea more before they begin teaching their students. His critique of the idea of courage undermined a provincial understanding of courage.

In John 18:33–40 Pilate asked Jesus to admit that he was king of the Jews. If Jesus would only admit that he were king, Pilate would give him a kingdom. Jesus rejects this Neolithic structure of human relationships and says, "My kingship is not of this world." Jesus, like Socrates, would not go along with the historical provincial leaders and thus he was killed. As Paul writes to the Christians at Philippi in Macedonia, "Our commonwealth is in heaven" (Phillippians 3:20).

The Buddha taught people to escape from all forms of attachment to this world. Attachment to this world leads ultimately to suffering in one form or another. Therefore the issue is not social rank but escape from all ranks to nirvana through the following of the Four Noble Truths. Confucius' thought was most related to the political order and in this sense his thought was different from the other Axial Age religious leaders, excepting Muhammad. But a closer examination shows that Confucius' example of the perfect king ultimately undercut the kind of kingship which had thrust China into long term war. The emperor was to lead by example, not power. The emperor should become a gentlemen (*chun tzu*). The emperor was to embody benevolence (*jen*) and the highest ritual order (*li*), which is music. Thus the ideal emperor was a learned musician who embodied benevolence in order to set an example for his people. Confucius, in the end, wanted a universal political order out of the feudal warring that was taking place. Lao Tzu, the founder of Taoism in China, like Confucius, emphasized social harmony and good government but paradoxically sensed that good government comes through *wu-wei,* which means "flowing with nature." Good government and social unity required a meditative and contemplative lifestyle in which the goal was to not act upon the world. After the death of Muhammed, Islam developed a political institution somewhat akin to kingship, the Caliphate. However, the Caliphate was different from kingship because Caliphates ruled by following the law as handed down by the one supreme god, Allah, not according to their own power. Caliphates preserved and maintained Muslim tradition. They possessed power only insofar as they followed the dictates of Allah as manifested in Islamic law.

Finally, all of the Axial Age religions have to do with behavior changes. Salvation and spiritual fulfillment are embodied within certain behaviors and courses of action. In the Acts of the Apostles, followers of Christ are first called Christian at Antioch. They were known by the way they acted. As one Roman put it, "see how they love each other." Buddhists inhabited their world of meaning through very specific actions. The monks begged for food and lived a monastic lifestyle, while lay persons were to feed the monks and to follow the five precepts. For Confucius the idea was to become a gentlemen who embodies benevolence through proper ritual behavior. Lao Tzu states that the saint flows with nature through inactivity, and Socrates' philosophy arises from being a *hoplite* soldier and member of the polis. The penetrating questions of Socrates related to how to be a proper member of the Greek community. Finally, Muhammad outlines the five pillars of Islam, which are the basis for participation in Muslim religious life. In all of these religions, followers inhabited the other world, the world of meaning, through modes of conduct.

Bibliography
Chapter 8 — The Axial Age

Allsen, Thomas T. *Commodity and Exchange in the Mongol Empire: A Cultural History of Islamic Textiles*. Cambridge, England and New York, 1997.
Banri, Namikawa. *Silk Road*. Tokyo-to, 1976.
Boulnois, Luce. *The Silk Road*. Trans. Dennis Chamberlin. London, 1966.
Cadonna, Alfredo. Editor. *Turfan and Tun-huang, the Texts: Encounter of Civilizations on the Silk Road*. Firenze, 1992.
Charlesworth, M.P. *Trade Routes and Commerce in the Roman Empire*. 2nd Ed. Cambridge, 1926.
Chevallier, Raymond. *Roman Roads*. Trans. N.H. Field. Berkeley, California, 1976.
Ch'e, Mu-chi. *The Silk Road, Past and Present*. Beijing, 1989.
Childe, V. Gordon. *What Happened in History*. New York, 1946.
Dunning, James. *The Roman Road to Portslade*. London, 1925.
Eisenstadt, S.N. Editor. *Origins and Diversity of Axial Civilizations*. New York, 1986.
Eliade, Mircea. *The Myth of the Eternal Return, or Cosmos and History*. Princeton, 1954.
Fisher, Moshe; Benjamin Isaac and Israel Roll. *Roman Roads In Judaea II: The Jaffa-Jerusalem Roads*. Oxford, 1996.
Franck, Irene M. and David Brownstone. *The Silk Road: A History*. New York and Oxford, 1986.
Friedlander, Ludwig. *Roman Life and Manners under the Early Empire*. 4 Vols. Trans. L.A. Magnus and J. Freese. New York, 1968.
Garraty, John A., and Peter Gay. Editors. *The Columbia History of the World*. New York, 1972.
Goldberg, Ellen S. *The Last Jews of Cochin: Jewish Identity in Hindu India*. Columbia, South Carolina, 1993.
Hand, Greg. "Annals of Ecumenism: Buddha, the Christian Saint." *Books and Religion* 14 (1986).
Hayashi, Ryoichi. *The Silk Road and the Shoso-in*. Trans. Robert Ricketts. New York, 1975.
Hedin, Sven Anders. *The Silk Road*. Trans. F.H. Lyons. New York, 1938.
Hopkirk, Peter. *Foreign Devils on the Silk Road: The Search for the Lost Cities and Treasures of Chinese Central Asia*. London, 1980.
Isaac, Benjamin, and Israel Roll. *Roman Roads in Judaea*. Oxford, England, 1982.
Jagersma, H. *A History of Israel from Alexander the Great to Bar Kochba*. Trans. John Bowden. Philadelphia, Pennsylvania, 1986.
Jaspers, Karl. *The Origin and Goal of History*. Trans. M. Bullock. London, 1953.

Kahane, Reuven, and David Shulman. Editors. *Orthodoxy, Heterodoxy, and Dissent in India*. Berlin and New York, 1984.

Kitagawa, Joseph M. "Primitive, Classical and Modern Religions: A Perspective on Understanding the History of Religions." *The History of Religions: Essays on the Problem of Understanding*. Joseph M. Kitagawa. Editor. Chicago, 1967.

Klimburg-Salter, Deborah E. *The Silk Route and the Diamond Path: Esoteric Buddhist Art on the Trans-Himalayan Routes*. Los Angeles, California, 1982.

Koester, Helmut. "The Historical Jesus and the Cult of the Kyrios Christos." *Harvard Divinity Bulletin* 24 (1995): 13–18.

Li, Ming-Wei. *Studies of the Silk Road and the Society and Economy of Northwest China*. Lan-chou, 1992.

Liu, Hsin-ju. *Silk and Religion: An Exploration of Material Life and the Thought of People*, A.D. 600–1200. Delhi, 1996.

Madsen, Axel. *Silk Roads: The Asian Adventures of Clara and Andre Malraux*. London, 1990.

Meek, Wayne A. *The First Urban Christians: The Social World of the Apostle Paul*. New Haven and London, 1983.

Myrdal, Jan. *The Silk Road: A Journey from the High Pamirs and Ili through Sinkiang and Kansu*. Trans. Ann Henning. New York, 1979.

Roetz, Heiner. *Confucian Ethics of the Axial Age: A Reconstruction under the Aspect of the Breakthrough Toward Postconventional Thinking*. Albany, New York, 1993.

Salisbury, Charlotte Y. *Tibetan Diary and Travels along the Old Silk Route*. New York, 1981.

Shafi, Iqbal M. *Silk Road to Sinkiang*. Lahore, Pakistan, 1988.

Toynbee, Arnold. *Civilization on Trial*. New York, 1948.

Tsai-wang, Shen. *The Silk Road in Southwest China*. Huang Chi-ping and Teng Hung-p'ing. Editors. Ch'eng-tu, 1992.

Viatores. *Roman Roads in the South-East Midlands*. London, 1964.

Vollmer, John, E.J. Keall and E. Nagai-Berthrong. *Silk Roads, China Ships: An Exhibition of East-West Trade*. Toronto, 1983.

Wach, Joachim. *Types of Religious Experience: Christian and Non-Christian*. Chicago, 1951.

_____. *The Comparative Study of Religions*. Joseph M. Kitagawa. Editor. New York, 1958.

Yung, Peter. *Bazaars of Chinese Turkestan: Life and Trade along the Old Silk Road*. Hong Kong and New York, 1997.

_____. *Xinjiang, the Silk Road: Islam's Overland Route to China*. Hong Kong and New York, 1986.

Chapter 9

Buddhism

Today the Indian national flag displays the Buddhist wheel of dharma although less than two percent of the population of India is considered Buddhist. To understand this anomaly we must examine Buddhist history in India, and that begins with the story of the Buddha himself. Buddha lived from approximately 560 to 480 B.C.E. Buddha's personal name was Siddhartha and his family name was Gautama. Born near Nepal's border with India, Gautama's family belonged to the ksatriya, or warrior caste. Buddha's father was a tribal chief and a member of the powerful Sakya clan, and for this reason the Buddha is often called Sakyamuni, or Sage of the Sakyas. Buddha is also often known as Tathagata, the meaning of which is unclear. It is sometimes translated as "one who follows in the foot steps of his predecessors" or "one arrived at truth."

During the Buddha's life, India underwent tremendous political, social and religious change. All over India the authority of the brahmins (priests) was being challenged and tribal kingdoms were being broken down and called into question. There were food and land shortages attributable to an increase in population. Iron became widespread and was increasingly used for war materials (Chakrabarti).

The story of the Buddha's life is shrouded in legend and mystery. Later mythology says that the Buddha's father had a vision that his son would grow up to be either a great world ruler or world renouncer. Interestingly, his father's vision was global in perspective, so already religion was becoming universal in scope. Buddha's father wanted very much for his son to become a great king and therefore took every precaution to lavish upon his son the good life so that he would remain with his household. It is said that the Buddha married at either 16 or 19 years of age and that he married a cousin who was a neighboring princess. Buddha's father built for him three palaces and surrounded him with young attendants so that he could alternate palaces with the changing of the seasons.

When young Siddhartha would go out riding, attendants would go in front of him and clear the highways of all poor, sick and elderly people. Because of that it is said that the Buddha grew up completely ignorant of the sorrows and vexations of human existence. Buddha's naiveté with respect to the negative side of human existence prompted the gods above to intervene and educate the Buddha on human reality. Thus evolved the story of the four passing sights, critical to the formation of Buddhism.

Four Passing Sights

One day when Buddha was outside, a god appeared to him on the side of the road in the form of a very old and feeble man. For the first time the Buddha learned of the frailty of old age. On another day he saw a man crippled with a terrible disease and knew then that physical illness could attend human existence. The third sight was that of a dead man being carried along to a funeral pyre; it was then that the Buddha experienced human mortality and death. These three sights caused the Buddha great spiritual turmoil and, indeed, in one of the oldest Buddhist writings, *Anguttara Nikaya*, Buddha exclaimed, "I also am subject to decay and am not free from the power of old age, sickness and death. Is it right that I should feel horror, repulsion and disgust when I see another in such plight? And when I reflected thus, my disciples, all the joy of life which there is in life died within me" (3.35). Upset at what he had seen, Buddha became depressed and pensive over the purpose of life. His father tried to cheer him up with dancing girls and other exotic entertainment forms, but the Buddha remained depressed. One day the Buddha saw an ascetic in a yellow robe walking towards him as he sat under a tree by the road side. From this person the Buddha learned that freedom from the miseries of old age, disease and death can be obtained. At that point the Buddha made up his mind to leave his home and to become a wandering monk.

Soon thereafter, the Buddha, after being entertained by dancing girls all night until they fell asleep, stepped over them and went in and looked at his sleeping wife with their infant son and bade a silent farewell. Leaping on his great white horse the Buddha rode away with his charioteer at his side to a place far away beyond a river. He shaved off his hair and beard and exchanged his clothes for a coarse yellow robe, said farewell to his charioteer and went off into the forest to begin a six year period of intense meditation. Buddha first went to study under two ascetic teachers who were living in hillside caves.

But the Buddha, dissatisfied, soon left them and took up severe bodily asceticism. So determined was he to reach enlightenment that he almost starved himself to death in an attempt to transcend bodily desire. Dressed in very irritating garments he would stand for days in a single posture. At one time he sat on a couch of thorns. Once he lay in a cemetery with rotting bodies and let his body become so dirty that the dirt fell off of him. At one point he even ate his own excrement in an attempt to show self discipline. Finally he reduced his daily diet to either a single hemp grain, rice grain or fruit. According to the *Majjhima Nikaya* he maintained this rigorous diet until he became so thin that, as he put it, "if I sought to feel my belly, it was my backbone which I found in my grasp" (1.80). At this time five other ascetics had joined him and the Buddha one day fainted from weakness.

Waking up he proclaimed that the way of self mortification had failed and that he would proceed to eat and drink to strengthen his mind and body. He accepted a bowl of rice from a young village girl, which so outraged his associates that they left him. Buddha then went to a grove now called Bodh-gaya and sat down at the foot of a fig tree. Meditating on enlightenment, the answer finally came. Human suffering was caused by desire, thirst and craving. Having realized this, Mara, the evil one, the god of desire and death, tempted him to try and give up enlightenment and succumb to the life of pleasure. Buddha was tempted by beautiful women, enemy assailants and finally a terrible storm and wind, but he sat immovable under the great fig tree and resisted the temptations of evil.

Fire Sermon

One last issue remained. Should the Buddha simply pass into nirvana or should he go out into the world and preach his message to other people? After much serious thought, the Buddha decided that he should postpone his attainment of nirvana to preach to other people. The Buddha then preceded to Deer Park located outside of Benares in present day Sarnath and sought out the five ascetics who abandoned him earlier. As he approached, they initially decided that they would scorn him, but the Buddha displayed such a radiant serenity that they approached him and a friendly discussion began. The Buddha then preached what has come to be called the Fire Sermon. According to the *Mahavagga* (1.6.17–30), he began by discussing the doctrine of the Middle Way. Enlightenment is to be obtained, the Buddha said, by charting a middle path between self indulgence and self mortification.

> There are two extremes, oh monks, which he who has given up the world ought to avoid. What are these two extremes? A life given to pleasures, devoted to pleasures and lusts; this is degrading, sensual, vulgar, ignoble and profitless. And a life given to mortifications; this is painful, ignoble and profitless. By avoiding these two extremes, oh monks, one who has arrived at truth has gained the knowledge of the middle path, which leads to insight, which leads to wisdom, which conduces to calm, to knowledge, to enlightenment, to nirvana.

Continuing, the Buddha preached to his followers how the middle path is lived. One follows the middle path by and through the eight fold path, namely: right belief, right aspiration, right speech, right conduct, right means of livelihood, right endeavor, right memory, right meditation. The eight fold path is considered progressive and sequential and parallels the life of the Buddha.

By following the eight fold path one touches nirvana with one's body. It is not the case that one experiences nirvana and then follows the eight fold path; rather, by becoming right behavior, right speech, right meditations and right thoughts, one embodies nirvana. Interestingly, early Buddhist philosophy arises out of the rules of behavior for Buddhist monks and lay people, and it is very pragmatic in scope.

Next, the Buddha, looking out at the five monks, disclosed the four noble truths of Buddhism. The first noble truth is that birth, decay, illness and death is suffering. Suffering comes from being near things we hate, and suffering comes from being separated from things that we love. Simply put, desire is suffering. The second noble truth is the cause of suffering. Thirst, desire and craving accompanied by pleasure and lust leads to rebirth and suffering. The third noble truth is the cessation of suffering. Suffering ceases with the cessation of thirst, passion and desire. Finally the fourth noble truth is the eight fold path which leads to the cessation of suffering. After preaching the four noble truths, the Buddha, taking a handful of rice and drawing a circle on the ground symbolizing the constant motion of samsara, used the metaphor of a flame to discuss the problem of rebirth and suffering.

The Buddha began by noting that all is burning, including sight, smell, taste, body and mind. All of those things are burning with "the fire of lust, with the fire of hate, with the fire of delusion;... burning with birth, aging and death, with sorrows, with lamentations, with pains, with griefs, with despairs." Once one realizes that, one becomes "dispassionate" with regard to body and mind and its sensations "pleasant or painful or neither painful nor pleasant." Continuing, the Buddha taught that one becomes detached by becoming dispassionate and therefore liberated. He knows that "birth is exhausted, the holy life has been lived" (*Samyutta-Nikaya*, XXXV:28).

Thus it is clear that Buddhism arises within the same context as did the Upanishads, in which the goal is to escape the suffering of this world by transcending the endless cycle of rebirths. Volumes have been written on the nature of nirvana, but the Buddha's own discussions of it were very practical and to the point. Indeed, the Buddha constantly emphasized the practical nature of his religious teachings and avoided speculation on matters which he did not feel were directly related to the achievement of enlightenment and nirvana.

At one time the Buddha was at Kosambi in a grove of sisu trees. Taking a few leaves in his hand, the Buddha told his disciples that his doctrines were few when compared with those things that he had not talked about. The Buddha explained that he had not talked about many other things because they were not related directly to living a religious life and do not lead to nirvana. The Buddha did talk about pain, the cause of pain, the cessation of pain and the way leading to the cessation of pain. Buddha did not talk about more philosophical or speculative matters because, as he put it in the *Samyutta-Nikaya* (v. 437),

> it is not profitable, does not belong to the beginning of the religious life and does not tend to revulsion, absence of passion, cessation, calm, higher knowledge, enlightenment, nirvana. Therefore, I have not declared it. And what, good monks, have I declared? This is pain, I have declared; this is the cause of pain, I have declared; this is the cessation of pain, I have declared; this is the way leading to the cessation of pain, I have declared; and why, monks, have I declared it? Because it is profitable it belongs to the beginning of the religious life and tends to revulsion, absence of passion, cessation, calm, higher knowledge, enlightenment, nirvana therefore I have declared it.

Nirvana

Once a student of the Buddha named Vaccha quizzed the Buddha on the realm of nirvana. Nirvana is like a fire going out or cooling off, the Buddha said. When the fire goes out one is neither reborn or not reborn, nor is one not both reborn and not reborn. Fire depends upon fuel; when the fuel is withdrawn the fire goes out. It does not fit the case to say whether the fire goes east, west, north or south, and thus the Buddha says any form by which one would postulate the existence of one who has reached nirvana does not make sense.

> "But where is the monk reborn, sir Gotama, whose mind is thus liberated?" "It does not fit the case, Vaccha, to say he is reborn." "Then, sir Gotama, he is not reborn." "It does not fit the case, Vaccha, to say he is not reborn." "Then, sir Gotama, he is both reborn and not reborn." "It does not fit the case, Vaccha, to say he is neither reborn nor not reborn...." "In this matter, sir Gotama, I feel in a state of ignorance and confusion, and the small amount of faith that I had in Gotama through a former conversation has now disappeared." "Enough of your ignorance and confusion, Vaccha, for deep is this doctrine, difficult to be seen and comprehended, good, excellent, beyond the sphere of reasoning, subtle, intelligible only to the wise. It is difficult to be understood by you, who hold other views, another faith, other inclinations, another discipline, and have another teacher. Therefore, Vaccha, I will ask you this, and do you explain it as you may please. Do you think, Vaccha, that if a fire were burning before you, you would know that a fire was burning before you?" "If a fire was burning before me, sir Gotama, I should know that a fire was burning before me." "And if some one asked you on what the fire burning before you depends, how would you explain it?..." "I should say that this fire which is burning before me depends on its clinging to grass and sticks." "If the fire before you were to go out, would you know that the fire before you had gone out?" "If the fire before me were to go out, I should know that the fire had gone out." "And if some one were to ask you, 'Vaccha, in what direction has the fire gone which has gone out, to the east, west, north or south,' you were thus asked, how would you explain it?" "It does not fit the case, sir Gotama, to say so, for the fire burned through depending on its clinging to grass and sticks, and through its consuming this, and not getting any other, it is without food, and comes to be what is called extinct." "And just so, Vaccha, that form by which one would assert the existence of a Tathagata has ceased, it is uprooted, it is pulled up like a taliput-palm, made non-existent, and not liable to arise again in the future. The Tathagata, who is released from what is called form, is deep, immeasurable, hard to fathom, and like a great ocean. It does not fit the case to say he is born again, to say he is not born again, to say he is both born again and not born again, or to say he is neither born again nor not born again" (*Majjhima-Nikaya*: I, 485ff.).

Nirvana is ultimately ineffable although volumes have been written on it. It is generally spoken of in negative terms, for it is nothing that can be labeled positively. It is the cessation of thirst, the cessation of illusion, the cessation of attachment, the cessation of ignorance. In response to the question of how does one know when one reaches it, the answer is simply that one knows when the fire of desire is extinguished.

The only thing that is absolute about nirvana is that there is nothing absolute. Only nirvana is substantial, and it is substantial insubstantiality. The Upanishads did away with the anthropomorphic gods of the Vedas through yoga and ended with the spiritual principle of Atman-Brahman. The Buddha goes behind even that. There exist only the dharmas that flash in and out of existence. The word human being is but a linguistic habit formed by the illusion of placing a name on a particular form. Nothing underlies the name or the form. If we examine the parts of a human individual separately one discovers that there is no "I" or, more specifically, that the individual neither is nor is not real. As the Buddha put it, "We are compound beings." In "The Simile of the Chariot," *Milindapanha* (25ff.) King Menander (Milinda) engaged Nagasena in a dialogue which is one of the best known treatises on the composite nature of humans. Nagasena tells the King that there is no permanent individual that corresponds to his or any other name. The name Nagasena is only a practical designation that does not correspond with any of the parts of the person, neither hair, nails, teeth, skin nor sensation nor consciousness.

A person is like a chariot. A chariot consists of poles, axle, wheels, frame, reins, yoke, spokes and goad, yet all of the separate parts together do not comprise a chariot. But neither is a chariot separate from its parts. Chariot, like a person's name, is a practical designation that is generally understood.

If there is, however, no reality underlining a person's name, then how can one be reincarnated? This question was addressed succinctly and to the point by Nagasena in another passage from *Milindapanha* (71).

> "Reverend Nagasena," said the King, "is it true that nothing transmigrates, and yet there is rebirth?" "Yes, your Majesty." "How can this be?... Give me an illustration." "Suppose, your Majesty, a man lights one lamp from another — does the one lamp transmigrate to the other?" "No, your Reverence." "So there is rebirth without anything transmigrating!"

Buddhism and the Axial Period

Buddhism is so antithetical to Christianity that it is similar. Jesus also is associated with the city. Jesus left the city of Jerusalem at one point and came back into Jerusalem to preach. But the message of Christianity is the opposite of the Buddha's. Christ wants all to be reborn in eternal life while the Buddha wants to eliminate rebirth. Yet Jesus claims that an individual obtains the real life by sacrificing one's self for his neighbors. Thus both Christianity and Buddhism fulfill the self by annihilating it. While the Buddha seeks to escape suffering, Christ affirms suffering (1 Peter 2:21;

1 Peter 4:13; James 1:12). Nevertheless, both religions are similar in that they go through individuality in order to ultimately undercut it. Buddha dissolves the self while Jesus sacrifices the self.

Both messages ultimately are soteriological and are addressed to those who are divorced from the cosmic rhythms. Both religious leaders emerge when the ceremonial center is no longer fundamentally a geographic place but rather an internal principle located inside each person. As the *Dhammapada* says, "If one man conquers in battle a thousand times a thousand men and if another conquers himself, he is the greatest of the conquerors."

It is difficult to understand any of the Axial Age religions apart from the cities of the ancient world. During the time of the Buddha, the Silk Road stretched from Chinese Turkestan all the way to Greece, and people from all over the world were meeting for the first time. City populations grew and were inhabited by people from different cultures and places. Thus tribal ethnicity was undermined as a blending of cultures took place through the establishment of a worldwide trade network. As these differing peoples came together, an emphasis was placed on ethics and religious orientation which transcended the differences between these people and focused on their common humanity. It is in this context that we should understand early Buddhist monasticism.

Sangha

After the Buddha preached to the first five disciples at Deer Park, they became monks (bhikkus) who formed the first Buddhist monastery (sangha). Very quickly sixty or more people joined the Buddhist monasteries and shortly thereafter thousands of converts joined Buddhist monasteries throughout India. Early Buddhism was linked very closely with monasticism. Buddhist monks followed some very simple rules: they wore yellow robes, shaved their heads, begged for their food with a begging bowl, meditated daily, and recited the three jewels, "I take refuge in the Buddha, I take refuge in the law or truth, I take refuge in the sangha (monastery)."

Furthermore all Buddhist monks undertook to follow the ten precepts: 1) do not destroy life, 2) do not steal, 3) do not be unchaste, 4) do not lie or deceive, 5) do not ingest intoxicants, 6) eat moderately and not after noon, 7) do not look upon dancing, singing or dramatic events, 8) do not use scents, perfumes or ornaments, 9) do not use high or wide beds, 10) do not accept gold or silver. The first five of these rules were also prescribed for the lay followers of Buddhism.

Soon there were a number of Indians who subscribed to the ideals of Buddhism but felt obligated to continue their life as householders. Very early a symbiotic relationship developed between the lay order of Buddhism and the monks such that each depended on the other in a profound way. Every day monks begged their food from the laity. Through begging, monks showed their dependence on others for their livelihood, and it was important that monks not beg from the same person every day.

Through the simple ritual of begging food, Buddhism showed the essential link between this world and the next world, or samsara and nirvana. The empty Buddhist begging bowl represented the void or nothingness of nirvana which the monks had obtained. Escape from samsara requires there to be a world, and the filling of the void of the begging bowl with food symbolizes the necessity of the world for the monks. The laity kept the world going by filling the begging bowl with food. In return, monks preached lessons to the laity which spiritually enriched their lives. Furthermore, it was understood that by helping the monks the laity acquired karmic merit which would help them in the next life. In exchange for giving matter (food) to spirit (monks), spirit (monks) fed matter (laity) a lesson. There must be world for there to be Buddhism; there must be samsara for there to be nirvana. Thus Buddhism, in one sense, is about the economy of begging. Through begging, Buddhism articulates a new valuation of human existence that can be exchanged universally.

Buddhist monks very early began to retreat from the city to caves in India. It is interesting to note that while Buddhism was born in the city, it took on older Indian fertility symbols from the very beginning. Indeed, the Buddha reached enlightenment under the fig tree, which is an Indian symbol of fertility that dates all the way back to Mohenjo-daro. Buddhism is a vehicle for symbols which are not thought out but which overwhelm the religion. Early Buddhists symbolized Buddhism by such symbols as the bo tree, the wheel of dharma, the stupa, footprints, the pillar encircled by flame and the empty throne. Sometimes these symbols were combined to form a symbolic Buddha body so that, for example, we see the stupa as footprints, pillar as the backbone and the wheel as the radiant head of the Buddha.

In these caves which served as some of the earliest monastic shelters there was constructed a *dagoba,* which marked the Buddha's death and rebirth into nirvana. Thus the Buddhist caves had a fertility theme and in fact were likened to the womb of earth. Following the lead of Buddhists, Hindus later on also undertake cave worship and replace the *dagoba* with the lingam. The lingam symbolizes the *axis mundi* or cosmic pillar which unites heaven, earth and the underworld and allows one to experience unity with the world. But the lingam also has a fertility structure. The lingam represents male fertility and the cave represents female fecundity. Thus in early Buddhism and Hinduism monastic and fertility structures were linked.

Asceticism and Fertility

As Buddhism grew, the need arose for large buildings because the small caves and temporary grass huts of the early Buddhists were not sufficient. Thus by the fourth century Buddhists stupas were built. Buddhist stupas are symbolic of the Buddha and also incorporate the older Indian fertility images. The stupa represents both the sky dome and a woman's breast, thus linking heaven and earth, as well as symbolizing Buddha's enlightenment. Furthermore, Buddhism, while it grows out of a religious vision that emerges with the decline of the ceremonial center, resuscitates the notion of the ceremonial center with the stupa. Recent stupas are built on top of older ones and stupas eventually take on meanings of the old Neolithic ceremonial center. Throughout Buddhism ascetic and fertility symbols are seen side by side. At first glance they may appear to be in conflict, but that is not the case.

The initial thrust of Buddhism is ascetic and world renouncing. Buddhism arises within the problematical rhythms of the city which it seeks to overcome. One of the fundamental problems that emerges within an urban environment in this time period is the doctrine of individuality. Traditional peoples define themselves primarily in terms of the cosmos and their own societies, with individuality being seen as essentially unimportant. Within the urban rhythms of the Axial Age humans became divorced from the cosmic rhythms and from their own tribal and ethnic communities and see themselves as individual persons. With the emergence of individuality comes a focus on things that are specifically human and made by human beings.

The city is the environment *par excellence* which maximizes human creations. The city is truly a "man made" world, and rebirth into the urban world with all of its specifically human problems was and is seen as problematical in India. Thus the initial thrust of Buddhism was to escape the rhythms of the city in order to return Indians to a proper mode of relationship with the cosmos, as was the case in earlier times. Thus Buddhism, while renouncing the urban world, very much affirms the archaic world of fertility and life. The world of the cosmos is a sacred world that is not made and sustained by human beings. By realigning Indians with the great cosmic rhythms, Buddhism overcomes the problematic nature of urbanity.

That helps us to understand the significance of Buddhist mathematics. Buddhism is credited with discovering the number zero. Greeks had only finite mathematics; their numbers included only one through nine. Buddhism discovered the zero and the zero meant emptiness and nothing on the one hand, yet it was also interpreted as *bindu*. *Bindu* means both seed (female) and semen (male), thus interrelating both asceticism and fertility structures. The Buddhist zero stands for both nothing and something, nirvana and samsara, because both meanings are ultimately true and presuppose one another within the Buddhist religious vision.

Buddhism emerged in an urban setting and was especially popular initially among urban peoples. Furthermore, Buddhism critiqued urban life and its corresponding emphasis on the significance of individuals. The eight fold path of Buddhism, like the ethics of other Axial Age religions, cleans up karma and makes people ethical, but ultimately is a means to escape karma-samsara. Thus Buddhism emphasizes ethical behavior while simultaneously positing the ultimate significance of another world of meaning. Buddhist law is like a boat crossing the river to the other side, which is nirvana. Once the boat crosses to the other side, once the disciple reaches nirvana, he realizes that there is ultimately no boat, no river, nothing. Thus Buddhist teachings are called "skillful means" which in themselves have no ultimate significance. Buddhist teachings are worthwhile insofar as they point one to enlightenment.

Early Buddhism

Early monastic Buddhists referred to themselves as "the five *Nikayas*." The *Nikayas* were a collection of *sutras* or teachings about Buddhist law (*dharma*) and the *vinaya* (monastic rules). The early monastic Buddhists were called Hinayana or "Lesser Vehicle" by the later Mahayana Buddhists or "Great Vehicle" school which arose between 100 B.C.E. and 100 C.E. In 280 B.C.E. at the Council of Pataliputra two important Buddhist schools emerged, the Sthaviras whose best known descendants are the Theravadins and the Sarvastivadins, and the Mahasanghikas.

The Mahasanghikas formulated the doctrine of the Bodisattva and added the doctrine of emptiness. It is from this school that the Mahayana school of Buddhism evolved.

An important Buddhist text, *The Small Perfection of Wisdom Suttra*, shows that Mahayana and Hinayana Buddhism were close initially. The

Mahayana ideal is the Bodisattva as compared with the Arhat of the Hinayana school of Buddhism. The Bodisattva is one who reaches the threshold of nirvana but withholds his own salvation so that he can spread the message to others in an attempt to help everyone reach enlightenment. This sutra says that the adoption of the Bodisattva was found in the story of the Buddha himself, who postponed his own final enlightenment so that he could preach the message to others.

The other important doctrine introduced in *The Small Perfection of Wisdom Sutra* was "emptiness" (*sunyata*). Hinayana Buddhists say that all of the world is suffering impermanence and not-self. To these three doctrines Mahayanists added the doctrine of emptiness. Emptiness means neither that the world exists nor does not exist; either extreme is considered heretical. The Middle Way according to the Mahanyanas is between being and not being. It denies that reality is either a unity or a plurality. Emptiness means simply that all terms used to describe ultimacy are themselves empty. Yet despite the doctrine of emptiness, Mahanyana Buddhists emphasize that Bodisattvas should show compassion (*karuna*) for all people in helping spread the Buddhist message.

Mahayana and Hinayana Buddhism

Twenty years after the dissemination of the *Small Perfection of Wisdom Sutra*, Mahanyana and Hinayana Buddhists were at odds with one another. Hinayana Buddhism was criticized for teaching that only monks reach nirvana. According to the *Lotus Sutra*, Theravadin Buddhists are concerned very little with lay people. Monks see themselves as flowers who are above the mud of the earth. However, the flower is one plant. If it is cut from the mud it dies. Practically speaking, lay persons feed the monks. If the lay people did not feed the monks, the monks would literally die. Spiritually speaking, the world and nirvana are not different. There must be samsara for there to be nirvana.

In the *Lotus Sutra* the Bodisattva no longer simply reaches the threshold of nirvana as in *The Small Perfection of Wisdom Sutra* but rather recognizes that all persons are already at nirvana. Everything is empty. The dharmas are empty; samsara and nirvana are empty; there is no difference between. The emptiness of nirvana and samsara is their suchness (*tathata*). Thus the message of the *Lotus Sutra* is not unlike that of *The Wisdom of the Further Shore Sutra*, where it is said that the teaching of the Buddha is a vehicle to get one from the shore of samsara across the river to the shore of nirvana. Once one arrives at nirvana one realizes there was no vehicle, there was no boat, there was no river, there was no samsara, there is no nirvana.

Nagarjuna

The greatest Mahayana Buddhist was Nagarjuna who lived about 200 C.E. Nagarjuna founded the Madhyamika school and the Middle Path. In the *Middle Stanzas* he showed that all the implications of his various opponents are unacceptable, and he does this through the fourfold proposition. Through the fourfold proposition Nagarjuna utilized the doctrine of emptiness to rid Buddhism of all theories. The fourfold proposition is as follows: 1) it is, 2) it is not, 3) it is and is not simultaneously, 4) it neither is nor is not simultaneously. To each of these propositions, Nagarjuna replied, "no peti," meaning, it does not apply.

In rejecting each of the propositions he found the middle-truth, which he said is a blend of the twofold truth, the covered-truth and the true-truth. The middle-truth is not half way between the covered-truth and the true-truth. Both are true at the same time. Nagarjuna thereby removed the distinction of samsara and nirvana by indicating that there is no difference between them. All positions are emptiness, yet emptiness is neither real nor unreal. Emptiness itself is empty says Nagarjuna. There is no Mahayana Buddhism ultimately, for it is only a tool to reach nirvana. Realizing the periodic cosmic cycles of creation and distraction, Mahayana Buddhism ultimately sees the emptiness of samsara. Therefore, in Mahayana Buddhism one reaches nirvana within samsara rather than fleeing it as though it is not real.

For Mahayana Buddhism, nirvana is not in the least distinct from birth and death. What is, has been, and will be. There is nothing new under the sun; there are no particulars, thus no suffering. Suffering results from the concept of individuality, itself the problem of division and multiplicity. Nagarjuna says that division and multiplicity are the result of ignorance. If nothing is the root of everything then there can be no ultimate division. Individuality raises the problem of an afterlife, which was not a problem in the Vedas where the afterlife was not discussed. People in archaic India were real to the degree that they were parts of the cosmos and community. Nagarjuna states that if one desires nirvana, one is still gripped by desire. By seeking to renounce the world, the world still traps one. Thus nirvana is no longer something to be sought but the realization of that which is already the case.

The emphasis on realizing a mode of existence that is already present influences another important school of Buddhism called the Yogacara, or "Mind Only," school, which emerges about 300 C.E. The earliest Yogacara doctrines were attributed to Maitreyanatha. In the fourth century his brothers gave the school its earliest form. Yogacarans were also influenced by an early Buddhist sect called the Sautrantikas, who said that karmic effects were transmitted from one life to the next as seeds. Yogacarans call these seeds the foundation of consciousness. Whereas the Madhyamika school of Nagarjuna posited two truths, covered and absolute, Yogacarans set up three natures — the absolute, relative and imaginary. The middle path of Yogacaran Buddhism takes one through three successive steps from imagination, to the relative, to the absolute. The imagination itself comes from reality, which is ultimately a construct of the mind.

Tantric Buddhism

Finally, in the sixth century C.E., Tantric Buddhism arose in India. In India and later Tibet, Tantric Buddhism became the Vajrayana, or Vehicle of the Diamond, or Thunderbolt school of Buddhism. Both the Vehicle of the Diamond and the Thunderbolt schools of Buddhism teach that nirvana is reached by using the senses to overcome the senses. Drawing heavily upon primitive folk religion and the Vedas, Tantric Buddhists felt that if properly understood, the deliberate breaking of morals helped one attain enlightenment. Thus Tantric Buddhists ate meat, drank alcohol and engaged in sexual activity — perhaps even ritual murder — in seeking enlightenment. Ironically, the yogin achieves salvation for behavior that consigns devotees of other religions to perdition.

By the eighth century Tantricism becomes more contemplative than ritualistic, and monks began to meditate on a symbolic design called a mandala in order to become one with the Buddha nature that was inherent inside. Monks engaged in a spiritual sexual union with the goddesses (*taras*) who inhabited the mandala, after which they returned to the everyday world vitalized with Buddha nature.

In Tantric Buddhism, as in Mahayana Buddhism, samsara and nirvana are one. As Saraha said, "Here there is no beginning, no middle, no end, no samsara, no nirvana. In this state of supreme bliss there is no self and no other. Just as water entering water becomes of the same taste so when the sage thinks vices and virtues the same there is no polarity" (qtd. in Robinson and Johnson 97). Thus Tantric Buddhism used the passions to dissolve the passions. The body itself is a microcosm, so that to know oneself is to know the universe and the Buddha nature inside. One overcomes desire through desire.

In Tantric Buddhism exploring the body of another sexually was likened to exploring a sacred geography. As one Tantric Buddhist put it, "The world is bound by lust and released by the same lust" (qtd. in Robinson and Johnson 97).

Tantric Buddhism is simply a recasting of the Buddha's middle way between self indulgence and self mortification. Self-indulgence is a way of life in which one succumbs to desire. Self-mortification is characterized by a strong desire to overcome desire. A life of self indulgence is immoral, while a life of self-mortification is very moral. Tantric Buddhism strikes a middle course between indulgence and mortification, immorality and morality. Tantric Buddhism is best described as amoral. It neither supports the senses nor rejects them; rather the senses are used as a vehicle by which they are overcome. The closest thing to Tantric Buddhism within the Christian tradition is perhaps the doctrine of "fools for Christ's sake" which also transcends the dichotomy of moral/immoral in order to locate religious meaning outside of a particular social class or group. Similarly, Tantric Buddhists do not locate religious meaning within any particular group, neither monks nor laity. Religious meaning transcends all human limitations and categories and is ultimately defined as being indefinable.

The Decline of Indian Buddhism

White Huns attacked northern India in the sixth century, and Buddhism steadily declined after the seventh century C.E. By the thirteenth century Buddhism was virtually gone from India in the north, and the same was true in the south by the fifteenth century. Today only 2 percent of Indians consider themselves Buddhists, yet the Indian flag today contains the Buddhist wheel of dharma.

Walter Fairservis wrote that Buddhism culminated Indian religion and then was exported to the surrounding countries. The Indian national flag symbolizes that the teachings of the Buddha were but tools to help one reach nirvana. Once enlightenment was obtained the tools were no longer necessary. Thus it could be argued that Indians today inhabit a world filled with Buddhist values, symbols and principles.

Richard Lannoy argued that the inclusiveness of traditional Indian religion ultimately engulfed Buddhism and overtook it. According to him, Buddhism represented a new development in Indian religion which itself was finally absorbed by the great cosmic cycles of birth, death and rebirth. The widespread legend of the Speaking Tree in India helps bring home this point. It was said that when Alexander the Great expanded his empire into

India that he announced his presence to the Speaking Tree. The Speaking Tree responded to Alexander the Great that his rule over India was temporary and that ultimately his kingdom would be absorbed by the great Indian cycles of time.

Another story also bears out Lannoy's point. In the fifth century a Chinese traveler named Fa-Hsien sojourned to India in order to visit various Buddhist monasteries. His purpose in making this trip was to learn more about true Indian Buddhism so that he could carry important original meanings and practices back to China. Having visited a number of well-populated Buddhist monasteries, Fa-Hsien stated that Buddhists and Hindus joined in ritual processions as though Buddhism were a branch of Hinduism (DuBary 1–11).

Maitreya Buddhism

In spreading from India, Buddhism came upon Manichism, Christianity and Zoroastrianism in an area called Chinese Turkestan. Around cities such as Kucha, Turfan, Taklamakan, Khotan and Kashgar, all of which were linked with the Silk Road, there arose a new strand of Buddhism called Maitreya. The Maitreya school of Buddhism, which is accepted by all Hinayana schools, states that a Buddha figure shall be born in the distant future. Buddha is portrayed as a historical figure who will come again. Unlike the other Buddhas before him, the Maitreya Buddha is viewed as alive and responsive to prayers. Thus he has a theistic element that makes him compatible with Western religions. Maitreyists see the world in a state of decline that will result in an apocalyptic restoration of a primeval harmony.

Followers of Maitreya Buddhism attempt to build up good karma so that they can be reborn in the good period. Later, this school centers around devotion where appeals to Maitreya are made to remove bad karma. In these later schools Maitreya can influence karma. Eventually the doctrine of rebirth is altered and is no longer seen as immediate. The Maitreya Buddha is thought to suspend reincarnation among his followers until he returns. Maitreya Buddhism takes on a historical dimension like Christianity and occasions increasing involvement of Maitreya Buddhists in political matters. Maitreya Buddhists in later schools begin to become actively involved in trying to reform the world to make it better. In some cases this has led to political activism although as with all Buddha sects the ultimate goal is transcendence from this world.

Conclusion

Whatever the case for the demise of Indian Buddhism, it is important to remember that Buddhism was ultimately a practical way of life aimed at overcoming the problems of suffering. Buddhism was first and foremost a vehicle to relieve suffering, a form of yoga that allows one to touch nirvana with oneself. In the *Majjhima-Nikaya I*, the Buddha explained the practical nature of his message through the parable of the arrow.

An elder approached the Buddha and told him that the Buddha had left a number of important theories unexplained, for example, whether the world is eternal or not eternal, whether the soul is the same as the body and whether the soul is one thing and whether a Buddha exists after death or does not exist after death. These unresolved issues left the elder perplexed, and he demanded that either the Buddha give him satisfactory answers or he would give up his training and return to a secular life. The Buddha first asked the elder whether he had ever represented to the elder that he would answer those questions for him, to which the elder answered no. Continuing, the Buddha stated that he did not address questions as to whether or not the world was eternal or not eternal because a person would die before those things would be explained.

Buddha explained that if a person were wounded by a poisoned arrow and refused to have the arrow removed until he learned whether he was wounded by one of the warrior, or Brahmin, or the agricultural, or the lowest caste; or what name or family he was from; whether he was tall, short or middle height; or whether he was black, dark or yellowish; or what village or city or town he came from; or whether the bow with which he was wounded was that of a chapa or kondanda; or whether the bow string was of swallow wart, bamboo fiber, sinew, hemp or of the milk sap tree; or whether the shaft was from a wild or cultivated plant; or whether it was feathered from a vulture's wing, or a heron's or a hawk's or a peacock's; or whether the arrow was wrapped around with the sinew of an ox, a buffalo, a ruru deer or a monkey; or whether it was an ordinary arrow, a razor arrow or an iron arrow or a calf tooth arrow, that man would die before he found the answers to these questions.

The cessation of suffering is not dependent on knowing whether or not the world is eternal or not eternal, whether the soul was different from the body or whether one lives or does not live after death. Because those matters are not concerned with a religious life and do not produce absence of passion, cessation of suffering, tranquillity, perfect knowledge and nirvana, they were not explained. The Buddha stated that what he has explained is suffering, the cause of suffering, the destruction of suffering and the path that leads to the destruction of suffering, and with that the elder applauded the words of the Buddha (Thomas *Buddhist* 64–67).

Bibliography
Chapter 9 — Buddhism

Basham, A.L. *The Wonder That Was India*. New York, 1955.
Bechert, Heinz, and Richard Gombrich. Editors. *The World of Buddhism*. London, 1984.
Chakrabarti, Dilip K. *The Early Use of Iron in India*. Delhi and New York, 1992.
Chalmers, Lord. Trans. *Further Dialogues of the Buddha*. London, 1926.
Ch'en, Kenneth. *The Chinese Transformation of Buddhism*. Princeton, 1973.
Conze, Edward. *Buddhism: Its Essence and Development*. Oxford, 1951.
_____. *Buddhist Meditation*. London, 1956.
_____. *Buddhist Texts through the Ages*. Oxford, 1954.
_____. *Buddhist Thought in India*. Ann Arbor, Michigan, 1967.
_____. Editor. *Buddhist Scriptures*. Baltimore, 1959.
DeBary, William Theodare. Editor. *The Buddhist Tradition in India, China and Japan*. New York, 1969.
Dumoulin, Heinrich, and John Maraldo. Editors. *Buddhism in the Modern World*. New York, 1976.
Eliade, Mircea. *A History of Religious Ideas: From Gautama to the Triumph of Christianity*. Chicago, 1982.
Eliot, Sir Charles. *Hinduism and Buddhism*. London, 1921.
Fairservis, Walter. *The Roots of Ancient India*. New York, 1971.
Foucher, A. *The Life of the Buddha According to the Ancient Texts and Monuments of India*. Trans. Siymone B. Boas. Middletown, Connecticut, 1963.
Gokhale, Balkrishna Govind. *Buddhism and Asoka*. Baroda, 1948.
Govinda, Lama Anagarika. *Foundations of Tibetan Mysticism*. York Beach, Maine, 1969.
Gregory, Peter N. Editor. *Traditions of Meditation in Chinese Buddhism*. Honolulu, 1986.
Grousett, Rene. *The Civilizations of the East*. Vol. 2, *India*. London, 1931.
_____. *In the Footsteps of the Buddha*. Trans. J.A. Underwood. New York, 1971.
Horner, I.B. *The Living Thoughts of Gotama the Buddha*. London, 1948.
Hubbard, Jamie. "Absolute Delusion, Perfect Buddhahood." *Buddha Nature*. Tokyo and Los Angeles, 1990.
I-Liang, Chou. "Tantrism in China." *Harvard Journal of Asian Studies* 8 (1945): 241–332.
Kapleau, Philip. *The Three Pillars of Zen*. New York, 1989.
Kitagawa, Joseph M., and Mark D. Cummings. Editors. *Buddhism and Asian History*. New York, 1989.
Kloetzli, W. Randolph. *Buddhist Cosmology*. Delhi, 1983.
Lamotte, Etienne. "Buddhist Controversy over the Five Propositions." *Indian Historical Quarterly* 32 (1956).

_____. *History of Indian Buddhism.* Trans. Sara Webb-Boin. Louvain and Paris, 1988.
Lannoy, Richard. *The Speaking Tree: A Study of Indian Culture and Society.* Oxford, 1971.
Law, B. C. Editor. *Buddhistic Studies.* Calcutta, 1931.
Ling, Trevor O. *The Buddha: Buddhist Civilization in India and Ceylon.* London, 1973.
Lopez, Donald S., Jr. Editor. *Buddhism in Practice.* Princeton, 1995.
Matsunaga, Alicia. *The Buddhist Philosophy of Assimilation.* Rutland, Vermont and Tokyo, 1969.
Müller, F. Max. Trans. *Sacred Books of the East.* Vol. X. *The Dhammapada.* Oxford, 1881.
_____, E.B. Cowell, and I. Takakusu. Trans. *Sacred Books of the East.* Vol. XLIX. *Buddhist Majjhima Text.* Oxford, 1893.
Nakamura, Hajime. *Ways of Thinking of Eastern Peoples.* Revised English Translation. Philip P. Wiener. Editor. Honolulu, 1964.
Overmyer, Daniel. *Folk Buddhist Religion: Dissenting Sects in Late Traditional China.* Cambridge, Massachusetts, 1976.
Pratt, J.B. *The Pilgrimage of Buddhism and a Buddhist Pilgrimage.* New York, 1928.
Rahula, Walpola. *What the Buddha Taught.* New York, 1959.
Rhys-Davids, T.W. and Hermman Oldenberg. Trans. *Sacred Books of the East.* Vol. XIII. *Vinaya Text.* Oxford, 1883.
Robinson, Richard H., and Willard L. Johnson. *The Buddhist Religion: A Historical Introduction.* 3rd Ed. Bellmont, California, 1982.
Snellgrove, David L. *The Image of the Buddha.* London, 1978.
Streng, Frederick J. *The Study in Religious Meaning.* New York, 1967.
Suzuki, Shunryu. *Zen Mind, Beginner's Mind.* New York, 1970.
Takakusu, Junjiro. *The Essentials of Buddhist Philosophy*, 3rd Ed. Wing-tsit Chan and Charles A. Moore. Editors. Honolulu, 1956.
Tambiah, Stanley J. *Buddhism and the Spirit Cults in North-East Thailand.* Cambridge, England, 1970.
_____. *World Conqueror and World Renouncer: A Study of Buddhism and Polity in Thailand Against a Historical Background.* Cambridge, England, 1976.
_____. *The Buddhist Saints of the Forest and the Cult of Amulets.* Cambridge, England, 1984.
Thomas, Edward J. *The History of Buddhist Thought.* New York, 1975.
_____. *The Life of the Buddha as Legend and History.* London, 1927.
_____. Trans. *Buddhist Scriptures.* London, 1913.
_____. Trans. *Early Buddhist Scriptures.* London, 1935.
Warren, H.C. *Buddhism in Translation.* Cambridge, 1896.
Wayman, Alex. *The Buddhist Tantras: Light on Indo-Tibetan Esotericism.* N.Y., 1973.
Welch, Holmes. *Buddhism Under Mao.* Cambridge, Massachusetts, 1972.
_____. *The Buddhist Revival in China.* Cambridge, Massachusetts, 1968.
_____. *The Practice of Chinese Buddhism, 1900–1950.* Cambridge, Massachusetts, 1967.
Zurcher, Erik. *The Buddhist Conquest of China: The Spread and Adaptation of Buddhism in Early Medieval China.* 2 Vols. Leiden, 1959.

CHAPTER 10

The Three Religions of China

Chinese religion and philosophy are first and foremost associated with the name Confucius, the Latin name for K'ung Fu-tzu (Kong Qui), or K'ung the Master. Confucius is spoken of reverently as the first teacher of China, and he influenced Chinese culture in an unprecedented manner. Born around 551 B.C.E. in Lu at the base of the Shantung peninsula, Confucius was apparently born into a modest home. Confucius states that he was without social rank as a child. Before Confucius reached the age of three his father died, and Confucius was raised by his mother. Because of his impoverished surroundings, Confucius worked very hard at menial tasks as a young man and always felt a certain compassion for the common folk of China.

Born in a time of great political and social strife, Confucius sought practical answers to a war-torn nation. The Chou dynasty began crumbling about the 8th century B.C.E., and China was divided into a number of warring states. Warfare itself in China had a long and honorable tradition in which certain rules of propriety were obeyed and carried out. Warfare in the age of Confucius devolved into something that was ruthless and depraved. All respect between warring armies was lost and whole populations were slaughtered by victorious conquerors. Mass killings of 60,000, 80,000 and even 400,000 people, including children, women and the elderly, are chronicled during the period of Confucius (Tsui; Williams; Fung).

China, during the time of Confucius, faced major political problems. The Chou emperor found that it was difficult to rule each province, in part because communication was by road and the roads were poor. The Chou emperor created a feudal system and delegated the rule of certain territories to subordinates who, for the most part, were relatives or chiefs of tribes that had assisted them in the conquest of the Shang dynasty. These feudal lords were free to govern their territories as they saw fit so long as they kept peace and paid tribute to the emperor. This system worked very well in the beginning. In time the feudal lords became settled into their territories and were accepted by the people that they ruled. Allegiances eventually were developed primarily towards the feudal lords rather than to the emperor. Stronger feudal lords warred against weaker feudal lords and various alliances were formed.

Finally, in 771 B.C.E. a coalition of tribes killed the reigning Chou king. The Chou capital was then established farther to the east, but the emperor had lost effective power over the various feudal territories. While it was generally recognized that China needed a strong king, no one could agree on who that should be, and thus a period of brutal warfare ensued. Furthermore, the decentralization of government continued as certain chief officials of feudal lords revolted against their feudal lords in the way that the feudal lords did against the emperor. For example, in Lu, Confucius's homeland, the duke still reigned in principle although most power was held by three of his relatives who were the principal officers of the government. In 517 B.C.E., when Confucius was 34, the reigning duke of Lu attempted to overturn the power of the three upstart officers but was unsuccessful and had to flee the state to live the rest of his life in exile.

This process of war and disagreement continued through all ranks of society so that when Confucius was 47, a high-ranking officer who turned against the duke of Lu was himself attacked by his own chief retainer. After imprisoning the officer and forcing him to swear by his commands, the retainer too was eventually overthrown and had to flee the territory. By the sixth century B.C.E. there were four large states of great political power in the Chinese world and a number of smaller states. Within many of these states the rulers were weak, and many times the noble clans would fight among themselves. Warfare and strife were so endemic to China that even families fought among themselves during this period.

Therefore, the thought of Confucius emerged during a time when the central problem facing the Chinese people was not nature but other human beings. The pivotal concern of the Chinese had become the problem of humans killing other humans rather than the struggle to wrest life from nature's rhythms. Nature was still considered fundamental in the time of Confucius, but Confucius' message emphasized that human mistreatment of other humans had upset the delicate balance of nature. Therefore, as with the other Axial Age religions, Confucius stressed ethics above all else. Within this context of human emphasis, individuality replaced the communal participation that typified the earlier Chou dynasty that Confucius so revered. Confucius was a nostalgic. He sought to restore the Grand Harmony which he said characterized the earlier Chou dynasty. Indeed, Confucius saw himself not so much as an innovator but as a renovator who sought to restore an earlier order. Confucius was fond of regarding himself as "a lover of the ancients" (*Analects* VII:1, 20).

But to get to a level of social and religious harmony which had characterized the earlier Chou dynasty, Confucius recognized that it would no longer suffice for the Chinese to rely on the unspoken dictates of ancient custom. Tribal and royal solidarities had broken down so that what was called for now was a consciously and rationally articulated system of behavior and principle which the people must be taught through education. Furthermore, the message taught must be global in scope because all of the people in the various provinces of China and the world beyond had lost the social glue that held them together. As Confucius noted when discussing the concept of goodness (*jen*), no national boundaries are recognized because "within the four seas all men are brothers" (quoted in Smith 180).

Thus Confucius pushes for a religious humanism that reverses the primacy of nature's power: "*Tao* is not far from man" (*Chung Yung*, IX:1). Whereas earlier Neolithic Chinese religion had emphasized the worship of ancestors, Confucius argued that it was more important to establish proper relationships between the living rather than the dead. As he put it, "We need to know of living before death" (*Analects*, XI:11). Ancestor worship still remained important in China as did the worship of the sacred powers of nature, but the relationships among living people took religious precedence. In a period of anarchy and injustice Confucius felt that the only solution was a radical reform of the government carried out by educated leaders.

Confucius himself never obtained a high political position and considered his own mission to be a failure at the end of his life. One legend says that Confucius was once offered a position as the chief minister by the duke of Lu but that he was too honest for the administration of this position and eventually resigned. At any rate, at the age of 55 he left the state of Lu and traveled widely through China unsuccessfully seeking political employment.

Confucius was not a religious leader but rather a person whose thinking was important religiously. But whether directly or indirectly, Confucius profoundly influenced on Chinese religion. Confucius stressed human virtue and the influence of human behavior on nature, writing, "Man makes the *Tao* great" (Analects XV:28). Nevertheless, Confucius also recognized the traditional significance of the *Tao* as influenced by heaven: "If the *Tao* is practiced that is because of the decree of heaven" (*Analects* XIV:38). Confucius recognized the ultimate significance of heaven, T'ien. T'ien is not withdrawn from the world. In fact Confucius believed that T'ien directed his own religious mission in life (*Analects* V:22; II:4).

The goal of a person under Confucian philosophy was to become the superior man, *chun tzu*, also translated as gentleman. It is important that heaven receive sacrifices, but it is even more important that people act properly and that there be good government. The concrete everyday problems of this world were the primary emphasis for the *chun tzu*. Therefore, philosophical debate concerning the nature of heaven or life after death is useless (*Analects* IV:12; VII:20; XI:11). Spirits, while real, are to be kept at a distance. For as Confucius put it, "If you cannot serve men how could you serve the spirits?" (*Analects* XI:11).

The education which develops the *chun tzu*, or gentleman, is intellectual, social and religious. The egalitarian and universal nature of Confucian thought is clearly shown in the Confucian ideal that anyone of any social rank could become a *chun tzu*. The chief principle in developing the *chun tzu* is noted by the term *li*, or ritual propriety. All life for Confucius should be properly lived. Ritual permeated intellectual, religious and social spheres of life.

Confucius enunciated the doctrine of the rectification of names which emphasized that the forms of the world should be properly described by language. One should speak correctly about the world because human beings define and describe the forms and rhythms of the environment through the use of names. In short, Confucius thought that it was important that the Chinese say what they mean and mean what they say.

Also important for ritual propriety was the *Doctrine of the Mean*. The two Chinese words for mean are *chung* and *yung*, which mean respectively "middle" and "constant." Therefore the mean is the way that is "constantly in the middle between life's extremes" (Smith 182). For Confucius, as for the ancient Chinese, proper human life should embody a balance between the opposites of the world. The gentleman inhabits the continuum between the bi-polar opposites of the world so that his life is one of harmony and balance. Such harmony was promoted by attention to the right forms of social life.

Confucius sought to re-create the right forms of social life by building upon that which already existed and had been handed down from the ancients. The most important of social relationships were the "five relationships" which were implicated in the *Analects* and were formalized after Confucius' death. The five most important human relationships are father/son, elder brother/younger brother, husband/wife, elder/younger, and ruler/subject. Interestingly and significantly three of the five basic relationships were family. Confucius strove to revolutionize and reorder Chinese society and religious life by restoring proper family relations. While he talked about the central significance of good government, Confucius clearly emphasized the fundamental significance of good families in building a new human society. The father should show kindness, while the son should show filial piety; the elder brother should demonstrate nobility, while the younger brother should show respect; the husband ought to show caringness, while the wife should show obedience; the elder should show humanness, while the younger man should show deference; and the ruler must be benevolent, while his subject should demonstrate loyalty.

Confucius addressed the problems associated with the rise of individuality in the Axial Age, and yet his response to the problems of the individual is relational. That is to say, Confucius ultimately solves the problematical nature of individuality by positing that individuals are members of relationships. The husband exists by virtue of his relationship to the wife, and vice-versa. Within these relationships ritual propriety requires reciprocity, *shu*. *Shu* is another fundamental concept within Confucian thought. In fact it is so significant that once a disciple asked Confucius, "Is there one word which may serve as a rule of practice for all one's life?" The Master said, "Is not reciprocity (*shu*) such a word? What you do not want done to yourself, do not do to others" (*Analects* XV:23). For Confucius the family relationships were basic, and in this he carried on the ancient Chinese understanding. In Chinese mythology the culture hero created Chinese people out of animal forms by inventing family. In other words, humanity and family emerged simultaneously according to Chinese mythology. In elaborating upon these familiar relationships Confucius demonstrated his interest in returning to the mythical beginnings of Chinese society in order to find that which is real and enduring.

The master said, "Tao is not far from man. If what one takes to be Tao is far from man, it cannot be considered Tao" (*Doctrine of the Mean* XIII:1). The Tao for Confucius was inextricably tied up with human conduct and righteousness. In the *Analects* Confucius said, "'My Tao is unified by a single [principle]'.... When the master went out the disciples asked, 'What did he mean?' Tseng Tzu replied, 'the Tao of our master is only *chung* and *shu*'" (*Analects* IV:15.1, 2). *Shu* is generally translated as reciprocity and *chung* as loyalty or conscientiousness.

The Doctrine of *li* is closely affiliated with *shiao* (filiality). In reply to a question as to what *shiao* is "The master said, 'While [the parents] are living serve them with *Li*; when they die bury them with *Li*; sacrifice to them with *Li*" (*Analects* II:5.3). And again from the same work, the master said,

> In serving his parents the filial son is as reverent as possible to them while they are living. In taking care of them he does so with all possible joy; when they are sick he is extremely anxious about them; when he buries them he is stricken with grief; when he sacrifices to them he does so with the utmost solemnity. These five [duties] being discharged in full measure then he has been able to serve his parents (*Doctrine of the Mean* I).

Under Confucius filial piety was not simply a philosophical ideal. Treating one's parents badly was a serious crime by law. A disrespectful child could be put to death or at least charged with criminal conduct, for which there was various prescribed punishments. Cursing one's parents was punishable by death.

But how does this emphasis on the family correspond with the Confucian emphasis on good government under the rule of the emperor? The answer is that, for Confucius, the emperor should lead by sacred example. By acting in conformity with the *Tao*, in other words, by the correct practice of rites, thoughts and customs (*li*) the emperor radiates sacred power that prompts the people to follow. Mentioning the famous philosopher King Shun, Confucius noted, "He simply stood there gravely and reverently with his face turned towards the south and that was all" (*Analects*, XV:4). Elsewhere he says, "With a correct behavior it is not necessary to give orders" (*Analects* XIII:6). And again, "To govern by virtue is as if one were the Pole Star: one remains in place while all the other stars circle around in homage" (*Analects* II:2).

Power was denoted by the term *te*. The Chinese Realists felt that the power by which people were ruled was a political power which was effectively handed down through physical might. In other words, for the Chinese Realist, might makes right. Confucius disagreed with that philosophy showing that, during the Ch'in Dynasty, all of China was conquered within nine years only to collapse before the generation was out. Thus Confucius was convinced that no government could physically force all of its citizens to obey its laws. Of economic sufficiency, military might and the confidence of the people, Confucius stated that trust of the emperor was by far the most important: "No state can exist without the confidence of the people" (*Analects* XII:7). Real power, *te*, resides in virtuous example.

The emperor set the standard for proper conduct in China, and if he acted appropriately the people would follow. Emperors should be people beyond personal ambition. Moreover, their worthiness to rule was not inborn. Nobility and distinction are not innate, said Confucius. They were obtained only through discipline and the development of certain gifts (*Analects* IV:5; VI:5). Thus when Confucius was asked whether certain criminals should be executed he answered, "What need is there of the death penalty in government? If you showed a sincere desire to be good your people would likewise be good" (Smith 186).

The emperor in his own life should fully develop *wen*, the arts of peace. Confucius valued the arts and especially music. The emperor, according to Confucius, should be a supreme musician, for music represents the highest achievement of excellence and orients humans to goodness. Chinese Realists disagreed with Confucius' ideas and felt that punishments for law breaking must be severe in order to keep the average person in line. Most people were simply incapable of acting properly unless they had to answer to a very powerful government.

At the other extreme was the philosophy of Mo Tzu (Mo Zi: ca. 468–390 B.C.E.), a contemporary of Confucius. Mo Tzu proposed that the solution to China's social problems was not force but love. Stressing that one must show love to enemy and friend alike, Mo Tzu felt that love should be universal. Mo Tzu's message, like Confucius', was directed at the incessant strife that characterized China at that time. There was war among states, disagreements among families and turmoil among individuals. Mo Tzu proposed that trouble at all these levels could only be overcome by and through unconditional love of one another.

> Take the present case of mutual attacks among states, mutual usurpation among families, and mutual injuries among individuals, or the lack of kindness and loyalty between ruler and minister, of parental affection and filial piety between father and son, and of harmony and peace among brothers. These are harms in the world. But when we examine these harms, whence did they arise? Did they arise out of want of mutual love?... They arise out of mutual love. At present feudal lords know only to love their own states and not those of others. Therefore they do not hesitate to mobilize their states to attack others. Heads of families know only to love their own families and not those of others. Therefore they do not hesitate to mobilize their families to usurp others. And individuals know only to love their own persons and not those of others. Therefore they do not hesitate to mobilize their own persons to injure others. For this reason, as feudal lords do not love one another, they will fight in the fields. As heads of families do not love one another, they will usurp one another. As individuals do not love one another, they will injure one another.... Because of want of mutual love, all the calamities, usurpations, hatred, and animosity in the world have arisen. Therefore the man of humanity condemns it. What is the way of universal love and mutual benefit? It is to

regard other people's countries as one's own. Regard other people's families as one's own. Regard other people's person as one's own. Because of universal love, all of the calamities, usurpations, hatred and animosity in the world may be prevented from arising. Therefore the man of humanity praises it. (Chan *A Source Book* 213–14).

Confucius did not subscribe to the thought of Mo Tzu and critiqued the doctrine of love on two grounds. First he felt that love itself could only be fostered through an establishment of proper relationships, thoughts, and behaviors. But more fundamentally, Confucius said that it is not appropriate to love another in every circumstance. When asked whether one should love one's enemy and those who do harm, Confucius replied, "Repay kindness with kindness, but repay evil with justice" (*Analects* XIV: 36).

We mentioned earlier how ancient Chinese religions seemed to focus upon the specifically human concerns of the world to an unprecedented degree. This concentration was manifested in Chinese creation mythology and finds its ultimate expression in the thought of Confucius. Confucius died thinking that he had little impact on China, but he could not have been more wrong. Confucius' thought became in effect China's state religion during the Han dynasty, 206 B.C.E.–220 C.E. In 130 B.C.E. it was made the basic discipline of training for government officials. In the Sung Dynasty the *Analects* became not merely one school book but *the* school book, the basis of all education in China. In 1934 Confucius' birthday was proclaimed a national holiday.

Taoism

Lao Tzu

It is said that the founder of Taoism lived during the time of Confucius. Lao Tzu (Laozi) is traditionally described as the founder of Taoism (Daoism), and many people say that he is the same person as Lao Tan(Lao Dan) of the sixth century. Some say that Lao Tzu was not a historical personage, and others state that he lived in the fourth century B.C.E. because that date has been attributed to his great book the *Tao Te Ching* (*Dao de jing*). The *Tao Te Ching* remains the most profound and mysterious book in Chinese religious literature, and no matter its origin it represents an important tradition in Chinese religious history.

For Lao Tzu, *Tao*, the underlying principle of the cosmos, is understood as mysterious and ineffable. The *Tao Te Ching* articulates well the inexpressible nature of this principle:

> The *Tao* that can be told of is not the eternal *Tao*; the name that can be named is not the eternal name. The nameless is the origin of heaven and earth; the named is the mother of all things. Therefore let there always be non-being, so that we may see their subtlety, and let there always be being so that we may see their outcome. The two are the same, but after they are produced, they have different names. They both may be called deep and profound, deeper and more profound, the door of all subtleties (quoted in Chan *The Way of Lao Tzu* 97).

In many ways Taoism is the antithesis of the philosophy of Confucius. Like Confucius, Lao Tzu of the *Tao Te Ching* was concerned in large part with advice directed to rulers and military leaders. Lao Tzu, however, states that the affairs of the state can best be managed only if rulers follow the way of the *Tao*. This is done, states Lao Tzu, if leaders practice *wu-wei*, which means "actionless action," "without doing," or "non-action." As the *Tao Te Ching* puts it, "The *Tao* forever remains without action, and there is nothing that it does not do" (37.1). Thus Taoist kings never intervened in an attempt to direct the affairs of the people.

Like Confucius, Lao Tzu advised rulers to lead by example. While Lao Tzu, like Confucius, states that political and military leaders should follow the *Tao*, the *Tao* is described by them very differently. Lao Tzu criticizes and rejects the Confucian system insofar as it stresses the importance of rights, social values and reason. As we saw, for Confucius benevolence and justice were important concepts, whereas Lao Tzu renounces their usefulness in goodness: "When one abandons the Tao one has recourse to benevolence; when one abandons benevolence one has recourse to justice; when one abandons justice one has recourse to rights. The rights are only a thin line of loyalty and faith and thus the beginning of anarchy" (*The Tao Te Ching* 38.9–14).

According to Lao Tzu, social values and discursive knowledge are illusory, and they destroy the natural unity of being and cause confusion by absoluting that which is relative. As Lao Tzu puts it, "That is why the holy man confines himself to inactivity and carries on wordless teaching" (2.10). As Confucianism wrestled with the internal political strife of China by attempting to reform government through proper ritual and social and educational means, Taoism emphasized ruling through inactivity and passivity. Strictly speaking, the Taoist preached a form of anarchism and felt that the promulgation and enforcement of laws itself caused disorder:

> As restrictions and prohibitions are multiplied in the empire, the people grow poorer and poorer. When the people are subjected to overmuch government, the land is thrown into confusion.... The greater the number of laws and enactments, the more thieves and robbers

there will be. Therefore the sage says, "so long as I do nothing the people will work out their own reformation. So long as I love calm the people will right themselves. If only I keep from meddling, the people will grow rich. If only I am free from desire, the people will come naturally back to simplicity" (Giles 38, LVII).

It has been said that the doctrine of yin-yang emerged in China around 1000 B.C.E. Yin represented the dark, passive, feminine powers and rhythms of the universe, while yang was light, active and male. Within that system of bi-polar opposites the thought of Confucius can rightly be considered yang while Taoism is yin. The *Tao Te Ching* describes the *Tao* as "the mother of the world" (Chapters 25, 52). And it is symbolized furthermore as the divinity of the valley "and the obscure female that does not die." Chapter 21 of the *Tao Te Ching* contains another passage that describes the *Tao* as "an imperceptible, indiscernible being" that "contains in its bosom" spiritual and fertile essences and beings. Developing this idea further, the *Tao Te Ching* says:

> The spirit of the valley never dies. It is called the mystic female. The door of the mystic female is the root of heaven and earth. Continuously it seems to remain. Draw upon it and it serves you with ease (quoted in Yutang *Wisdom of China* 586, VI).

Tao is feminine and passive and yet is the greatest power in the universe; "the *Tao* is ever inactive, and yet there is nothing that it does not do" (*Ta-kao* XXXVII). The Tao is often likened to water, for water is primordial, pliable and yet powerful.

> There is nothing in the world more soft and weak than water, yet for attacking things that are hard and strong there is nothing that surpasses it.... The soft overcomes the hard; the weak overcomes the strong. By acting passively in the world the leader is able to rule. The sage relies on actionless activity,... puts himself in the background; but is always to fore. Remains outside; but is always there. Is it not just because he does not strive for any personal end that all his personal ends are fulfilled? (Waley *The Way* Chapters 2, 7).

The *Tao* flows naturally through life like water. In this way one is able to work without working. As Chapter 15 of the *Tao Te Ching* says, "Those who flow as life flows know they need no other force; they feel no wear, they feel no tear, they need no mending, no repair" (quoted in Smith 206). The Taoist idea of a proper kingdom would be a small village state, quiet, self-contained and self-sufficient.

> Take a small country with a small population. It might well be that there were machines that saved labor ten times or a hundred times,

and yet the people would not use them.... They would not immigrate to distant countries. Although there might be carriages and boats, no one would ride in them. Although there might be weapons of war no one would issue them....

Make the people's food sweet, their clothes beautiful, their houses comfortable, their daily life a source of pleasure. Then the people will look at the country over the border, will hear the cocks crowing and the dogs barking there, but right down to old age and the day of their death, they will not trouble to go there. An important Taoist value is humility as is shown in the following ancient saying, "Be humble and you shall remain entire — Can this be regarded as mere empty words?" (*Ta-kao* XXII).

Humility is also important for leaders. Lao Tzu states that emperors are most successful when unnoticed: "A leader is best when people barely know that he exists.... Of a good leader who talks little when his work is done his aim fulfilled they will all say 'we did this ourselves'" (Chapter 17).

While the Confucian ideal was to be a cultivated gentleman, the Taoist ideal was to be uncultivated. The Taoist ideal is sometimes symbolized as an uncarved block of wood. A key for understanding Lao Tzu's philosophy is naturalness. Whereas Confucius stressed the promulgation and following of many rules, Lao Tzu emphasized acting spontaneously. Lao Tzu was critical of *li*: "Now propriety (*li*) is a superficial expression of loyalty and faithfulness, and the beginning of disorder" (Chapter 38).

Chaung-Tzu

Second only to Lao Tzu in importance among the Chinese Taoists was the philosopher Chaung-Tzu (Zhuang Zhou), who lived approximately from 365 to 290 B.C.E. Like Lao Tzu, Chaung-Tzu rejects discursive knowledge and social values. Life and death are but two modalities of a single ultimate reality and it was this notion that helps us understand the ease with which Chaung-Tzu discussed death.

The universe carries me in my body, toils me in my life, gives me repose with old age, and rests me in death. What makes my life a good makes my death a good also. If we take the universe as a great melting pot and nature as a great foundryman, what place is it not right for us to go? Calmly we die; quietly we live (quoted in Giles *Chuang Tzu* Chapter 6).

For Chaung-Tzu, there is a unity of all things within the universe and there are no absolutes. Thus one should not fear death. Chaung-Tzu said that one should simply, calmly inhabit the natural rhythms of the universe.

It has been said that when his wife died his friend Hui Tzu, a musician, went to see him according to custom and found him singing and beating time on a metal bowl. Shocked at this sight Hui Tzu said to him:

> To live with your wife and see your eldest son grow up to be a man, and then not to shed a tear over her corpse—this would be bad enough but to drum on a bowl and sing; surely this is going too far.
> "Not at all," replied Chaung-Tzu. "When she first died, how could I help being affected, but then on examining the matter, I say that in the beginning she had originally been lifeless. And not only lifeless, but she had originally been formless. And not only formless but she had originally lacked all substance. During this first state of confused chaos, there came a change which resulted in substance. This substance changed to assume form. This form changed and became alive. And now it has changed again to reach death. In this it has been like the passing of the four seasons, spring, autumn, winter and summer and while she is thus lying asleep in the great house, for me to go about weeping and wailing would be to show myself ignorant of fate therefore I refrain" (quoted in Fung 237).

The holy man understands that everything emerges from an origin and must return to its beginnings in the natural order of things. Lao Tzu said,

> Stretch a bow to the full. And you will wish that you had stopped in time; temper a sword-edge to its very sharpest, and you will find it soon grows dull. When bronze and jades fill your hall, it can no longer be guarded. Wealth and place breed insolence that brings ruin in its train. When your work is done, then withdraw! All things come into existence, and thence we see them return. Look at the things that have been flourishing. Each goes back to its origin, returning as the motion of the *Tao* (*Ta-kao* XL).

For Chaung-Tzu, life and death, consciousness and unconsciousness are the rhythms of a ceaseless flow of change. Consciousness itself is a relative state as shown by this well known anecdote: "Long ago I, Chaung-Chou (Tzu) dreamed that I was a butterfly, a butterfly on the wing, and I was happy; I did not know that was Chou. Suddenly I waked, and I was myself, the real Chou. And I do not know if I was Chou dreaming that he was a butterfly, or a butterfly dreaming that it was Chou" (Eliade 32).

Whereas Confucius sought to participate actively in and reform government and died disappointed at his political status, Chaung-Tzu wanted nothing to do with politics. Once when he was fishing on the River Pu, the leader of Chu sent two officials to offer Chaung-Tzu the post of minister. Chaung-Tzu, without turning his head, and continuing to fish said, "I have heard that in Ch'u there is a sacred tortoise which has been dead now some three hundred years. And that the prince keeps this tortoise carefully enclosed in a chest on the alter of his ancestral temple. Now would this tortoise rather be dead and have its remains venerated, or be alive and wagging its tail in the mud?" "It would rather be alive," replied the two officials together. "Then," cried Chaung-Tzu, "be gone. I too would rather wag my tail in the mud" (quoted in Giles, H.A. XII, 5). Thus Chaung-Tzu emphasized that the spontaneous life of the simple person is more important than political power and status. For Taoists human life should be simple and natural. As Chaung-Tzu put it,

> In the days when natural instincts prevailed, men moved quietly and gazed steadily. At that time there were no roads over mountains, nor boats, nor bridges over water. All things were produced, each for its own proper sphere. Birds and beasts multiplied; trees and shrubs grew up. The former might be led by the hand; you could climb up and peep into the ravens nest. For then men dwelt with birds and beasts, and all creation was one. There was no distinction of good and bad men. Being all equally without knowledge, their virtue could not go astray. Being all equally without evil desires, they were in a state of natural integrity, the perfection of human existence.
> But when sages appeared, tripping people over charity and fettering with duty to one's nature, doubt found its way into the world. And then with their gushing of her music and fussing of a ceremony, the empire became divided against itself (quoted in Giles, H.A. *Chaung Tzu* VIII, 2).

Thus Taoism ultimately yearns for the mythological age of paradise which is shared by all archaic people. Chaung-Tzu sought to return to the primordium, when humans and animals lived side by side and there were no social distinctions between people. In its goal to transcend the urban world of social stratification and human achievements, Taoism reemphasized a mythological orientation that is characteristic of primal people all over the world. Confucians argued that people must have many rules in order to follow the *Tao*. Taoists noted that a person who follows the *Tao* needs no rules. Rules are created by humans who have lost unity with the world. Taoism recovers that unity and hence has no need of rules.

Taoist literature is full of examples of dialogues and debates with Confucian thinkers. In one of the most famous, Chaung-Tzu, the Taoist, and Hui Tzu, a Confucian, were walking one day on a bridge over the Hao River. Chaung-Tzu said, "The white fish are swimming at ease. This is the happiness of fish." "You are not a fish," said Hui Tzu. "How do you know its happiness?" "You are not I," said Chuang-Tzu. "How do you know that I do not know the happiness of the fish?"(quoted in Chan *A Source Book* 209–210).

Taoism and the Quest for Immortality

During the first century B.C.E. in the Han dynasty, Taoism produced at least one school in which the goal was to obtain immortality on earth. The *Tao Te Ching* and the *Chaung Tzu* both make vague references to the attainment of immortality, and later Taoists drew upon these in seeking eternal life *(hsien)*. Some scholars think that Lao Tzu and Chaung-Tzu were indifferent to the question of personal immortality as they emphasized living in spontaneous harmony with the natural order in the present world. Others point to passages which refer to the transcendence of death as proof that early Taoists were concerned with the attainment of personal immortality.

Some Taoists emphasized a life in harmony with the natural forms and rhythms of the world, while others sought immortality in addition to health and long life. Immortality was to be achieved through alchemy, breathing exercises, hygiene, diet and the help of the gods. There is ample support in the *Tao Te Ching* for both views. For example, it is said, "I have heard that he who possesses the secret of life, when traveling abroad, will not flee from rhinoceros or tiger; when entering a hostile camp, he will not equip himself with sword or buckler. The rhinoceros finds in him no place to insert its horn; the tiger has nowhere to fasten its claw; the soldier has nowhere to thrust his blade. And why? Because he has no spot where death can enter" (quoted in Giles, Lionel *The Sayings of Lao Tzu* 50). Again in another place the *Tao Te Ching* says, "He who attains Tao is everlasting. Though his body may decay he never perishes" (*Ta-kao* 50).

Chaung-Tzu, drawing upon the *Tao Te Ching*, told the story of a sage who was able to transcend the realm of life and death: "In three days he could transcend this mundane world … then he could transcend all material existence. After he could transcend all material existence … he could transcend all life. After he could transcend all life, then he had the clear vision of the morning and after that he was able to see the solitary. After seeing the solitary he could abolish the distinctions of past of and present. After abolishing the past and present he was able to enter where life and death are no more" (Yutang in *Wisdom 't China* 660–61). The last sentence of this quote is one reason why the later Taoists cite Chaung-Tzu as favoring the quest for immortality.

Some groups searched for an elixir of eternal life distilled from the five elements. Alchemy was also employed as a way of finding a way to prolong human life. In the third century B.C.E. the quest for immortality became an open interest of the imperial court, and a number of emperors were attracted to this form of Taoism. Common people also began to pursue this search for eternal life by following dietary means to prevent the body's decay. Important here was a basic Chinese principle that human beings shared certain essential elements with the cosmos. Every part of the great *Tao* of heaven was reproduced in each human being, and all of these elements were broken into five classes. Through breath control one attempted to slow down the body's activity in order to reach a state of embryonic respiration akin to existence in the womb. Here diet was very important. It was believed that one must live on fruits, berries, roots or tubers and give up meats and cereals. Sexual rites akin to Tantric Buddhism were also performed by these Taoists who would attempt, at the moment of ejaculation, to return semen back to the body where, mixed with breath, it could ascend to the brain in order to nourish it.

Yet with all of Taoism's success, it never became the official religion of the Chinese state. Taoism, at least on the surface, was often overshadowed by Buddhism and the thought of Confucius, the latter greatly influencing Chinese education. Today Taoism, on the surface, seems very much in decline although the Chinese inhabit a world filled with Taoist principles and values.

Chinese Buddhism

China suffered more than thirty years of internal strife and foreign invasions before they again achieved political unity during the brief but significant Sui dynasty (581–618 C.E.) The Sui undertook an ambitious program of canal building in order to link traditional Chinese centers on the northern plain with newly emerging areas in the Yellow River Valley. However, an unsuccessful war with Korea caused the Sui to fall from power. They were followed by the Tseng dynasty (618 to 907 C.E.), during which time Chinese civilization prospered. Concluding the canal system begun by the Sui, the Tseng divided up many large estates and distributed lands to the peasants and otherwise reformed the central government's administration. As the empire expanded, local areas were able to retain their leaders as long as they viewed the Tseng emperor as the ultimate political power. Literature and arts flowered, and throughout all of East Asia Tseng culture was imitated.

The two most significant aspects of the Tseng culture were the emergence of Buddhism among intellectual and artistic circles and the development of international trade. The Chinese capital of Chang-An became linked with India and Mediterranean markets through caravans. Moreover, Christian, Jewish and Muslim communities were established in China during that time. Chinese responses to Buddhism were unique in all of Asia. On the one hand, Buddhism was persecuted as in no other Asian country. On the other hand, China developed Buddhist symbols that made Buddhism attractive to the Koreans, Japanese and Vietnamese. The ancient Chinese disliked the Buddhist upheaval of indigenous Chinese family values.

In one sense it is a wonder that Buddhism could penetrate "China's wall" given Buddhism's ascetic flavor. However, Buddhism was able to introduce itself into China in three major stages. Earlier, texts were translated and introduced from 148 to 654 C.E. in central Asia in the cities along the Silk Road. This has been called the period of the "Buddha Taoist" because scholars discussed Buddhism within the language of Taoism. The initial break into the wall of China came at the beginning of the third century, 220 C.E. War had divided China into north and south regions and six dynasties. People looked for a new religion. Neo-Taoism arose proclaiming that everything seemingly comes and goes, which keeps one from the eternal *Tao*. In the fifth century in the north the Chinese were controlled by the Wei barbarians, who were non–Chinese and non-traditional. They thought Buddhism was as good to them as they were to the Chinese. The Wei did not want to embrace Taoism or the thought of Confucius, so they imported many Buddhist monks. The Chinese were attracted to the efficacy of meditation and the notion that the truth is here and now, and this helped pave the way for Buddhism in the north.

In 508 C.E. the north and south merged; from 581 to 618 the Sui dynasty existed, and the Tseng followed from 618 to 907 C.E. The Chinese had many Buddhist texts translated into Chinese during the Sui and Tseng dynasties. Efforts were made to fashion their understanding of Buddhist symbols within Chinese tradition. After China restored unity, the Chinese were ripe for the Mahayana principle of "all in one and one in all," and the *Lotus Sutra* became the main text. Ch'an (Zen) Buddhism arose in the fifth century, although not much is known about its introduction into China.

We do know that early Chinese Buddhist scriptures contain a great deal of market place language and very little metaphysics, reflecting the Silk Road influence. Buddhism in China first and foremost appealed to the merchants. Eventually a new strand of Ch'an developed that was acceptable to monks and traditional Confucians who were dissatisfied with Buddhist principles. Eventually there were at least ten schools of Buddhism in China, many of which overlapped. Finally, the Ching-t'u ("Pure Land" sect) and the Ch'an schools came to dominate. In the Ching-t'u salvation was promised to those who called in faith on the name of the great Buddha, *Amit'o* (Amitabha). This sect dominated popular devotion as expressed in temple worship. Those Chinese who were more concerned with inter-mystical experience gravitated towards the Ch'an school of Buddhism. The Pure Land sect, sometimes called Amida Buddhism, was founded in China by Hui-Wuan in the latter part of the fourth century. In this sect of Buddhism one relies on the grace of the divine power to save one through the utterance of his name.

It is more difficult to say when the Ch'an movement started, but tradition says that it was first brought to Canton in 520 C.E. by a famous Indian monk, Bodhidharma. The emphasis of the Ch'an school is anti-intellectual; enlightenment does not come from learning or education. One famous Ch'an school picture shows a monk tearing up the Scriptures. Ch'an developed two methods called *wen-ta* and *kung-an* to produce illumination. *Wen-ta* means "question and answer" and *kung-an* means "riddle." Literally *kung-an* means "public document"; the riddles emerged from dialogues between masters and pupils. The enlightenment generated by riddles could not be learned from textbooks. Illumination that comes from such exercises is sudden or spontaneous and is like an awakening or sudden conversion (*tun wu*).

Neo-Confucianism

Not all the Chinese responded well to Buddhism, and, as a result, Neo-Confucianism emerged very quickly in an attempt to revitalize the teaching of Master K'ung. Two different strategies emerged among those Chinese who wished to resuscitate the teachings of Confucius. One was to resist Buddhism, and the other was to attempt to make Buddhism more Chinese in character.

During the Tang, two men, Han Yu (768–824 C.E.), a poet, and Li Ao (fl. 798), a government official, both gave Confucianism new life and helped keep it from being eradicated. Both made a frontal attack on Buddhism and Taoism. They demonstrated dislike of Buddhist ritual, which was seen as superstitious and non–Chinese, and they were especially critical of the way Buddhism and Taoism neglected the centrality of family. Han Yu was also critical of the Taoist doctrine of *wu-wei*. He was credited as saying, "Until the sages die off the robbers will not disappear," and "If we were animals we could live Taoism but we are humans." Both Han Yu and Li Ao argued that the way of Confucius could not prevail unless Taoism and Buddhism were stopped. Given the human condition, they asked how could the Chinese follow Taoist non-action(*wu-wei*) and the silence of the Buddha?

Neo-Confucianism thrived from the twelfth to the sixteenth centuries, and its most famous proponent was Chu Hsi (Zhu Xi), who lived from 1130 to 1200 C.E. For Chu Hsi, *li* was the basis of all truth, value and purpose. Neo-Confucianism developed sophisticated metaphysical arguments in order to stand up to Buddhist thought. Ironically, it did so by borrowing many Buddhist terms. Chu Hsi argued that there was an immaterial principal (*li*) in all things which combines with material energies (*chi*) to form everything. *Li* and *chi* are part and parcel of the absolute reality which transcends them. Chu Hsi affirmed the reality of the phenomenal world and in this way brought about a critique of the doctrine of Buddhist emptiness. Chu Hsi also pushed for the investigation of things, which he said was an exercise of solemnity. By exploring the world in a serious way one can attain much morality, wisdom and calmness.

The other major Neo-Confucian school is called the Lu Wang after Luttsiang-Shan (1139–1192 C.E.) and Wang Yang-ming (1472–1529 C.E.). One must clear one's mind of all impurities and arrive at a pure state which is *li*. According to Luttsiang-Shan, "the universe is in my mind and my mind is in the universe." He critiqued the detachment of Buddhism by stating that one should deal seriously with the world. Wang Yang-ming had great influence on his time. He argued that *li* and mind existed as a unity and that everything is present in the mind. In contrast to Chu Hsi, Wang Yang-ming argued that intuitive knowledge exists apart from the material world. And finally, he stated that there is a unity of knowledge and action. Knowledge is the beginning of action, which completes knowledge.

The Three Become One

Although Confucianism, Taoism and Buddhism are often referred to as the three teachings (*san jiao*) of China, it is important to remember that at least since Sung times, the last thousand years approximately, the distinctions between those three religions was not as important as the distinction between the religious orientation of common masses and those of the educated aristocracy.

Recent scholarship calls into serious question the discussion of Chinese religion since late imperial times in terms of three separate traditions (Lopez). Even as early as the sixth century one Chinese scholar, Li Shan, wrote that "Buddhism is the sun, Daoism the moon, and Confucianism the five planets" (Lopez 3). Thus the three teachings are separate but interrelated parts of Chinese religious life. Chinese life interweaves aspects from these three religions in a complex pattern that cannot be accurately described by the terms "Confucian," "Taoist," or "Buddhist." For example, as the historian of religions Russell Kirkland has shown, Ch'uan-chen Taoism originated and blended with both Ch'an Buddhism and Neo-Confucianism (432). Numerous other examples of the fusion and parallel development of the three religions of China exist (Ebrey and Gregory; Lopez).

Bibliography
Chapter 10 — The Three Religions of China

Ames, Roger, and D.C. Lau. *Tracing Tao to Its Source (and Other Essays from Han Dynasty Taoism)*. London, 1981.

de Bary, William Theodore. Editor. *The Unfolding of Neo-Confucianism*. New York, 1975.

Bell, Catherine. "Ritualization of Texts and Textualization of Ritual in the Codification of Daoist Liturgy." *History of Religions* (1988): 366–392.

Bokenkamp, Stephen. *Early Daoist Scriptures*. With Contribution by Peter Nickerson. Berkeley, California, 1997.

Boltz, Judith. "Lao-tzu." *Biographies of Spirit Immortals*. Frankfurt, 1987.

Boltz, William G. "Kung-kung and the Flood: Reverse Euphemerism in the *Yao tien*." *T'oung pao* 67 (1981): 141–153.

Bynners, Whitter. *The Way of Life According to Lao Tzu*. New York, 1944.

Chai, Ch'u, and Winberg Chai. Trans. and Editors. *The Humanist Way in Ancient China: Essential Works of Confucianism*. New York, 1965.

Chan, Wing-Tsit. *Chu and Neo-Confucianism*. Honolulu, 1986.

_____. "Chu Hsi's Completion of Neo-Confucianism." *Sung Studies*. 2 (1973): 59–90.

_____. "Confucian Thought: Foundation of a Tradition." *Encyclopedia of Religion*. Vol. 4. Mircea Eliade. Editor-in-Chief. New York, 1987: 15–24.

_____. *Wang Yang-ming yu Chan*. Tai-pei shih, 1984.

_____. Trans. *A Source Book in Chinese Philosophy*. Princeton, 1963.

_____. Trans. and Editor. *The Way of Lao Tzu (Tao Te Ching)*. New York, 1963.

Chang, Carsun. *The Development of Neo-Confucian Thought*. New York, 1957.

Ch'en, Kenneth. *Buddhism in China: A Historical Survey*. Princeton, 1964.

_____. *The Chinese Transformation of Buddhism*. Princeton, 1973.

Ching, Julia. "Confucius." *Encyclopedia of Religion*. Vol. 4. Mircea Eliade. Editor-in-Chief. New York, 1987: 39–42.

_____. *To Acquire Wisdom: The Way of Wang Yang-ming (1492–1529)*. New York, 1976.

Creel, Herrlee G. *Confucius and the Chinese Way*. New York, 1960.

_____. *What is Taoism?* Chicago, 1970.

Dean, Kenneth. *Taoist Ritual and Popular Cults of South East China*. Princeton, 1993.

De Groot, J.J.M. *The Religious System of China: Its Ancient Forms, Evolution, History and Present Aspect, Manners, Customs and Social Institutions Connected therewith.* 6 Vols. Leiden, 1892–1910; reprinted Taipei, 1982.

Dumoulin, Heinrich. *A History of Zen Buddhism.* New York, 1963.

Ebrey, Patricia Buckley, and Peter N. Gregory. Editors. *Religion and Society in T'ang and Sung China.* Honolulu, 1993.

Eliade, Mircea. *A History of Religious Ideas.* Vol. 2. Trans. W. R. Trask. Chicago, 1982.

Fung, Yu-lan. *A History of Chinese Philosophy.* 2 Vols. Trans. Derek Bodde. Princeton, 1952–1953.

Giles, H.A. *Chuang Tzu: Mystic Moralist and Social Reformer.* Shanghai, 1889.

Giles, Lionel. Trans. *The Sayings of Lao Tzu.* London, 1905.

_____. *The Sayings of Confucius.* London, 1917.

Girardot, N.J. *Myth and Meaning in Early Taoism.* Berkeley, 1983.

_____. "Behaving Cosmologically in Early Taoism." *Cosmology and Ethical Order.* R.W. Lovin and Frank E. Reynolds. Editors. Chicago, 1985.

Hansen, Valerie. *Changing Gods in Medieval China: 1127–1276.* Princeton, 1990.

Henricks, Robert G. Trans. *Lao Tzu: Te Tao Ching.* New York, 1989.

Israeli, Raphael. *Muslims in China: A Study in Cultural Confrontation.* London, 1978.

Kaltenmark, Max. *Lao Tzu and Taoism.* Stanford, California, 1969.

Kao, Karl S.Y. *Classical Chinese Tales of the Supernatural and the Fantastic: Selections from the Third to the Tenth Century.* Bloomington, 1985.

Kirkland, Russell. "Book Review of Terry F. Kleeman's *A God's Own Tale: The Book of Transformations of Wenchang, the Divine Lord of Zitong.*" *Journal of the Academy of Religion* LXIV (1996): 430–432.

Kohn, Livia. *Early Chinese Mysticism.* Princeton, 1991.

Lagerwy, John. *Daoist Ritual in Chinese Society and History.* New York, 1997.

Latourette, Kenneth Scott. *A History of Christian Missions in China.* London, 1929.

Lau, D.C. *Mencius.* New York, 1970.

Legge, James. *The Analects of Confucius.* Vol. 1. *The Chinese Classics.* 2nd Ed. Oxford, 1893–1895.

_____. *The Chinese Classics.* Hong Kong, 1960.

_____. Trans. *The Texts of Confucianism.* Part 1. *The Sacred Books of the East.* Vol. III. Oxford, 1879.

_____. Trans. *The Sacred Books of China: The Texts of Taoism.* New York, 1962.

Liu, Wu-chi. *A Short History of Confucian Philosophy.* New York, 1955.

_____. *Confucius: His Life and Time.* New York, 1956.

Lopez, Donald. Editor. *Religions of China in Practice.* Princeton, New Jersey, 1996.

Maspero, Henri. *Taoism and Chinese Religion.* Trans. Frank A. Kierman, Jr. Amherst, Massachusetts, 1981.

Mitchell, Stephen. *Tao Te Ching.* New York, 1989.

Okada, Takahiko. "The Chu Hsi and Wang Yang-ming Schools at the End of the Ming and Tokugawa Periods." *Philosophy East and West* 23 (1973): 139–162.

Overmyer, Daniel L. *Folk Buddhist Religion: Dissenting Sects in Late Traditional China.* Cambridge, Massachusetts, 1976.

Robinet, Isabelle. *Taoism: Growth of a Religion*. Trans. Phyllis Brooks. Palo Alto, California, 1997.
Roth, Harold D. *Who Compiled the Chuang Tzu?*. LaSalle, 1991.
Schipper, Kristofer. *The Taoist Body*. Palo Alto, California, 1993.
Shaughnessy, Edward L. *Before Confucius: Studies in the Creation of the Chinese Classics*. Albany, New York, 1997.
Smith, D. Howard. *Confucius*. London, 1973.
_____. *Chinese Religions*. London, 1968.
Smith, Huston. *The Religions of Man*. New York, 1958.
Stein, Rolf A. "Religious Taoism and Popular Religion from the Second to Seventh Centuries." *Facets of Taoism: Essays in Chinese Religion*. Holmes Welch and Anna Seidel. Editors. New Haven, 1979.
Strickmann, Michel. "History, Anthropology and Chinese Religion." *Harvard Journal of Asiatic Studies* 40 (1980): 201–248.
_____. "The Mao Shan Revelations: Taoism and the Aristocracy." *T'oung Pao* 63.1 (1977).
Ta-kao, Ch'u. *The Tao Te Ching*. Trans. Buddhist Society. London, 1982.
Thompson, Lawrence G. *Chinese Religion: An Introduction*. Belmont, California, 1969.
Tsui, Chi. *A Short History of Chinese Civilization*. New York, 1943.
Waley, Arthur. *The Analects of Confucius*. Boston and London, 1938.
_____. *The Way and Its Power*. London, 1934.
_____. *Three Ways of Thought in Ancient China*. London, 1939.
Watson, Burton. Trans. *Chaung Tzu: Basic Writings*. New York and London, 1964.
Wei-ming, Tu. *Confucian Thought: Selfhood as Creative Transformation*. Albany, New York, 1985.
Welch, Holmes, and Anna Seidel. Editors. *Facets of Taoism: Essays in Chinese Religion*. New Haven, Connecticut, 1979.
_____. *The Practice of Chinese Buddhism, 1900–1950*. Cambridge, Massachusetts, 1967.
Williams, S. Wells. *The Middle Kingdom*. New York, 1899.
Wilson, Thomas A. *Genealogy of The Way: The Construction and Uses of the Confucian Tradition in Late Imperial China*. Stanford, California, 1995.
Wright, Arthur F. *Buddhism in Chinese History*. New York, 1965.
_____. *Confucianism and Chinese Civilization*. New York, 1967.
Yang, Ch'ing-K'un. *Religion in Chinese Society*. Berkeley, California, 1961.
Yu-Lan, Fung. *The History of Chinese Philosophy*. Trans. Derk Bodde. Princeton, 1952.
Yutang, Lin. *The Wisdom of China and India*. New York, 1942.
_____. *The Wisdom of Confucius*. New York, 1938.
Zurcher, E. *The Buddhist Conquest of China: The Spread and Adaptation of Buddhism in Early Medieval China*. Leiden, 1959.

Chapter 11

Christianity

Christianity is the most widespread religion in the world with somewhere between 800 million and 1 billion followers. It is also the most written about religion and the most critically examined. Most biblical scholarship has concentrated on attempting to discern the historical accuracy of the Bible, which has generated numerous questions.

Although the present calendar of the Western world would place the birth of Jesus at the beginning of the first millennium C.E., historical studies date Jesus' birth 6–4 B.C.E. Matthew 2:1 says that Jesus was born "in the days of Herod." Since Herod died in 4 B.C.E., Jesus must have been born sooner. Furthermore Luke 3:1–2 and 23 say that John the Baptist began preaching in the fifteenth year of the emperor Tiberius, which would have been 26–27 C.E. Jesus was baptized shortly thereafter when he was "about thirty years old." Thus, working back in time, Jesus' birth date probably was between 6 and 4 B.C.E. That date conflicts with Luke 2:1–4, which states that Jesus was born during a census ordered by Augustus Caesar when Quirinius was governor of Syria (6–9 C.E.). However there is evidence that Quirinius was in the service of the government sometime before his governorship. Thus Luke may be referring to a time when Quirinius was sent to Judea to conduct a census some ten or twelve years prior to his taking office as governor.

Unfortunately, our uncertainty about the knowledge of Jesus' life does not end there. Very little is known about the life of Jesus of Nazareth. According to Matthew and Luke, Jesus was born in Bethlehem, "the city of David." His parents lived in Nazareth of Galilee, and it was there that Jesus grew up and lived most of his life up until his 30th birthday. Jesus' childhood and youth are shrouded in mystery. His parents apparently belonged to the common people who were religious enough, according to Luke, every year to go to Jerusalem to observe the Passover. Jesus knew the Torah and the Jewish prophets well enough to be able to quote them at will. Jesus knew enough of the prophetic tradition to develop a healthy suspicion of the formalism and intolerance that characterized the Pharisees and scribes. Trained as a carpenter, Jesus grew up in a large family in which there were at least six other children, including four boys — James, Joses, Simon and Jude.

Luke 2:41–52 gives us an important glimpse into the religious bent of the young boy Jesus. When Jesus was 12 his parents went to Passover in Jerusalem as they did every year. At the end of the feast his parents began to journey home and had traveled for a day before they realized that Jesus was not in their company. Returning to Jerusalem, they searched for three days before they found him in the temple, "sitting among the teachers, listening to them and asking them questions and all who heard him were amazed at his understanding and his answers" (46). After being scolded a little bit, Jesus puzzled his parents with a response and then returned to Nazareth, "and was obedient to them and his mother kept all these things in her heart" (51). In this brief episode we learn that Jesus gained favor with God (52). We hear virtually nothing about Jesus during the next 18 years, until his 30th birthday, and a number of scholars have assumed that during this period Joseph, his father, died and that Jesus as the oldest son took over the duties of the household.

But when he was about thirty years old Jesus went through a profound experience involving John the Baptist. John the Baptist was an ascetic who "wore clothing made of hair cloth and had a leather belt around his waist and he lived on dried locusts and wild honey" (Matthew 3:4). Suddenly he appeared on the banks of the Jordan River with an urgent proclamation that the people repent, "for the kingdom of heaven is coming." A long-prophesied Messiah of the Jewish people who was to judge the world was about to appear. Those who were not repentant would be cut down and "thrown into the fire" (Matthew 3:10). John the Baptist made clear that the time was near: "even now the ax is laid to the root of the trees" (10).

John the Baptist began baptizing people by submerging them in water. As he baptized others, he mentioned that one was coming after him who was mightier than he and whose followers would be gathered unto him as "wheat into a granary," but the unrepentant "chaff he will burn with unquenchable fire" (12). John the Baptist went all over the region around Jordan preaching "a baptism of repentance for the forgiveness of sins" (Luke 3:3). Repentance for John the Baptist was tied up inexorably with proper ethics. He was asked by the multitudes, "What then shall we do?"

(Luke 3:10). John the Baptist answered, "He who has two coats, let him share with him who has none; and he who has food let him do likewise" (10).

The Gospel of Mark also discusses John the Baptist. John the Baptist tells the people that he baptizes with water but that the one coming after him will "baptize you with the Holy Spirit" (Mark 1:8). Jesus of Nazareth came to John the Baptist in those days and was baptized by John the Baptist, "and when he came up out of the water, immediately he saw the heavens opened and the Spirit descending upon him like a dove; and a voice came from heaven, 'Thou art my beloved son; with thee I am well pleased.'" (Mark 1:10–11). Next, Jesus was led by the Spirit into the wilderness where he fasted for 40 days, after which, while hungry, he was tempted by Satan.

Matthew and Luke cover the temptations well. First the devil attempted to have Jesus turn stones into loaves of bread. But Jesus made clear that God's message cannot be reduced to economic concerns of food: "Man shall not live by bread alone but by every word that proceeds from the mouth of God" (Matthew 4:4). Next the devil took Jesus to the Holy City, put him on top of the temple and asked Jesus to throw himself down so that the angels could rise him up in order to demonstrate his great power. But Jesus, being fully human and humble, refused to tempt God's power in that way. Finally, the devil took him to a very high mountain and showed him "all the kingdoms of the world and the glory of them and he said to him, 'All these I will give you if you will fall down and worship me'" (Matthew 4:8–9). But again Jesus refused the temptation, saying that "you shall worship the Lord your God and Him only shall you serve" (Matthew 4:10). And, in this way, Jesus preached that the Kingdom of God was not of this world.

Next, Jesus heard that John the Baptist had been arrested. He then withdrew into Galilee and dwelt in Capernaum by the sea in order to fulfill what was spoken by the prophet Isaiah (Matthew 12–14). Elsewhere Jesus again said that he had come to fulfill the message of the Jewish prophets. "Think not that I have come to abolish the law and the prophets; I have come not to abolish them but to fulfill them" (Matthew 5:17). As he walked by the Sea of Galilee, Jesus saw Simon, who was called Peter, and his brother Andrew. He recruited them as his first disciples. From there he saw two other brothers, James and John, and they left their fishing nets and followed him.

From Matthew we hear that Jesus "went about all Galilee teaching in their synagogues and preaching the gospel of the kingdom and healing every disease and every infirmity among the people" (Matthew 4:23). Jesus' fame spread throughout Syria, and great crowds began to follow him from Galilee, Jerusalem, Judea and from beyond the Jordan. Seeing these great crowds, Jesus ascended a mountain and there delivered his most famous sermon, the Sermon on the Mount.

> Blessed are the poor in spirit: for theirs is the kingdom of heaven. Blessed are they that mourn: for they shall be comforted. Blessed are the meek: for they shall inherit the earth. Blessed are they which do hunger and thirst after righteousness: for they shall be filled. Blessed are the merciful: for they shall obtain mercy. Blessed are the pure in heart: for they shall see God. Blessed are the peacemakers: for they shall be called the children of God. Blessed are they which are persecuted for righteousness' sake: for theirs is the kingdom of heaven. Blessed are ye, when men revile you, and persecute you, and shall say all manner of evil against you falsely, for my sake. Rejoice, and be exceeding glad: for great is your reward in heaven: for so persecuted they the prophets which were before you (Matthew 5:3–12).

The Sermon on the Mount's appeal to people all over the world is widespread, and even Mohandas Gandhi stated during his life that he found great solace in the Sermon on the Mount. For Jesus, one's thoughts were as important as one's acts. It was important not only to follow the law but also to have a good heart and to think the right thoughts. Thus Jesus said that one who is angry with his brother shall be liable to judgment just as one who kills another human being (Matthew 5:21). Similarly, Jesus admonished that one should not commit adultery, and that "everyone who looks at a woman lustfully has already committed adultery with her in his heart" (Matthew 5:28). Jesus recognized no ultimate significance between any class of people (James 2:1–8). He associated with all types of people, Samaritans from other places, tax collectors, Pharisees, criminals, prostitutes and the poor (Matthew 9:9–13; Mark 2:13–17; Luke 5:27–32). And he asked others to follow his example: "When you give a feast, invite the poor, the maimed, the lame, the blind, and you will be blessed" (Luke 14:13–14). His message transcended all differences and applied to everyone. Jesus was impatient with those who would exalt one class of people over another: "Truly I say unto you that the tax collectors and the harlots go into the Kingdom of God before you" (Matthew 21:31).

Good News

But the most fundamental aspect of Jesus' teaching was the proclamation of the Gospel, or Good News. According to Mark, after John was arrested, "Jesus came into Galilee preaching the gospel of God and saying 'The time is fulfilled and the Kingdom of God is at hand, repent and believe in the gospel'" (1:14–15). Jesus' tone was urgent and he made it clear that there was little time to waste. The end of time was approaching very quickly according to Jesus' message: "Truly I say to you there are some standing here who will not taste death before they see the Kingdom of God come with power" (Mark 9:1). And again in Mark 13:30–33, "Truly I say to you this generation will not pass away before all these things take place. Heaven and earth will pass away, but my words will not pass away. But of that day and that hour no one knows, not even the angels in heaven, nor the Son, but only the Father. Take heed, watch; for you do not know when the time will come."

The end of the age was imminent. The Kingdom of Heaven was soon to follow. A number of passages in Luke underlined the exigency of the situation. One man invited to follow Jesus said, "Lord let me first go and bury my father." But Jesus said to him, "Leave the dead to bury their own dead but as for you go and proclaim the Kingdom of God" (9:59–60). Another man said to Jesus, "I will follow you Lord; but let me first say farewell to those at my home." Jesus said to him, "No one who puts his hand to the plow and looks back is fit for the Kingdom of God" (9:61–62).

Jesus preached at a time of extreme political tension. Rome had conquered Palestine and the Jews found Roman rule intolerable. Not since Egypt had the Jews suffered such oppression. The Jews and the Romans were worlds apart and a spirit of revolt was in the air. Galilee had to pay a number of direct personal taxes for administrative expenses as well as additional taxes in the form of customs, duties, toll booths at bridges and harbors and a salt tax. In 6 C.E. Quirinius, the governor of Syria, ordered a census taken of the inhabitants of Palestine in order to work out an even more thorough form of tax assessment.

Emotions boiled swiftly into insurrection and a Jewish faction called Zealot formed. Zealots attacked the city of Sepphoris and seized the armory and held it until the Roman general Veras regained the city with the help of two Roman legions. Thousands of Zealots were crucified, which flamed the fuels of discord even more. However, not all Jews were supportive of the Zealots. For example, the Essenes were opposed to violence in principle and waited very patiently for the Messiah to return. Pharisees also stayed out of political conflict. They were by far the largest party in Galilee and were led by scribes and rabbis who felt that the only way to hasten the coming of the Messiah and to save Judaism was to be rigid in religious practice. Thus they set out to keep each of the Sabbath laws and the Jewish festivals and to be very particular about ceremonial purity and dietary rules. Sadducees were less influential but even more conservative. They maintained rigid adherence to the old customs.

In this context one can appreciate even more the radical and profound nature of Jesus' emphasis on love of everyone: "You have heard that it was said, 'You shall love your neighbor and hate your enemy,' but I say to you love your enemies and pray for those who persecute you so that you may be sons of your Father who is in heaven; for he makes his sun rise on the evil and on the good, and sends rain on the just and the unjust" (Matthew 5:43–45). And again Jesus said, "So whatever you wish that men would do to you, do so to them; for this is the law and the prophets" (Matthew 7:12).

When asked by a Pharisee lawyer what was the "great commandment in the law?" Jesus said to him, "You shall love the Lord your God with all your heart, and with all your soul, and with all your mind. This is the great and first commandment. And a second is like it, you shall love your neighbor as yourself. On these two commandments depend all the law and the prophets" (Matthew 22:36–40).

An essential element in the love of neighbor for Jesus was forgiveness. A number of significant Biblical passages stress its importance for the early Christian message (Matthew 6:29–30, 18:15, 18:21–22; Luke 7:3–4). In Matthew 5:38–40, Jesus said, "You have heard that it was said, 'an eye for an eye, and a tooth for a tooth.' But I say to you, do not resist one who is evil. But if anyone strikes you on the right cheek, turn to him the other also; and if anyone will sue you and take your coat, let him have your cloak as well; and if anyone forces you to go one mile, go with him two miles" (Matthew 5:38–41).

Retaliation against transgression leads to further strife, violence and discord. Responding to violence and power in kind only creates more trouble, discord and difficulty in the world. Jesus sought to overcome the discord in the world between people and his message of forgiveness, in a very practical way, stopped violence before it ever started. In Matthew 5:25, Jesus said, "Make friends quickly with your accuser while you are going with him to court." Throughout the Gospels Jesus preaches a message of forgiveness and reconciliation in order that people might live in harmony together.

One of the basic tenets of Christian forgiveness is the prohibition against judging other people. Jesus makes it clear that no one is perfect and no one is in a position to stand in judgment of other people (Matthew 10:24–25, 15:14; Luke 37–38). As Jesus put it,

> Judge not that you be not judged. For with the judgment you pronounce you will be judged, and the measure you give will be the measure

you get. Why do you see the speck that is in your brother's eye, but do not notice the log that is in your own eye? Or how can you say to your brother, "Let me take the speck out of your eye," when there is the log in your own eye? You hypocrite, first take the log out of your own eye and then you will see clearly to take the speck out of your brother's eye (Matthew 7:1–5; see also James 2:1–8, 5:9).

Christian teaching makes clear that all are equal in God's eyes: "There is no difference between us because all have sinned and fall short of the glory of God" (Romans 3:23).

Here too we see that Jesus, like the Buddha, Confucius, Lao Tzu and the Jewish prophets directed his message to each individual. The greatest enemy that one faces in this life is oneself, and one should attempt to conquer the evil within before undertaking to do so in another.

In stressing the universality of his message, Jesus made clear that ethnic, regional and even family ties are ultimately transcended in the Christian community. Mark recorded that once Jesus' relatives had come to Capernaum in order to hear him speak: "And his mother and his brother came; and standing outside they sent to him and called him. And a crowd was sitting about him; and they said to him, 'Your mother and your brothers are outside asking for you' and he replied, 'Who are my mother and my brothers?' and looking around on those who sat about him, he said, 'Here are my mother and my brothers, Whoever does the will of God is my brother and sister and mother'" (3:31–35).

Jesus and his disciples traveled throughout the country, and at one point they went to the villages of Caesarea. On the way Jesus asked his disciples to tell him who other people thought that he was. "Peter answered him, 'You are the Christ' and he charged them to tell no one about it" (Mark 8:29–30). Jesus then began to instruct his disciples that he would be rejected by the elders and chief priests, killed, and after three days, he would rise again (Mark 8:31). It was time for Passover and Jews from all over the world went into Jerusalem. Jesus rode into town on a donkey, accompanied by his disciples. He was greeted with shouts of joy and the Galileans spread palm branches in his way.

Then Jesus did a startling thing. He went to the temple and began overturning the tables of the money changers and all those who were buying and selling things, and he cried out, "Is it not written, my house shall be called a house of prayer for all the nations, but you have made it a den of robbers" (Mark 11:17). At this time the chief priests and scribes sought a way to destroy him because they feared his teaching and because the multitude was astonished at his teachings.

Finally, when Jesus foresaw his own death, a simple ceremony was performed: "And as they were eating he took bread and blessed and broke it and gave it to them and said 'Take, this is my body,' and he took a cup and when he had given thanks he gave it to them and they all drank of it and he said to them, 'This is my blood of the covenant which is poured out for many'" (Mark 14:22–24). Jesus was then arrested and brought before the Sanhedrin and, after an examination, was turned over to Pontius Pilate. Pilate passed Jesus to Herod Antipas, the governor of Galilee, who sent Jesus back to Pilate. Pilate sought to have Jesus released by offering him as the one criminal who should be released that year. But the crowd shouted that Barabbas should be released instead, and so Jesus was turned over to the Roman soldiers to be crucified.

At three o'clock P.M. Jesus died on a cross, surrounded by women who would not forsake him. To avoid the body hanging on the cross on the Sabbath day, Joseph of Arimathea, a member of the Sanhedrin, made available his own tomb, and Jesus' body was taken there.

Resurrection

Three days later Mary Magdalene and Mary, the mother of James and Salome, went to the tomb when the sun had risen, and they noticed that the entrance to the tomb was rolled back: "In entering the tomb they saw a young man sitting on the right side dressed in a white robe and they were amazed. And he said to them, 'Do not be amazed; you seek Jesus of Nazareth who was crucified. He has risen; he is not here: see the place where they laid him. But go tell his disciples and Peter that he is going before you to Galilee and they will see him as he told you'" (Mark 16:5–7; see also Luke 24:1–12).

Jesus later appeared before his disciples. At first they were startled and frightened and Jesus said to them, "'Why are you troubled and why do questionings arise in your hearts?...' Then he said to them, 'These are my words which I spoke to you while I was still with you, that everything written about me and the law of Moses and the prophets and the Psalms must be fulfilled.'" Then he opened their minds to understand the scriptures and said to them, "Thus it is written that the Christ should suffer and on the third day rise from the dead and that repentance and forgiveness of sins should be preached in his name to all nations beginning from Jerusalem" (Luke 24:36–38, 44–47).

The resurrection of Christ is the cornerstone of the Christian faith. Christianity promises eternal life to those who believe and have faith in Christ. Just as Christ was resurrected from the dead, so too Christians are promised the gift of eternal life. It was this gift of life everlasting that made Christianity so attractive to the urban people of the Middle East. Other Neolithic religions, such as Cybele-Attis and Isis-Osiris, promised some form of resurrection, but they did not speak to the disenfranchised people of the urban world during the first millennium. Christianity spoke powerfully to those individuals who no longer inhabited Neolithic ethnic and tribal worlds.

A fatalistic outlook on life was endemic within the Roman Empire during the time of Christianity. Christianity offered salvation, a turning around of life in new terms, something not found in earlier religions. Christianity provided answers for the problems of the city that were related to astrology. Within the Roman Empire cities were linked with the sky and sky was connected to the concept of fate, a totally impersonal power. As the doctrine of fate became pervasive, the city-state became secular and separated from the gods. The stars were seen as despots who ruled the world in a fatalistic manner that ultimately occasioned a pessimistic outlook on life. Christianity offered freedom from this fatalistic pessimism by and through resurrection.

Christianity and Judaism

The Christian Church began as a sect within ancient Judaism and Christians differed from Jews only in that they believed Christ to be the Messiah who was raised from the dead and who would return to redeem the world. Paul's letters, especially Galatians 2 and the early chapters in Acts, depict Jewish Christians in Jerusalem attending the temple regularly and obeying Jewish law with respect to circumcision, food taboos and the Sabbath rest. Jerusalem and the Temple were directly under Roman control and the high priests of Judaism held their position only by Roman fiat. Jews looked for the son of David to free them from this oppressive political situation, and they were anxious to follow anyone who proclaimed war against Rome. Jewish Christians shared all of this but believed that Jesus was the appointed Messiah. One of the prominent features of early Palestinian Christianity was prophecy. Like the earlier Jewish prophets of Jerusalem, Christians were very conscious of the prophetic tradition. According to Ernst Kásenmann, prophets were among the leaders in early Christianity, which was dominated by the apocalyptic hope for the coming of the Messiah.

While Christianity itself began as a sect within Palestinian Judaism, and although Jesus himself was a Palestinian Jew, the social context in which Christianity arose was the network of urban centers strung along the Silk Road. The conquests of Alexander the Great created a culture from the Isthmus of Corinth to the Indus Valley and from the Black Sea to the Red Sea. The cities around Palestine were especially influenced by the Greeks and Greek was the common language. From the very beginning of its days in Jerusalem, the Christian Church contained among its members active Greek-speaking Jews who were most influential in spreading Christianity throughout the Hellenistic world (Acts 6). The Acts of the Apostles exemplified the missionary fervor with which Hellenistic Christians spread the Good News of Christianity.

The fall of Jerusalem to the Romans in the destruction of the Temple in 70 C.E. paralleled the spread of Christianity throughout the world. Jerusalem and its temples were holy to Christians as well as to the Jews. Paul's letters make it clear that Jerusalem had special significance for the Christian community. Therefore, the destruction of Jerusalem and the Temple by the Gentiles caused reverberations throughout the Jewish Christian world whose effects would be difficult to overstate (Perrin *The New Testament* 40–41). The Christian Gospels had not yet been written. Prior to the fall, Christianity had emphasized the place of Jerusalem as a sacred land. With the fall of Jerusalem the connection with sacred place was lost, and Christians began to emphasize the temporal aspect of Christianity. It was the emphasis on sacred time that generated the production of the Christian Gospels.

Of all Hellenistic Jewish Christians, the most famous was Paul, who is often called a second founder of Christianity. Indeed the majority of the books constituting the New Testament are letters written by Paul to various churches within the Roman Empire. Interestingly, all of this happened after Paul began an earlier career of opposition to Christianity. Paul was a non–Palestinian Jew born about the same time as Jesus in the town of Tarsus in Cilicia. Paul (born Saul) was a devoted Jew in his early years and went to Jerusalem to study with Gamaliel, a leading Pharisee of Tharisaic. Paul joined in the persecution of early Christians, but according to Acts 9:2–4, "as he journeyed he approached Damascus and suddenly a light from heaven flashed about him and he fell to the ground and heard a voice saying to him, 'Saul, Saul, why do you persecute me?'" Blinded by a vision of a bright light, Paul was led into Damascus where for three days he could not see. He had seen the resurrected Jesus and from that time on he became a disciple of Christ. Paul traveled extensively through the Roman Empire visiting churches and establishing churches at Perga, Antioch, Pisidia, Iconium, Lystra and Derbe.

Paul was the author of 1 Thessalonians, which is considered the oldest surviving Christian document (50–51 C.E.) In 1 Thessalonians, Paul discussed eschatology and especially whether God will raise those who are already dead. Early Christians were very much concerned about the return of Christ to redeem the world, which they felt would be within their own lifetime.

Christianity differed from other religions in the Hellenistic world, such as Gnosticism. While both Gnostics and Christians believed in human salvation, Gnostics perceived that enlightenment came by freeing the true self, a pre-existing spark of light. Salvation for Christians was different. Christians did not achieve salvation by releasing a previously existing eternal spark, but by receiving eternal life as an act of the grace of God.

Early Jewish Christians were much concerned with resurrection, and thus the question arose in the church at Thessalonica as to whether God would raise those who were already dead. Paul makes it clear that those who died prior to the Second Coming of the Christ will be resurrected. As he put it,

> For since we believe that Jesus died and rose again, even so, through Jesus, God will bring with him those who have fallen asleep. For this we declare to you by the word of the Lord that we who are alive, who are left until the coming of the Lord shall not precede those who have fallen asleep. For the Lord himself will descend from heaven with a cry of command with the archangel's call and with the sound of the trumpet of God. And the dead in Christ will rise first; then we who are alive and who are left shall be caught up together with them in the clouds to meet the Lord in the air and so we shall always be with the Lord (1 Thessalonians 4:14–17).

The other question that was very much on the minds of the early Christians, who were living a generation after the death of Christ, concerned the time of his return. First Thessalonians answers that question as follows: "But as to the times and the seasons brethren you have no need to have anything written to you. For you yourselves know well that the day of the Lord will come like a thief in the night" (5:1–2).

Elsewhere in the New Testament other passages made it clear that no one could predict when Jesus would return (Acts of the Apostles 1:6–7; Luke 17:20; Matthew 24). Paul wrote primarily to small churches. During the life of Paul, Christians were a small group within the Roman Empire consisting mainly of merchants. Once it became apparent that no one knew when Christ would return and that it might be some time, important ethical questions emerged within the Church. How were Christians to treat one another while awaiting the resurrection? Thus, Paul called Christianity "The Way" and wrote numerous letters about how Christians were to behave.

Paul often asked churches to show Christian love through action. In Galatians 5:14, Paul stated, "For the whole law is fulfilled in one word, 'You shall love your neighbor as yourself,'" and in 2 Corinthians 13:11–14, Paul discussed how Christ's grace leads to the love of God, which produces the fellowship in humans. But ethics does not exist apart from faith in Christ. Paul makes it clear that works without faith are dead, just as faith without works is dead. In Galatians 5 and 6, Paul spoke of "faith working through love." Again in Galatians 6:1–10, Ephesians 4:25–32 and Colossians 3:12–14, charitable acts among Christians are stressed by Paul.

Behaving charitably to another, a Christian embodies faith in Jesus Christ. As James 2:18 put it, there can be no faith without works, but one may embody faith through one's actions: "Show me your faith apart from your works, and I by my works will show you my faith." First John 3:18 similarly states the relationship between love and behavior this way: "Little children, let us not love in word or speech but in deed and truth." Proper behavior is important, but it must embody Christian love to bear fruit. As Paul wrote in 1 Corinthians 13:3, "If I give away all I have and if I deliver my body to be burned but have not love, I gain nothing." For early Christians the gain was eternal life.

Again we see the similarity between Christianity and the other Axial period religions. Paradoxically, early Christianity stressed both ethics and salvation from a problematic world. In 1 Corinthians 7:29–31, Paul spoke of participating in a world with a certain inner-detachment because "the form of this world is passing away." And in Romans 14:17, Paul stated, "For the Kingdom of God does not mean food and drink but righteousness and peace and joy in the Holy Spirit." Christians are not citizens of this world; rather they are citizens of Heaven (Phillipians 3:20).

And Paul was not the only early Christian who emphasized the interrelationship of faith and works (James 1:22–25, 2:14–26; John 13:35). The Jewish Christians were in daily expectation of the Second Coming of Christ, the Parousia. The end of history was upon them and the eschaton was imminent: "There are some standing here who will not taste death before they see the Kingdom of God come with power" (Mark 9:1). The Kingdom of God was most often projected in the Synoptic Gospels as a future event that would occur at the end of time (Matthew 6:10). This world was fading away very rapidly but would be redeemed when Christ returned on earth.

On the other hand, some biblical passages speak as though the Kingdom of God was already present in Christ and Christians have eternal life now: "We know that we have passed out of death into life" (1 John 3:14) and, "The Kingdom of God is within you" (Luke 17:21; Luke 10:18, 11:20).

For John and Luke the Resurrection of Jesus was the final event that brought about the new life now. In actuality, both interpretations of God's kingdom existed side by side and were emphasized at different moments.

Early Christian Life

Early Christian life was simple. Christians, as shown by the Acts of the Apostles, tried to follow the teachings of Jesus very closely. Jesus, having been fully human, laid down the pattern of existence which Christians sought to imitate in order to experience eternal life now and in the future. In *New Testament* times Christianity was known as "The Way" (Acts 19:9). Those that followed Christianity were required "to be dead unto sin, live unto God and Christ Jesus" (Romans 6:2). The ethical dimension of Christianity was important: "As obedient children, do not be conformed to the passions of your former ignorance, but as he who called you is holy, be holy yourselves in all your conduct; since it is written, 'You shall be holy for I am holy'" (1 Peter 1:14–16). Christians were exhorted to live constantly in the divine presence. Christian life was characterized by joy, faith, hope and love. These principles were not simply internal dispositions but were manifested outwardly in all actions.

Ceremonial life was simple also for early Christians. Early Christian churches stressed two rituals, Baptism and the Eucharist. Baptism was based on the baptizing of Jesus by John. Being submerged under water at a river, one was initiated into the new Israel which is the church. Baptism was also a ritual of rebirth which infused one with the Holy Spirit and raised one from the death of sin so that one might have eternal life.

The Eucharist, or the breaking of bread (Acts 2:24), was the fundamental ritual act of early Christians. The bread represented the body of Christ and the wine represented his blood. This ritual re-actualized the presence of Christ and hence his kingdom and simultaneously heralded the Messianic end of time. It had a number of meanings. It reaffirmed salvation and represented the remission of sins. It also symbolized mystical union with Christ since all Christians became one body through the one bread of Christ (1 Corinthians 1:16; Romans 12:5; Ephesians 4:12). Finally, the breaking of bread seems to have provided spiritual sustenance for the early Christian community.

Age of Martyrs

When it first began, Christianity was but a small sect among many others within the Roman Empire. And yet it was uniquely different from all the others in speaking to its followers at the level of their estranged and alienated individuality. Christians were known very early on by their acts. Charity so inhabited their interactions with one another that Christians were known by the way they behaved. As an early observer noted, "See how they love each other." Early Christianity has sometimes been called the Age of Martyrs. Christians were often called atheists for not worshipping the Roman gods and especially the emperor. Early Christians were so faithful to their religion that they refused to worship the emperor as a god. Christians were not revolutionary as shown by Jesus' response when asked whether Christians should pay taxes: "Render to Caesar the things that are Caesar's and to God the things that are God's" (Mark 12:17). The Romans sometimes called Christians cannibals because they went underground into catacombs for secret services.

Christians were persecuted and killed in the Roman arena, but they faced up to death and had faith in God to resurrect them. During this period of persecution, the Christians' own symbol became the fish, which represented the Good News. Fishes were scratched into the ground or on the sides of walls of houses to point the way towards the place where the local Christian group held its underground meetings. The fish was one of the favorite symbols because the Greek letters of the word fish are also the first letters of the words Jesus Christ, Son of God, Savior. The fish thus represented the Good News of Christ.

One of the famous early Christian martyrs was Polycarp of Smyrna, who lived in the second century C.E. During the time of Polycarp, Christians were routinely tortured in the Roman arena. Polycarp was an old Christian, 86 years old, when his name was finally called by the Romans. His supporters persuaded him to leave the city, and he went to a farm outside of Rome with a few friends. Soldiers searched for him for days and he was eventually found three days later. To his captors, he was very cheerful and invited them in to eat. He asked permission only to pray for about an hour. After praying aloud, he was taken to the arena. Caesar was emperor and gave Polycarp many chances to repent. Polycarp stated that he was a Christian. When Polycarp was threatened with burning at the stake, he said he feared only the eternal fire of damnation. With that, Caesar ordered that Polycarp die.

Interestingly, the more the Christians were persecuted, the more their religion spread. Eventually Christianity emerged as the largest religion within the Hellenistic world. The last major persecution of Christians occurred under Diocletian in 303 C.E. Diocletian killed thousands of Christians and burned entire villages. He was followed by Constantius Chlorus, who died in 306.

Constantine

Constantius Chlorus had a son named Constantine who ruled the Roman Empire from 306 to 337. In 311 Constantine issued the Edict of Toleration, which officially ended the persecution of Christians. In 313 Constantine proclaimed the Edict of Milan, giving Christianity equal status with the other religions of the Roman Empire. Constantine himself favored Christianity but never made it the official religion of the Roman Empire. While strongly supportive of the Christian religion, perhaps because his mother converted to Christianity, he was not baptized until he was on his deathbed.

Constantine's conversion resulted ultimately in Christianity's becoming the official religion of the empire. Christian symbols began to appear on Roman coins as early as 315, and the Church began to receive a privileged status in that the state recognized decisions of the Christian courts even in civil affairs. Christians attained the highest political offices and restrictions against the pagans increased in number. However, it would be too much to say that Christianity flourished in Rome because of Constantine's conversion. By 300 the Christian community was the largest religious group in Alexandria. The unshakable faith of Christians as demonstrated in their courage to face up to death and torture no doubt contributed to its spread. Moreover, the social solidarity of Christians was striking. The church offered the only hope for many people who suffered from alienation, loneliness and urban malaise. Anyone could become a Christian and thus this religion overcame all barriers related to race, society or ethnicity. Christ's message transcended all ethnic territories as well as particular spiritual and ceremonial centers. Jesus, at one point, was confronted by a woman who asked his position about competing loyalties to ceremonial shrine: "Sir, I perceive that you are a prophet. Our fathers worshipped on this mountain; and you say that in Jerusalem is the place where men ought to worship." Jesus said to her, "Woman believe me, the hour is coming when neither on this mountain nor in Jerusalem will you worship the Father.... God is spirit and those who worship him must worship in spirit and truth" (John 4:20–22).

Constantine granted land to the church, built churches and declared Sunday to be a holiday. Moreover, he personally intervened in internal disputes within the Christian community. It was in that spirit that Constantine convened an ecumenical council at Nicea in Asia Minor in 325 C.E. The term ecumenical derives from the Greek word *oikoumene,* which means the inhabited world. For the first time Christian bishops from all over the world gathered together to discuss certain creeds.

The fundamental question which they addressed was the status of Christ. A priest named Arius, who belonged to an Egyptian church, put forth the idea that Christ was created by the Father in history. In other words, only God the Father was eternal; Christ was not. This concept was summed up in the famous quote of Arius, "There was when he was not." According to Arius' opponent, Athanasius (296–373 C.E.), the son (Christ) is "true God from true God, begotten, not made, of the same substance with the Father." According to him, although the two persons were different they possessed the same substance (homoousios). At Nicea the council eventually adopted the position of Athanasius.

Under Constantine great numbers of people converted to Christianity. There are stories of whole tribes being baptized at one time. One story tells of a single tribe which stood downstream from an official baptism so that the baptismal waters would wet them. It is important to note that some of the Christians who converted during the time of Constantine denied their allegiance to Christ during the brief rule of Julian (361–262), and Christians themselves began to talk about true Christians as opposed to false Christians. As Christianity became aligned with the political power of the Roman Empire, its character began to change.

Augustine

The great Christian thinker Augustine (354–430 C.E.) wrote the *Apologia* in order to justify Christianity's incorporation of political power as it spread throughout the urban world. In the *City of God*, Augustine divided the world into the City of World (*Civitas Terrenae*) and City of God (*Civitas Dei*). The essence of the City of God is love of God, while the essence of the world city is self love which can be practically effective but not perfect. Augustine said that the City of God is not realized until the next life, after the return of Christ. Because the world of fallen humans is so imperfect, political force and power is necessary for order in this world.

Early Christians would clearly have disagreed with Augustine's justification of political force as they practiced total nonviolence and submission to political power. Others have argued that early Christians had no political power and felt that the Parousia was imminent. Once it became apparent that no one knew when Christ was coming back, it became important for Christians to establish effective ways of living in this world while awaiting the Second Coming of Christ.

It has been said that Augustine laid the groundwork for the adoption of infallibility of the Catholic church. Augustine said that there were three levels of humanity: 1) *posse non peccare*, 2) *non-posse non peccare* and 3) *non-posse peccare*. The first stage represented Adam before the Fall, when human beings were not able to sin because they had no knowledge of good and evil. The second stage represented Adam after the Fall but before the sacrifice of Jesus to redeem sins, during which time humans were not able to not sin. The third stage represents Christians, who Augustine said cannot sin. Augustine felt that the doctrine of infallibility applied both to Christ and the Church and that, therefore, the Church cannot sin.

This doctrine later supported the doctrine of the infallibility of the Pope at the council of Chalecedon 451 C.E., where Leo I was tapped the first Pope of the church. At Chalecedon the doctrine of the incarnation was again discussed and Nicea's position was reaffirmed. Adopting the viewpoint of Athanasius, the council proclaimed that Jesus was fully human and fully divine. Thus, at Chalecedon, the doctrine of docetism, which said that Jesus was fully God, and ebiontism, which says Jesus was purely man, were both rejected.

Middle Ages

The Middle Ages roughly extends from the decline of the Roman Empire in the fifth century to about 1500. It was primarily a Western European phenomenon and was a time that produced many of the characteristics associated with the contemporary Western world. Historians sometimes overemphasize the Greco-Roman roots of the Western world while failing to properly recognize the influence of the Middle Ages. For example, the Middle Ages saw the emergence of depository banks, election of representatives to a national government, reliance on English common law precedent, establishment of universities, growing interest in the study of science, worship in Gothic churches and the widespread printing of books (Strayer). Even the modern debate between church and state had its roots in the Middle Ages.

The period from about 410, when the Huns sacked Rome, until 800, when Charlemagne was crowned Holy Roman Emperor, has been called the Dark Ages. This was a time of Christian isolationism when feudalism and monasticism first developed. Very little change took place within Christianity during this time except that Christianity spread westward and became very much a Western European phenomenon rather than simply a Middle Eastern phenomenon. Development of monks became very prominent during the Dark Ages, and indeed Pope Gregory I, who ruled 590–604, was the first monk to become a pope. Pope Gregory I was a great administrator who exerted political influence in Italy, France, Spain and England. In 622 Islam emerged in Saudi Arabia and spread incredibly rapidly across the ancient world. Christians found themselves trying to hold off Muslims in Spain while simultaneously attempting to convert Germanic tribes, Franks and Saxons.

Charles Martel defeated the Saxons, converted them and succeeded in thwarting the advance of the Muslims. He supported Rome and protected the popes from the Saxons, and thus, in Rome on Christmas Day 800 C.E., Pope Leo III crowned Charles the Holy Roman Emperor. With the support of the Catholic Church, Charles, who became Charles the Great, and later Charlemagne, unified the Western European Germanic tribes. During this era Christianity spread very quickly throughout the Western European steppe and, at Charlemagne's death, great problems arose as to how the empire was to be divided. More importantly, a power struggle emerged between church and state.

Church and State

In the eleventh century Pope Gregory VII and the Holy Roman Emperor, Henry IV, had a dispute over the issue of the primacy of power. Specifically, each claimed that he had the power to appoint German bishops. Henry IV, who was German, claimed that the "temporal sword" had primary power over the "religious sword." For making this statement Pope Gregory VII excommunicated Henry IV, and Henry almost immediately lost his political power. Forced to beg for forgiveness, he visited the Pope at a castle in Canossa in 1077, where he stood in the snow for three days until the Pope received him. The resulting peace was only temporary. Henry, with the help of an anti-Pope, overran Gregory three years later and dethroned King John of England for refusing to appoint Henry's candidate for the archbishop of Canterbury. Gregory and Henry's successors, Henry Calixtus II and Henry V, reached a compromise, and thereafter Pope Urban reestablished the power of the Church over the Holy Roman Emperor.

France began to wield more power than Italy and soon Pope Boniface VIII (1294–1303) and Phillip the Fair fell out. Phillip called together the first French State General, consisting of clergy, nobility and masses. In response to their support of Phillip, the Pope issued a proclamation that every creature who is to be saved must be subject to the Roman pontiff. Another French States General convened labeling the Pope as criminal, heretical and immoral. The Pope eventually imprisoned Phillip. A succession of French popes (1305–1377) brought fear of revolt in Italy so the

Popes retired to Avignon, France. There the French king and the Pope ran into conflicts, so another Pope was elected, and then a third in 1409. Called the Great Schism, this period saw France and England become increasingly independent, hurting papacy power.

Crusades

Pope Urban also launched the first and only successful Crusade in 1096. Thereafter, Christians and Muslims fought through the thirteenth century until the last Crusade in 1291. The historian Lamb wrote that although on the surface the Crusades were an attempt to take back Jerusalem and Holy Land from the Muslims, the biggest cause of the Crusades was the decline of the Church (Eliade). Despite the negative dimensions of the Crusades, it was an important fact for medieval history. As Steven Runciman has said, "It was out of the Crusades that the establishment of western Europe's modern history began" (quoted in Eliade 93).

The Crusades were fraught with several layers of significance. As Alphonse Dupront has shown, the center of the Crusade consciousness was the duty to liberate Jerusalem. The re-taking of Jerusalem was linked with eschatology so that clergy and laity during the period of the Crusades felt that time would be fulfilled with the recapture of Jerusalem. The Crusades helped Europe gain knowledge of Greek philosophy and science through Muslims. Christian apologists said that the Crusades gave a very powerful Christian empire the only viable mode of martyrdom, but most scholars argue that the Crusades were an attempt to transfer the problems between church and state onto an external negative other (Eliade). Other scholars such as H.R. Davidson emphasize that the Crusades showed the influence of the Anglo-Saxon warrior tradition on Christianity.

A number of Christians who went to Jerusalem to fight in the Crusades contracted leprosy and upon returning to Europe were viewed as outcasts whose lack of faith caused the disease (Foucault). Christians designated lepers as social outcasts and built leprosariums to house these unholy, sinful infidels. As many as 19,000 lazar houses were spread throughout Christendom. Not until the fifteenth century, with the gradual disappearance of this disease, did these houses begin to empty. Lepers revealed both the presence and wrath of God. Punished because they refused to keep the faith, lepers nevertheless manifested God's presence. It was understood that lepers could achieve salvation only through being abandoned by the rest of society. Thus their exclusion manifested God's ultimate grace. As we shall see later on, the structure of social otherness continued to thrive within the Western world long after leprosy had disappeared.

Sacred Reason

Thomas Aquinas (1225–1274) was the greatest Christian thinker of the Middle Ages. He attempted a great medieval synthesis using Aristotelian logic and reasoning which was borrowed from the Muslims. Aquinas attempted to synthesize reason and faith, Aristotle and Christ. Theology was called the "Queen of the Sciences," and all other disciplines were ultimately subordinated to theology. However, reason took on a special sacred significance for Aquinas because he held that God wills the good because it is rational. Reason itself became divine, and indeed Aquinas constructed several complex arguments in which he attempted to use reason to prove God's existence.

Christendom during the Middle Ages was an attempt to unify all aspects of life under Christianity. Force was used when necessary to abolish diversity. Christianity in this period became a concept and a very limited way of life that gave birth to the Inquisition. Using race as the measure, the Inquisition attempted to find "true" Christians. Thus we can see how Christianity evolved from a small cult of peaceful, submissive people to a politically dominant, self-defined group. As we shall see in the last chapter, Christianity underwent another dramatic transformation during the Renaissance, the Reformation and especially with the discovery of the New World.

Sacred Kingship and Chivalry

For most Germanic tribes, kingship had a sacred origin and nature; the ancestors of royal dynasties descended from the gods, especially Wodan. Even after conversion to Christianity this genealogical link with Wodan retained importance. Of the eight royal dynasties in England, seven claimed descent from Wodan (Chaney 29). After conversion, the king becomes known as *Christus Domini*, "the Lord's anointed." As an eleventh century author put it, "A Christian king is Christ's delegate in the midst of his people" (quoted in Eliade 90).

A similar synthesis took place with respect to chivalry. Among the ancient Germans, it was shameful for the chief in battle to be surpassed in bravery and for his soldiers to be less brave than he. The chief (*princeps*) must be defended by his companions: "The chief fights for victory; his companions for the chief" (Eliade 91). After the conversion of the Germanic tribes to Christianity, this institution was preserved. A sense of loyalty to the chief formed the basis of chivalry and also feudalism. In 791 Charlemagne's oldest son, Lewis, received the warrior's sword from his father. Forty-seven years later Lewis dubbed his 15-year-old son with "manly arms, the sword," thus originating the initiatory ritual of chivalry.

Chivalry played a major role in the social, religious and cultural history of the West. However, it did not blossom into its classic form until the ninth century, with the introduction into France of large horses capable of carrying heavy armor. From the beginning the knight's duty was to show not only loyalty to his lord but also to defend the poor and the Church. By the twelfth century the Church's influence on knighthood became important. It was then that the institution reached its greatest heights. Conversion to Christianity never fully eclipsed the pagan dimension of this military initiation. But by the twelfth century the ceremony unfolds under the control of the Church. Following a confession, the squire would spend the night in prayer inside a church. Then in the morning, he would take Communion and, while being dubbed, would swear an oath of respect for the code of chivalry and also say a prayer. Interestingly, after the first crusade, two military organizations were established in the Holy Land to defend pilgrims and to care for the sick: the Templars and the Hospitalers.

Byzantium and Rome

The differences in the Eastern and Western Church were already evident by the fourth century. There are a number of reasons for this difference: there was a mutual ignorance of each other's language, one culture was Greco-Oriental, the other Romano-Germanic, and there were differences in religious practices. For example, Eastern priests could marry; Western priests could not. The Western Church used unleavened bread; the East, leavened bread. The Eastern Church's doctrine of *theosis* held that a human could obtain divination while here on earth, and that doctrine was rejected in the West. At the Council of Constantinople in 381 C.E. the Eastern Church proclaimed that it had the relics of St. Andrew, "the first called," who therefore was considered to have precedence over St. Peter. In so doing, Constantinople claimed equality with Rome.

Also spawning the split between the churches was the addition of the *filioque* of the Nicene creed. In 589 C.E. a Western council meeting in Spain at Toledo added to the Nicene creed (381 C.E.) the word *filioque*, "and from the son," saying that the Holy Spirit proceeds from the Father and the Son. The East maintained that the Holy Ghost proceeded from the Father. Another theological controversy centered on the belief in Purgatory, which was taught in the West but rejected in the East.

It was not until 1014 at the demand of Emperor Henry II that the Nicene creed with the *filioque* was chanted in Rome, thus marking the beginning of the Great Schism. However, 1054 is the traditional date given for the final break between East and West. In 1053 Pope Leo IX sent Cardinal Humbert and others to Constantinople to reestablish relations in order to repel the Normans who were seeking to occupy southern Italy. But the Byzantine patriarch, Michael Cerularius, refused to compromise any disagreements, and on July 15, 1054, Leo's legates deposited an excommunication sentence on the altar of Santa Sophi against Cerularius, accusing him of ten heresies, including the removing of the *filioque* clause from the Nicene creed and the approval of marriages of priests.

Animosity between the Occidentals and the Greeks continued until 1204 when the final irreparable rupture occurred. The armies of the Fourth Crusade attacked and pillaged Constantinople, breaking icons and throwing relics into filth. The Greeks never forgot this tragic episode although, probably because of Turkish menaces, the Orthodox Church did resume negotiations with Rome after 1261. Negotiations took place over the next two centuries and finally at the Council of Florence, in 1439, the Eastern Church accepted Rome's conditions. This union was, however, immediately invalidated by clergy and lay people alike. Moreover, in 1453 Constantinople was occupied by the Turks, and the Byzantine Empire ceased to exist. However, its basic religious structures continued to live for the next three centuries in eastern Europe and Russia.

Bibliography
Chapter 11 — Christianity

Adam, Karl. *The Spirit of Catholicism.* New York, 1954.
Atiyah, Aziz Suryal. *Eastern Christianity.* London, 1968.
Attwater, Donald. *The Christian Churches of the East.* 2 Vols. Milwaukee, 1947–1948.
Augustine of Hippo. *The City of God.* Edinburgh, 1934.
Barrett, C.K. Editor. *The New Testament Background: Selected Documents.* New York, 1961.
Bays, Daniel H. Editor. *Christianity in China: From the Eighteenth Century to the Present.* Palo Alto, California, 1996.

Bettenson, Henry. Editor. *Documents of the Christian Church*. 2nd Ed. Oxford, 1963.
Borg, Marcus. *Jesus: A New Vision*. San Francisco, 1988.
Bornkamm, G. *Jesus of Nazareth*. Trans. Irene and Fraser McLuskey and James Robinson. New York, 1960.
Bowman, John W. *The Intention of Jesus*. Philadelphia, 1943.
Breen, John, and Mark Williams. Editors. *Japan and Christianity: Impacts and Responses*. London, 1996.
Browne, Lawrence E. *The Eclipse of Christianity in Asia: From the Time of Muhammad till the Fourteenth Century*. Cambridge, 1933.
Bultmann, Rudolf. *Primitive Christianity in Its Contemporary Setting*. Trans. R.H. Fuller. New York, 1956.
Chadwick, Henry, and Owen Chadwick. Editors. *Oxford History of the Christian Church*. 2 Vols. Oxford, 1977.
Chadwick, Owen. Editor. *A History of Christianity*. New York, 1995.
_____. Editor. *The Pelican History of the Church*. 6 Vols. Harmondsworth, 1960–1970.
Chaney, William. *The Cult of Kingship in Anglo-Saxon England: The Transition from Paganism to Christianity*. Berkeley and Los Angeles, 1970.
Cochrane, C.N. *Christianity and Classical Culture: A Study of Thought and Action From Augustus to Augustine*. Oxford, 1940.
Colish, Marica L. *Medieval Foundations of the Western Intellectual Tradition*. New Haven, Connecticut, 1997.
The Confessions of St. Augustine. Trans. Edward Pucpusey. New York, 1948.
Corbishly, Thomas. *Roman Catholicism*. New York, 1950.
Cross, F.L. Editor. *The Oxford Dictionary of the Christian Church*. 2nd Rev. Ed. London, 1974.
Cullmann, Oscar. *Early Christian Worship*. Trans. A. Steward Todd and James B. Torrance. London, 1953.
Cumont, Franz. *The Oriental Religions in Roman Paganism*. Authorized Trans. Chicago, 1911.
Davies, W.D., and D. Daube, Editors. *The Background of the New Testament and Its Eschatology*. Cambridge, 1956.
_____. *The Gospel and the Land: Early Christianity and Jewish Territorial Doctrine*. Berkeley, California, 1974.
_____. *Paul and Rabbinic Judaism*. London, 1948.
Dodd, C.H. *The Founder of Christianity*. London and New York, 1970.
_____. *The Interpretation of the Fourth Gospel*. Cambridge, 1953.
Dunkerly, Robert. *Beyond the Gospels*. Harmondsworth, 1957.
Dupré, Louis, and James Wiseman, Editors. *Light form Light: An Anthology of Christian Mysticism*. New York, 1988.
Ehrman, Bart D. *The New Testament: A Historical Introduction to the Early Christian Writings*. New York, 1997.
_____. *The New Testament and Other Early Christian Writings*. New York, 1998.
Eliade, Mircea. *A History of Religious Ideas: From Muhammad to the Age of Reform*. Vol. 3. Trans. A. Hiltebeitel and D. Apostoloc-Coppadona. Chicago, 1985.

Enslin, Morton Scott. *Christian Beginnings.* Parts I and II. New York, 1956.
Forell, George W. *The Protestant Faith.* Columbus, Ohio, 1975.
Foucault, Michel. *Madness and Civilization: A History of Insanity in the Age of Reason.* Trans. Richard Howard. London, 1967.
Grant, Frederick C. *The Gospels: Their Origin and Their Growth.* New York, 1953.
Grant, Robert. *Augustus to Constantine: The Thrust of the Christian Movement.* New York, 1970.
The Holy Bible: Revised Standard Version. New York, 1953.
Huizinga, Johan. *The Waning of the Middle Ages.* London, 1927.
John, Eric. Editor. *The Popes: A Concise Biographical History.* New York, 1970.
Johnson, Paul. *A History of Christianity.* New York, 1977.
Jonas, Hans. *The Gnostic Religion: The Message of the Alien God and the Beginnings of Christianity.* Boston, 1963.
Kidd, V.J. *A History of the Church to 461.* 3 Vols. Oxford, 1922.
Knox, A.D. *Saint Paul.* New York, 1938.
Knox, John. *The Man Christ Jesus.* Chicago, 1941.
Lang, Bernhard. *Sacred Games.* New Haven, Connecticut, 1997.
Latourette, Kenneth Scott. *A History of Christian Missions in China.* London, 1929.
_____. *A History of the Expansion of Christianity.* Vol. 1. *The First Five Centuries.* New York and London, 1957.
Leff, Gordon. *Medieval Thought: St. Augustine to Ockham.* London, 1960.
Long, Charles H. "Primitive/Civilized: The Locus of a Problem." *History of Religions* 20 (1980): 43–61.
Macmullen, Ramsay. *Christianity and Paganism in the Fourth to Eighth Centuries.* New Haven, Connecticut, 1997.
Malina, Bruce J. *The Social World of Jesus and the Gospels.* New York, 1946.
Manson, T.W. *The Teachings of Jesus.* 2nd Ed. Cambridge, 1937.
McLeod, Hugh. *European Religion in the Age of Great Cities.* New York, 1996.
Metzger B.M., and Herbert May. Editors. *Holy Bible: Revised Standard Version.*
Molland, Einer. *Christendom.* New York, 1961.
Nock, A.D. *The Old and the New in Religion from Alexander the Great to Augustine of the Hippo.* Oxford, 1933.
The Oxford Dictionary of the Christian Church. 2nd Ed. Oxford, 1983.
Ozment, Steven. *The Age of Reform.* New Haven, Connecticut, 1980.
_____. *The Reformation in the Cities.* New Haven, Connecticut, 1975.
Pelikan, Jaroslav. *Christianity and Classical Culture.* New Haven, Connecticut, 1993.
_____. "Christianity: An Overview." *Encyclopedia of Religion.* Vol. 3. Mircea Eliade. Editor-in-Chief. New York, 1987: 348–362.
_____. *The Illustrated Jesus Through the Centuries.* New Haven, Connecticut, 1997.
_____. *Jesus through the Centuries.* New York, 1987.
Perrin, Norman. *The Kingdom of God and the Teaching of Jesus.* London, 1963.
_____. *The New Testament: An Introduction.* New York, 1974.
_____. *Rediscovering the Teaching of Jesus.* New York, 1967.
Ramsey, Paul. *Basic Christian Ethics.* New York, 1952.
Richardson, Darryl C. Editor. *Early Christian Fathers.* Philadelphia, 1953.
Riley-Smith, Jonathan. *The Crusades.* New Haven, Connecticut. 1990.

Southern, R.W. *The Making of the Middle Ages.* New Haven, Connecticut, 1961.
Strayer, Joseph R. *Western Europe in the Middle Ages.* New York, 1955.
Taylor, V. *The Life and Ministry of Jesus.* London, 1954.
von Harnack, A. *The Mission and Expansion of Christianity in the First Three Centuries.* Trans. and Editor. James Moffat. London and New York, 1901.
Walker, Williston. *A History of the Christian Church.* New York 1918.
Ward, John W.C. *A History of the Early Church to A.D. 500.* 4th Ed. New York, 1973.
Ware, Timothy. *The Orthodox Church.* New York, 1986.

CHAPTER 12

Islam

Of all the founders of the great Axial Age religions we have the most biographical information about Muhammad, the prophet of Islam. While the historical accuracy of these sources is called into question somewhat because they are written from the perspective of pious Muslims, we nevertheless have a good overall picture of the life of this religious man. Born in Mecca between 567 and 572, Muhammad belonged to a very powerful tribe, the Quraysh. His childhood was very difficult. His father died prior to his birth, his mother died when he was six years old, and his grandfather, whom he lived with next, died when Muhammad was nine. After his grandfather's death, he was taken into the home of his uncle where he worked very hard minding his uncle's flocks.

Described as pure of heart and sensitive, Muhammad was always ready to help others, especially those less fortunate than him. He had a great sense of loyalty and duty, which helps explain his later titles as "The True," "The Upright" and "The Trustworthy One." Nevertheless, like Jesus, Muhammad always seemed somewhat detached from the secular affairs of the Arabic world in which he grew up. He thought often and hard about the widespread warfare between Arabian tribes, the lack of social justice and the immorality that characterized urban life in Mecca.

As a young adult, he became involved in the caravan business. Mecca was a commercial center along the Silk Road in one of the staging posts on the great caravan routes that crossed the desert. Muhammad was every bit an urban person. Mecca was no backwoods community; it was a wealthy commercial town that virtually monopolized the trade between the Indian Ocean and the Mediterranean. Its citizens had acquired wide knowledge of cities and peoples along the Silk Road.

At 25 Muhammad began working for a wealthy widow named Khadija. They eventually fell in love and were married although she was 15 years his senior. Their marriage was happy. Muhammad married nine women after Khadija's death, but she was his only spouse during her lifetime. They had seven children, including three sons who died at a young age.

Outside of Mecca was a huge rock known as Mount Hira, which jutted upward towards the Arabian sky from the desert below. In this rock was a cave which Muhammad frequented for some fifteen years after his marriage to Khadija. There he would reflect and meditate on the violence, injustice and immorality that were so rampant in Arabia. It is probable that Muhammad was influenced by the nightly prayers and meditations of certain Christian monks whom he had known or heard speak during his journeys along the Silk Road. Furthermore, one of Khadija's cousins was a Christian. However, the religion of central Arabia does not seem to have been influenced by Christianity during the time of Muhammad.

Mecca was the religious center of Arabia. Mecca was mentioned in the *Ptolemaic Corpus* of the second century C.E. as Makoraba, a word derived from Makurabi meaning "sanctuary." A ceremonial center, the middle of Mecca's sacred area contained the sanctuary of the *Ka'ba*, meaning literally "cube." The *Ka'ba* was a monument opened to the sky which contained the famous Black Stone. Just as it is today, circling the *Ka'ba* was a major ceremony during pre–Islamic times. The divinity of the *Ka'ba* was Allah ("the God"). As was the case with other Neolithic communities Allah had ceased to be the high god. He was periodically offered grains and animals which were given to him simultaneously with various other local divinities. More important than Allah were the three goddesses of central Arabia: Manat ("Destiny"), Allat (feminine form of Allah), and Al'Uzza ("the Powerful"). All three were regarded as the "daughters of Allah."

As Muhammad continued to meditate at Mount Hira one important truth began to make itself clear to him: Allah was *the* God. Allah was not one god among many but was the one and only deity, and this revelation was to eventuate in the most powerful phrase in the Arabic language: *La Ilaha Illa Allah* ("There is no God but Allah"). Once, when Muhammad was asleep in the cave, the angel Jebril came to him holding a book and ordered him to read. Muhammad, out of fear, at first refused to read, but the angel pressed the book so tightly against him that he was almost suffocated. After asking what he should read, the angel answered, "Recite: In the name of my Lord who created man from a blood clot. Recite: And thy Lord is the most generous, who taught by the pen, taught men that he knew not" (Quran 96:1-5). Muhammad then awoke from his sleep but continued to envision Jebril no matter where he looked. For about three years Muhammad communicated these first visions only to Khadija and to several friends, such as his cousin Ali, his adopted son Zaid, and the two future Caliphs, Uthman and Abu Bakr.

Finally, in 612, Muhammad had a vision that commanded him to go public with certain messages. It is then that Muhammad became an apostle. God, Muhammad said, was a merciful God who created people from a blood clot and who created the heaven, the mountains, earth and the camels(96:1; 88:17–20). His message stressed the transient nature of human existence in contrast to the eternal majesty of the Creator: "All that dwells upon the earth is perishing, yet still abides the face of the Lord, majestic, splendid" (55:26–27).

Muhammad also preached the imminence of the Judgment Day and the resurrection of the dead: "For when the trumpet is sounded that day will be a harsh day, for the unbelievers not easy" (74:8–10). Numerous references are found in the old "Suras" of the Quran, but the most complete description of the end of time occurs in a later "Sura," 84:1–12. Muhammad described the end of the world in very explicit terms. The mountains will be reduced to ashes and dust, the vault of heaven will burst and the fire of the stars and the moon will be put out (55:35). Then at the second sound of a trumpet the dead will rise and ascend from their tombs. This will occur in a blink of an eye. Men will then be brought before Allah, who sits on a throne, and judgment will be passed before them. The unrepentant will be condemned to hell, while the faithful will live in paradise. Paradise for Muslims is described in very vivid material terms. There will be clear rivers, trees laden with fruit, meats of all sort, beautiful young men and chaste virgins (56:26–43).

Once convinced that he was a prophet, Muhammad started to relay the message he received to his fellow Meccans. One of the first things that he told them was to stop selling figurines of the many gods of the region. This brought him in direct conflict with a number of merchants. Muhammad called for a unity of community and ethics due to the unity of God. His message was more about ethics than idolatry. Thus he mentioned the unity of God only once in the Quran (51:51). Muhammad was not as interested in the theological questions of the day as he was the ethical problems of life along the Silk Road.

Muhammad and his few followers, which included his wife, were ridiculed, laughed at, and later beaten, stoned, whipped and imprisoned. Often his followers were stripped and taken to the desert where they were offered water only if they would worship idols. They refused to do so. According to tradition, it is said that verse 20 of "Sura" 53 described the three goddess Al'Uzza, Allat and Manat as sublime goddesses who may mediate between the people and Allah. Later Muhammad took the stance that these words were inspired in him by Satan and thus that verse was retracted. The position of Muhammad and his followers became worse. The powerful political leaders in Mecca decided to exclude them from their own tribal rituals. Muhammad eventually lost his rights as a member of the Qurash tribe. Interestingly, Muhammad stated that his own tribe's refusal to embrace the monotheism of Allah was itself decreed by Allah, that Allah had decided that certain people would be blindly attached to the worship of many gods (16:39; 10:75; 6:39). Thus it was inevitable that Muhammad break with these disbelievers (109:1–2).

After about ten years of hard work, Muhammad had gathered only a small band of devoted followers. It was then that he realized that only a firm break with his kin would help bring about the universal community of people that he sought. Then Muhammad got an opportunity. About 250 miles to the north of Mecca the city of Yathrib (then Medina) was suffering from a prolonged war between rival Arab tribes. These tribes requested that Muhammad come and attempt to resolve their differences. Negotiations ensued for one or two years until finally, in the autumn of 622, Muhammad fled secretly from Mecca to Medina, followed by pursuers. This is called the *hijra*, or immigration. In Medina the teachings of Muhammad took on an even greater concern with the organization of the community of the faithful (*ummah*). The theological underpinnings of Islam had been clearly established in Mecca, and now Muhammad's message turned especially to the rules concerning prayer, fasting, alms giving and pilgrimages. From the beginning Muhammad demonstrated a keen political acumen. Quickly he brought together the Mecca Muslims and the new converts in Medina and proclaimed himself their sole leader. In so doing Muhammad began the process of abolishing tribal loyalties. From that point forward there existed only the community of Muslims.

In 623 Muhammad decreed that both the Mecca and Medina Muslims formed a single people distinct from all others. However, he did make clear that there were important rights and privileges to other claims and also to the three Jewish tribes in Medina. While not everyone in Medina shared Muhammad's views, his success in bringing about a harmonious community solidified his position. Muhammad continued to receive revelations from the angel Jebril which added to his determination. Muhammad's biggest disappointment was his failure to convert the three Jewish tribes.

He originally chose Jerusalem as a point of orientation for prayer and borrowed other Israelite rituals. Had the Jews recognized Muhammad as their prophet he would have continued to allow them to practice their own rituals. But the Jews never recognized Muhammad because of his lack of knowledge of the Hebrew scriptures. Then on February 11, 624, the prophet received a new vision directing him to orient prayers towards Mecca (2:136). This was based on the vision that the *Ka'ba* had been built by Abraham and his son Ishmael (2:127). Simultaneously, Muhammad founded a sanctuary more ancient than Jerusalem while maintaining its connections with the Jewish heritage. Muhammad's influence on Yathrib is shown in the change of the name of the city to Medinat un-Nabi, "the city of the Prophet," and then finally to Medina, "the City."

Muhammad and his followers began to undertake raids against Meccan caravans. All booty taken from these raids was distributed evenly among all the combatants. After an initial victory at Badr in March 627, the Muslims suffered a serious defeat at Uhud the following year. In this skirmish Muhammad himself was injured. In the Battle of the Ditch 4,000 Meccans attempted to take Medina over a two week period. However, a tornado appeared and scattered the army. In April 628 Muhammad received a new revelation: the faithful could return to Mecca for a pilgrimage to the *Ka'ba* (48:27). Although the Medina converts suffered a partial loss and were not allowed to enter the city at this time, Muhammad was able to get his followers to swear him an absolute oath of fidelity (48:10).

Finally, in 629 Muhammad entered the city of Mecca accompanied by two thousand faithful followers. Thereafter numerous tribes and even some representatives from the Quraysh began to convert. Then in 631 Muhammad undertook a total war against the worship of many gods (9:3-6). In February or March 632 Muhammad undertook his last pilgrimage to Mecca. On this occasion he outlined in detail the ritual of the *hajj*, which is still followed to this day. Turning to Medina on the last days of May 632, Muhammad fell ill. He died in the arms of his favorite wife, Aisha, on June 8th. There was great distress within the Muslim community. Muhammad's body was interred in a room in Aisha's apartment where there still stands a funeral monument that is considered almost as sacred as the *Ka'ba*.

Islam After Muhammad

Abu Bakr was elected Caliph (successor) to the prophet. Addressing the rumor that Muhammad ascended to heaven as did Jesus, Abu Bakr proclaimed, "If one venerates Muhammad, Muhammad is dead; but if one venerates God, Muhammad is living and does not die" (Eliade 76). The death of Muhammad unleashed a potential crisis which was nevertheless averted. Muhammad had not designated a successor when he died. A number of factions developed and each selected a candidate to succeed Muhammad. Eventually Abu Bakr, father of Muhammad's favorite wife, Aisha, was chosen. Many think that Muhammad probably would have hand-picked Ali, the husband of his daughter Fatima and the father of his grandsons Hasan and Husayn. But Ali and his partisans accepted the election of the elderly Abu Bakr in order to preserve the unity of the community (*ummah*).

Abu Bakr immediately undertook political and military expeditions to subdue the Bedouin tribes who were beginning to detach themselves from the community. Immediately thereafter raids were organized against Syria. Abu Bakr died after succeeding Muhammad for only two years. He had already named his successor, Umar, who was one of his generals. Umar was Caliph for ten years (634–644), and under his brilliant leadership Muslim victories were gained very quickly. The Byzantine Christians abandoned Syria in 636. The Sassanid Empire collapsed in 637, as did Antioch. Egypt was conquered in 642.

Nevertheless, during this time of great success the unity of the community was gravely threatened. Having been fatally wounded by a Persian slave, Umar designated six companions of the Prophet to elect his successor. The six chose the Prophet's other son-in-law Uthman (644–656). Only after Uthman was assassinated by Bedouins from Egypt and Iraq was Ali proclaimed Caliph.

According to the Shi'ites, Ali was the first true Caliph, as they recognize no successor outside the family of the Prophet. Aisha and a number of Meccan chiefs accused Ali of conspiring to assassinate Uthman. These two factions confronted one another at the Battle of the Camel. Following that battle, Ali established his capital in an Iraqi town, but his caliphate was contested in battle by the governor of Syria, Mu'awiya, who was a cousin of Uthman. As a result of Ali's failure to hold onto the gains acquired through this battle, certain militants known as Kharijites, "the Secessionists," broke off and formed a new faction.

Ali was assassinated in 661, and his followers, few in number, named his eldest son Hasan as Caliph. The Syrians had elected Mu'awiya as Caliph in Jerusalem, and he succeeded in convincing Hasan to abdicate the position in his favor. Mu'awiya was a very competent military chief and politician. He reorganized the Muslim empire and founded the first dynasty of the Caliphs, the Umayyads (661–750). But the *ummah* failed to achieve unification when Husayn, the second son of Ali, was killed in 680 in Iraq along with most of the members of his family. The Shi'ites never forgot this incident, which incited revolts for several centuries.

Thus thirty years after the death of Muhammad the *ummah* found itself divided into three parties which still exist today. The majority of Muslims are called the Sunnis, that is, partisans of the *sunnah* (practice or tradition). The second group, the Shi'ites, are faithful to the lineage of Ali, claiming that Ali was the first true Caliph. Third are the Kharijites, or Secessionists. They feel that only the community has the right to elect its leader and to remove him from office if he is guilty of misconduct.

Under the Umayyad dynasty the Muslim conquest continued; Carthage fell in 694. Before the end of the seventh century, Islam reigned over North Africa, Syria, Palestine, Asia Minor, Mesopotamia and Iraq. Only the Byzantine Christian empire resisted, although its territory was greatly reduced. Within a century of the death of Muhammad, Arab conquests extended into Morocco, Spain, France, the Gates of Constantinople and across Central Asia up to the Indus River.

Muslims remained unyielding and even hostile to those who would resist, and yet showed an incredible sense of tolerance of diversity within their own community. More astonishing than the speed of the conquests was their orderly character. Although the Muslims left some ruin in their wake, by and large they were able to conquer their surrounding countries in a way that led to a new integration of peoples and cultures. Life for those people under Muslim rule changed little as they were allowed to maintain a number of their own cultural and social institutions. There was no persecution and no forced conversions. Military expansions continued until 715 when the Arabs were finally forced by the Turks to abandon a region of the Oxus. Then in 717 a second naval expedition against Byzantium failed.

Finally, in 733 Charles Martell, king of France, crushed the Arabs near Tours and forced them to withdraw to the other side of the Pyrenees Mountains. Martell's victory marked the end of Arab conquests. From that point on Muslim expansion would be done by people with other ethnic backgrounds. Still the success with which Islam spread across the Ancient Near East in its early days is historically unprecedented. Muslims give a simple explanation for these amazing victories — they were willed by Allah.

The Umayyad dynasty was overthrown in 750 and replaced by another important Meccan family, the Abbasids. The new Caliph, with the aid of the Shi'ites, emerged victorious. The first four Caliphs had kept the seat of the caliphate at Medina, but Mu'awiya established the capital of the empire at Damascus. After that, Hellenistic, Persian and Christian influences increased throughout the entire Umayyad dynasty. The results of this influence reveal themselves chiefly in religious and secular architecture. The Abbasids (750–1258 C.E.) prolonged and developed this process of incorporation of oriental and Mediterranean cultural heritages.

Islam created an urban civilization based on commerce, bureaucracy and tolerance. In 762 a new capitol in Baghdad marked the end of a preponderantly Arab Islam. Caliphs became ever more isolated and turned over the handling of daily problems to the *ulama*, theologians and specialists in sacred law. The Abbasids incorporated many Persian traditions and recruited an army with Iranian military background. During this period the works of Greek philosophers, doctors and alchemists were translated for the first time.

Islamic civilization climaxed in breadth and creative effort in the ninth and tenth centuries. As H.A.R. Gibb noted, industry, commerce, architecture, arts and philosophy flourished as Persia, Mesopotamia, Syria and Egypt began to contribute to the cultural make up of the Muslim community (Mohammedanism). Along Baghdad's many miles of waterfronts were many types of sea vessels. Baghdad was very much a central stop along the Silk Road. From China came porcelain, musk and silk; from India and the Malay islands, spices, dyes and minerals; from the Turks in Central Asia, rubies, lapis lazuli, slaves and fabrics; from Russia and Scandinavia, honey, wax, furs, and white slaves; and from Eastern Africa, ivory, black slaves and gold. Various goods were sent to Baghdad from Umayyad provinces: rice, linen and grain from Egypt; glass, fruits and metalware from Syria; pearls, weapons and brocade from Arabia; and silks, perfumes and vegetables from Persia (Hitti).

From Baghdad and other centers merchants shipped fabrics, jewelry, metal mirrors, glass beads, and spices to the Far East, Europe and Africa. Arab coins have been found as far north as Russia, Finland, Sweden and Germany.

Muslim merchants became international traders, superseding Christians, Jews and Zoroastrians. The ports of Baghdad, Basrah, Siraf, Cairo and Alexandria became commercial centers. Muslims traveled all the way to China in the east and Morocco and Spain in the west. Muslim merchants carried with them dates, sugar, woolen and cotton fabrics, steel tools and glassware.

Intellectual activities also flourished during this period under Greek, Persian and Indian influence. The older Muslim sciences of history and language study were broadened and became more secular. Greek medical and mathematical sciences became accessible through various translations, and this was especially true in algebra and trigonometry. Geography flowered in all its branches. Some Islamic leaders saw their spiritual foundation being brought into question Hellenistic thought. A struggle to subordinate intellectual thought to religious principles continued for a number of centuries.

The greatest science in the Muslim world was that of law (*fiqh*), not theology, which was the "Queen of the Sciences" in medieval Christendom. Law was said to embrace all aspects of human life, and nowhere was its study pursued with more vigor, with perhaps the exception of the Jews. Islamic law was very far reaching and structured all aspects of Muslim life. Muslim law made possible a unified community in a changing political world. With the decline of the Abbasids and caliphates in the tenth and eleventh centuries, the door was open for anarchy and disintegration. The authority of the law was maintained and thus the community continued to prosper.

After 750 Islam was threatened by its confrontation with a number of tribes in outlying regions. The first Barbarians were Turkish tribes from Central Asia. Islam had grown up within the framework of a urban civilization but now was faced with the task of making a religious order effective in areas where tribal cultures predominated. From the eleventh century on this was done through the teachings of Muslim mystics who called themselves Sufis because they wore *suf,* or wool. Mystics became the most important and successful missionaries for Islam and were the leaders in converting outlying tribal peoples to Islam. It is through their work that Islam became successful in extending itself into Africa, India, Indonesia, Turkistan, China and parts of Southeastern Europe. The Sufi movement was never fully coordinated with the Orthodox Scholastic tradition and maintained an independence from the caliphates.

Muhammad was considered the last prophet or the "seal of the prophets." A fighting prophet, he strove not to defend Islam but to proselytize its message. The Muslim message concerned itself with bringing about the will of God by force. The unity of the Muslim community was not based on the blood of the Jews or the love of Christians, but rather on the power of Allah. Jews and Christians were considered closely related to the Muslims and were called "people of the book." They had a special place within the Muslim community and were considered Muslim spiritual ancestors. Indeed, as Muhammad said in one passage, "The Torah and the Gospel, and what was sent down to them from their Lord.... Surely they that believe, and those of Jewry and the Sabaeans and those Christians, whosoever believes in God in the last day, and works righteousness — no fear shall be on them, neither shall they sorrow" (5:68–69).

Muhammad did not consider that he was establishing a new religion so much as he was bringing about a unity of community based on the unity of God. Earlier, Jews and Christians had failed to achieve a cohesive society. Islam disagreed with Christianity in holding that Jesus was a prophet, not a god. Still Islam had great respect for the Christian message. God, through Jesus, had attempted to bring about a proper world order based on forgiveness of sins and love of one's neighbor. However, humans had not lived up to this great standard and thus God sent Muhammad to use force if necessary to bring about submission to God. Islam means "surrendering."

The Muslim holy war, or *jihad,* was not so much about belief in God as it was about bringing the institutions of the human community under the will of God. The public life must be ruled by Allah as told to Muhammad. Allah was primarily concerned about justice along the Silk Road and thus Islam contained many rules. One of the problems with Christianity was that Jesus gave few rules on how to actually bring about a sacred community. Conversely, Muhammad was instructed precisely on the way in which human behavior was to be regulated. The Quran dealt primarily with justice and ethics. If one believed that Allah is God and Muhammad his Prophet, then one could live happily within a Muslim community as long as one followed Muslim law. The Christian doctrine of sin gave people the power to disobey the will of God. Muslim law, *Shar'iat,* made sin intolerable. The Quran was written as commands and imperatives rather than parables and suggestions. God manifested a direct relation with human beings through the dictates of the Quran. The historian of religions Marshall Hodgson insightfully characterized the Muslim emphasis on holy law as "Shari'ah-mindedness" (Hodgson, Vol. I, 238).

Quran

The Quran is a relatively short work, about four fifths the length of the New Testament. It is divided into 114 chapters or "Suras" which are arranged in decreasing length except for the first "Sura." *Quran* means "to read or recite." Muslims make it clear that one cannot fully appreciate the sacrality of the Quran unless one has heard it recited. Perhaps the most significant point about the Quran is that it formulates the world's most absolute monotheism. Allah is God; he is the only God. Allah is creator of the earth and heavens and of all that exists. He continues to create the universe according to His will (35:1). It is because of His continual creation that night follows day, rains fall from heaven, and that the ship "sails on the sea" (2:164). Allah thus is a God of both cosmic rhythms and of history. Allah acts freely and his freedom allows him to act arbitrarily and contradict himself.

The Quran is considered to be the literal word of God as enunciated through the voice of Jebril. Thus the Suras are prefixed with "God has said," not "the Prophet said." It is not clear if the monotheism of the Quran is derived from Jewish and Christian traditions of which Muhammad was somewhat familiar, although not intimately, since his references to the Bible are rarely precisely accurate. H.A.R. Gibb argued that Muslim monotheism was derived from an obscure Arabian tradition represented by the so-called Hanifas. Whatever its origin it is clear that the Quran is concerned primarily with the fear of God's wrath to come. God is the omnipotent Master of the creatures called human, and these creatures are ever in danger of incurring his wrath on the final Judgment Day. Only by following the five pillars of Islam and the law can a Muslim obtain the grace of God and gain eternal bliss in the next world.

The Five Pillars

Nothing in the world escapes the will or judgment of God; however, Allah is simultaneously a compassionate god who gives Muslims hope. Muslim worship does not require a church or a priesthood. One may practice its basic rites anywhere. Interestingly, the famous *shahada* or profession of faith, *La Ilaha Illa'llah Muhammadun Rasulu'llah* ("There is but one God, Muhammad is the apostle of God") is not found in that precise form anywhere in the Quran. However, both halves of the message are found separately, and the outline of the *shahada* is found in "Sura" 4:135. The Arabic word Allah is a shortened form of *al-ilah* meaning, "the God." God is referred to in many names in the Quran and is called the "Hearer, Seer, Bestower, Recognizer, Pardoner, Keeper and Guide" (Gibb *Mohammedanism* 37). But perhaps the most impressive description of Allah is found in "Sura" 2:256:

> God — there is no God but He, the living, the self subsistent. Slumber seizeth him not, neither sleep. To him belong it whatsoever is in the heavens and whatsoever is in the earth. Who is there who shall intercede with him save by his will? He knoweth what is present with men and what shall befall them, and not of his knowledge do they comprehend, save what he willeth. His throne is wide as heavens and the earth, and the keeping of him wearyeth him not. And he is the high, the mighty one.

Being a Muslim requires giving one's whole allegiance to the one God (*ikhlas*). This is contrasted with the worship of many gods (*shirk*). *Shirk* literally means "associating," that is to say, associating one thing with another so that the two are placed on the same level. In Islam *shirk* constitutes the one unforgivable sin: "Verily God forgiveth not the giving of partners to him; other than this will he forgive to whom he pleaseth, but whosoever giveth a partner to God hath conceived a monstrous sin" (4:51). God has existed for all times and he is the only reality (28:88). While God is singular the Quran does mention angels who are represented as God's messengers. Above all there is Jebril, God's chief messenger, who communicated the Quran to Muhammad (81:19–21). Alongside the doctrine of angels is the doctrine of *jinn*, which are spirits. Rebellious *jinn* are called *shaitans*, and they may lead men astray and oppose the prophets.

The Quran always mentions the last day as a cataclysmic event which will come suddenly at a time known only to God. At the Judgment Day the blessed and pious Muslims will be gathered up and placed in a mansion with flowing rivers while reclining on silk couches and enjoying heavenly food and drink in total bliss. Paradise can only be gained by God's grace, and God's grace can be gained only by following the five pillars of Islam.

The second pillar, *salat,* is also not specifically mentioned in the Quran, but the practice of prayer was firmly established by the time of Muhammad's death. Muslim prayer consists of gratitude and supplication, with thanksgiving being primary. Thus a Muslim is quick to thank Allah for creating the universe, helping the sick, relieving the distressed, consoling the broken-hearted and forgiving sins. Following such a prayer of thanksgiving, the devout will then continue to beseech God for love of others, righteous behavior and firm faith and direction. It is common also to pray for forgiveness for faults and for the strength to resist them and to ask for mercy.

Five times a day a Muslim should face Mecca and go through a prescribed set of ritual gestures and prayers. Each prayer consists of a fixed number of bowings (*rak'ah*). Each bowing consists of seven specific ritual gestures and recitations. First, facing Mecca, the Muslim recites the phrase, *Allahu akbar,* "God is most great," with hands opened on each side of the face. Next is recited the *fatihah,* or opening "Sura," of the Quran: "Praise belongs to God, Lord of the worlds, the compassionate, the merciful, King of the day of judgment. Tis thee we worship and thee we ask for help. Guide us in the straight path, the path of those whom thou hast favored, not the path of those who incur thy anger nor of those who go astray." Following the *fatihah* another passage is recited while standing upright. Next, the supplicant bows from the hips, straightens up and glides to the knees, prostrating his or her face to the ground. Then he sits back on his haunches and touches his head to the ground a second time.

This ritual is conducted at daybreak, noon, mid-afternoon, after sunset and the early part of the night. One might perform this ritual anywhere, although it is preferably performed in a congregation at a *masgid* (place of prostration) under the leadership of an *Imam*, a ritual leader. Prior to praying one should either wash one's face, hands, arms to the elbows and wipe one's head and feet, lesser ablution (*wudhu*), or completely wash the body, greater ablution (*ghusl*). If no water is on hand, one should simply wipe one's hands and face with fine clean sand. Furthermore one is excused from praying if one is sick or in a foreign country that would cause one to be persecuted.

While there is nothing that approaches the Christian Sunday, Friday most nearly approximates a holy day for Muslims. It is significant that the original "Sura" in the Quran which is recited during *salat* makes reference to the straight path. Islam is primarily concerned with the embodiment of piety to Allah as manifested through proper behavior. While Jesus was a great prophet and exhorted people to live a righteous life, it was left to Muhammad, the "seal of the prophets," to show how God's will should be lived.

The third pillar of Islam is *zakat* or alms giving. This too is an outward sign of piety which gains a Muslim salvation. Those who are blessed with material abundance should help those who are less fortunate. Muhammad set a figure of two and one-half percent of one's total wealth. Thus poor people owe nothing while middle and upper class people annually distribute among the poor one-fortieth of the value of all they possess. The Quran is very specific in outlining to whom alms should be given: the poor, the needy, those employed in its collections, slaves, prisoners, debtors and wayfarers ("Sura" 9:60). Almsgiving is not considered a tax but is a returning to God of that which was initially his.

Fasting (*sawm*) is the fourth pillar of Islam. During the ninth month of the lunar year (Ramadan) Muslims observe a period of fasting with complete abstinence from food and drink during the hours of daylight. Ramadan was the month when Muhammad received his initial appointment as prophet from the angel Jebril and ten years later made the *hijra* from Mecca to Medina. Fasting teaches self-discipline, compassion for those who are less fortunate and recognition of one's dependence on the fruits of Allah's creation.

Islam's fifth pillar is pilgrimage, *hajj*. This occurs during the twelfth lunar month. Every Muslim is exhorted to make this trip once during his life if he is physically and economically able. The pilgrimage begins in Mecca at the *Ka'ba*. After circumambulating this sacred black stone twelve times, the pilgrims walk 14 miles to the east to Arafat in order to meditate on the plain. From there they walk to Mina and then back towards Mecca where they stone a monument representing the devil. From there the pilgrims return to the *Ka'ba* to circle it a last time. This entire ritual takes about ten days to complete. Meat and camels are sacrificed at Mina on the way back to Mecca. To make the pilgrimage, worshippers must be in a state of ritual consecration (*ihram*). This involves shaving one's head and discarding one's ordinary clothing before entering the region of Mecca. One wears two plain unsewn sheets leaving only the head and face uncovered. From that point on, the pilgrim may not hunt, cut hair or nails, use perfume, cover the head unless female, or have sexual relations until after the sacrifice at Mina, when they resume their normal life. National leaders and the homeless participate in this ritual side by side, demonstrating in a concrete manner how all are equal before Allah.

After the initial rite of circumambulation, pilgrims perform the *sa'y*, running between two low hills near the *Ka'ba*. This reenacts another story connected to Abraham. According to Muslim tradition, Sarah, in a jealous rage, persuaded Abraham to expel his concubine Hajar, who produced Abraham a son, Ishmael. The two were dying of thirst and Hajar ran back and forth between two low hills crying for divine assistance. Allah provided her with the well of Zamzam. Thus this ritual also is a symbol of humanity's dependence upon God, who is ready to respond. The culmination of the *hajj* takes place at Arafat, a plain 14 miles east of Mecca. Here the pilgrims perform the right of standing (*wuquf*) before God in worship. It was on the hill adjacent to the plain of Arafat that the prophet addressed his people shortly before his death. This ritual lasts from noon until sundown. During that time the Mountain of Mercy is covered with pilgrims. At Mina the pilgrim stones three pillars. This is a holdover from a pre–Islamic custom that is usually interpreted as a resistance to the devil.

The *hajj* is the single largest ritual in the world. There is no gathering of followers on a global scale in any other religion that can compare to the Muslim *hajj*. For example, while all Christians worship Christmas and Easter, they do so within the confines of their own churches and denominations. There is simply no universal Christian ceremony which parallels this Muslim gathering.

Sunni and Shi'ite

A split within the Muslim community, Ummah, was created following the rupture of the Sunnis, who followed the Sunna (traditional practice), and the Shi'ites, who claimed Ali was the first true Caliph. Sunnism continues to represent the Islamic mainstream. It is characterized primarily by its literalist interpretation of the Quran and the emphasis it placed on the law, the *Shari'at*. Muslim law is broader in scope and deeper in function than it is in Western jurisprudence. The law for Muslims contains not only the relationships between people but also concerns itself with community's relationship with God. Furthermore, the *Shari'at* is seen as a divine revelation. The Muslim law has many sources, including the Quran, the Sunna, or tradition, the *ijma,* or consensus of the testimonies of Muhammad's companions, and personal reflections on issues where the book and Sunna are silent (*ijtihad*). The Sunni community recognizes four schools of law which we shall not concern ourselves with here.

Annmarie Schimmel, a historian of religions, has written that Shi'ite Muslim was originally Arabic in origin and resulted from the rejection of the power of the third caliph by Ali and the descendants of Muhammad. The Shi'ite division of Islam was initially an Arab dispute that in part revolved around the moving of the capital from Kufa to Damascus. Arabs of Kufa opposed the Arabs of Syria. Kufa Muslims wanted the caliphate returned to the house of Ali. Very soon Shi'ite Islam became a lens through which was refracted the doctrine of the Persian Imam (from Ali's house) as well as Persian light mysticism and love poetry. With the emergence of Shi'ite Islam came Ayatollahs who are mediating links with Allah. Shi'ite Islam has given birth to a number of different sects and schisms.

Shi'ite Muslims feel that their religious leaders, who are directly related to Muhammad, function somewhat as intermediaries between the people and Allah. The orthodox Muslims call the idea of the Imam *ghuluw*, which means exaggeration more than heresy. For Sunni Muslims only the *Shar'iat* mediates Allah and the people. The *Shar'iat* is the law but it is more than a law. The *Shar'iat* is a whole way of life that includes everyday ordinary activities in addition to rites of passage and major seasonal or cosmogonic rituals. *Shar'iat* is a practical utilitarian mode of piety that shows submission to Allah. Sunni Islam shows how the normality of society reveals piety to Allah, and it makes Islam the first religion, or perhaps the second religion after Confucianism, to develop the social life theologically.

According to Sunni Muslims, every human has the law of God written on his or her heart. Allah created everybody, but many people have forgotten this fact. To be born, according to Sunni Muslims, is to be born a Muslim, for birth itself is submission to Allah. Thus the *Shari'at* is a doctrine of society that is based on the doctrine of creation. In the end Muslims act in history, but their acts are ahistorical because Allah does not arise from historical revelation as did Jesus, but from the creation of the world itself. The *Shari'at,* in a sense, is about the establishment of a City of God on earth in contrast to Augustine, who looked for the City of God in heaven. Probably John Calvin's Puritans at Geneva came closest to the establishment of a Christian order on earth. In a treatise titled *On Civil Government,* Calvin tried to wed love to justice, especially through the Psalms. Aquinas in the Middle Ages similarly tried to translate love into law in order to establish a Christian kingdom on earth. But in the end Christians have only managed to approximate Christ's teachings.

Sufism

As early as the Umayyad period (661–750 C.E.) devout Muslims begin to protest the corruption of Islamic society. Drawing on elements from early Christian ascetics, such as the Anchorites, some Muslim mystics began to devote themselves to fasting and meditation on the Quran. Furthermore, in imitation of Christian ascetics, some began to wear course wool, *suf,* which later gave rise to the name Sufism. Muslim ascetics (*Zahid*) extolled asceticism as a way of transcending humanity's attachment to material joys and pleasures. According to the Sufi Masruq, a *Zahid* is one who is controlled only by God.

The first Muslim mystic ascetic was Hasan al-Basri (died 728). Famous for his profound melancholy spawned by constant meditation on the Day of Judgment, he was followed by Ibrahim ibn Adham, who defined three phases of asceticism: 1) renouncing the world; 2) renouncing the happiness of knowing that one has abandoned the world; and 3) realizing completely the world's lack of importance so that one no longer even regards it.

However, in the eighth and ninth centuries Sufis began to transcend the negative asceticism of the early ascetics in order to state their spiritual quest in more positive terms. Their life was characterized by their love of God (*hubb* or *mahabbah*). Thus later Sufis emphasized love of God, which also manifests itself in love of other human beings.

Tradition says that Muslim mysticism began with Muhammad. Before Muhammad announced his role as Prophet he was considered a friend of God (*wali*). Muhammad was reputed to have gone into trances when he was visited by Allah through Jebril. Trance was a sign of the impact of God's transcendence. It is said that Muhammad had face to face communions with God and that this laid the ground work for Muslim mysticism. The great Sufi theologian and mystic al-Ghazzali (1059–1111) declared that human fulfillment was found in the conquest and complete possession of the human heart by the love of God. Sufis believe that the mystical path begins by following the *Shari'at*, which brings about spiritual discipline and the avoidance of sin. Once one obeys God, one can gather around a *shaykh* (spiritual master) who will direct one's actions in attempting to seek the inner spiritual dimensions of the law (*tariqah*). Sufism proceeds from a process of freeing oneself from the material world, the consciousness of the material world, and then of oneself so that one is absorbed totally in God. Over time Sufis developed a ritual called *dhikr*, which entails the remembrance of God in repetition of his name. Through the repetition of this ritual one is able to abandon one's self and become one with God.

This is not the place to talk about the extent to which Sufism drew upon Shi'ite and Persian elements. Suffice it to say that Sunni Sufis always maintained the transcendence of Allah from themselves. A famous Persian mystic, al-Hallaj, who was born in the southwest of Persia in 857, proclaimed that the ultimate human goal was mystical union with God, which was affected by love (*'ishq*). Thus he pronounced in ecstasy the famous words "I am the truth (God)," which led to his execution. While al-Hallaj in reality may have denied that he was equating himself with Allah, the statement potentially eclipsed the absolute monotheism and separateness of Allah, and thus he was accused of *shirk* (polytheism) and put to death. A later mystic, Sohrawardi, who was born in 1155 in a town in northwest Persia, drew heavily from Persian light mysticism in developing a religious orientation centered around the "Light of Lights."

But it was al-Ghazzali who brought respectability and acceptance among the doctors of law. Sufism then experienced great popularity. Sufism flourished originally in the Near East and Northern Africa but soon spread into India, Central Asia, Indonesia and East Africa. Indeed Sufism became so popular that Gibb suggests that the eclipse of Shi'ism was primarily the result of the popularity and missionary spirit of the Sufis. Be that as it may, it is certain that Sufism contributed greatly to the renewal of the Muslim religious experience. Sufism's cultural contribution was also considerable, for it influenced music, dance and especially poetry. In order to make sure that Sufism never developed outside of the law, the *ulama* developed colleges called *madrasas* for theological education. By the fourteenth century hundreds of these schools had been developed and were used to influence theological developments.

Islam today has over 400 million followers and claims one out of seven people in the world as a follower. Pakistan, a new Muslim state, was founded in 1947. It is said that where Islam and Christianity are competing for converts in Africa, Islam is gaining at a rate of ten to one. In the 1950s and 1960s Elijah Muhammad (1897 to 1975) called himself a messenger of Allah and announced that American blacks were descended from the ancient tribe of Shabazz that originally had settled in Mecca. While black Muslims developed doctrines that were considered heretical to Orthodox Muslims, they were nevertheless permitted to make the pilgrimage to Mecca.

Another religion, Bahai, developed in the late nineteenth century from another messenger of Allah named Bab, who said that his name should be added as the thirteenth Imam, a Shiite doctrine. Bahai takes the universality and monotheism of Islam one more step and argues that there is only one God, although he has many names. Thus, according to the Bahais, everyone ultimately worships the same God. This religion has produced extreme tolerance and brotherhood among all peoples including those who claim allegiance to other religions such as Christianity, Hinduism and Buddhism. It too is a rapidly growing religion especially in Third World countries.

In the end Islam arose out of the ancient urban world and helped create the Mediterranean world of the Middle Ages. Muhammad's message was directed primarily to those people who lived in the cities along the Silk Road. Teaching that cities could and must change, Islam does not critique urbanity as does Buddhism or Christianity. Walking a straight path by following the law of God creates right relations among people based on God's unity. This doctrine, coupled with Islam's tolerance for other religious traditions, helps explain its success in the Third World. One can be a traditional African as long as one professes belief in one God, Allah, and Muhammad as his Prophet. Marshall Hodgson perhaps best showed that Islam pulled together the diverse religious, political, linguistic and ethnic groups that lived in the great urban and trade centers between the Nile and Oxus rivers (Vol. 1). Through sound law and fair dealing Islam established an international urban community that was remarkably stable for several centuries. With its great sense of tolerance one cannot help but wonder if the modern world would not have been different if Muslim explorers had discovered the New World rather than western Europeans, and it is to that discovery that we now turn.

Bibliography
Chapter 12 — Islam

'Ali, Amere. *The Spirit of Islam*. London, 1967.
Ali, Muhammad. *The Religion of Islam*. Lahore, Pakistan, 1950.
Andrae, Tor. *Mohammed: The Man and His Faith*. London, 1936; reprint New York, 1960.

Arberry, A.J. *Sufism*. London, 1950.
_____. *The Koran Interpreted*. 2 Vols. London, 1955.
Bell, Richard. *The Origin of Islam in Its Christian Environment*. London, 1926.
_____. *The Qur'an*. 2 Vols. Edinburgh, 1937–39.
Bravmann, M.M. *The Spiritual Background of Early Islam*. Leiden, 1972.
Coulson, Noel J. *A History of Islamic Law*. Vol. 2. *Islamic Surveys*. Edinburgh, 1964.
Cragg, Kenneth. *The House of Islam*. Belmont, California, 1975.
_____. *The Mind of the Qur'an: Chapters in Reflection*. London, 1973.
Danner, Victor. *The Islamic Tradition*. Amity, New York, 1988.
Dawood, N.J. Trans. *The Koran*. 4th Rev. Ed. New York, 1974.
Denny, Frederick Mathewson. *An Introduction to Islam*. New York and London, 1985.
Donaldson, Dwight M. *The Shi'ite Religion*. London, 1933.
Donner, Fred M. *The Early Islamic Conquests*. Princeton, New Jersey, 1981.
Eliade, Mircea. *A History of Religious Ideas: From Muhammad to the Age of Reforms*. Vol. 3. Trans. A. Hiltebeitel and D. Apostolos-Cappadona. Chicago, 1985: 62–84; 113–151; 302–306; 307–309.
Geertz, Clifford. *The Religion of Java*. Glenco, Illinois, 1964.
_____, and Hildred and Lawrence Rosen. *Meaning and Order in Moroccan Society*. Cambridge, England, 1979.
Gibb, H.A.R. *Mohammedanism: A Historical Survey*. London and Oxford, 1953.
_____, and J.H. Kramers, Editors. *Shorter Encyclopedia of Islam*. Leiden, 1961.
Goldziher, Ignaz. *Introduction to Islamic Theology and Law*. Trans. Andras and Ruth Hamor. Princeton, New Jersey, 1981.
Guillaume, Alfred, Trans. *The Life of Muhammad: A Translation of (IBN) Ishaq's "Sirat Rasul Allah."* London, 1955.
Hitti, Philip P. *History of the Arabs*. 10th Ed. New York, 1970.
Hodgson, Marshall. *The Venture of Islam: Conscience and History of a World Civilization*. 3 Vols. Chicago, 1974.
Hourami, A.H., and S.N. Stern, Editors. *The Islamic City*. Oxford, 1970.
Ibn Ishaq, Muhammad ibn Yasar. *The Life of Muhammad*. Trans. A. Guillaume. London, New York and Toronto, 1955.
Israeli, Raphael. *Muslims in China: A Study in Cultural Confrontation*. London, 1978.
Jeffrey, A. *Materials for the History of the Text of the Qur'an*. Leiden, 1937.
_____. Editor and Trans. *A Reader on Islam*. Mouton, 1962.
Lawrence, Bruce B. *Defenders of God: The Fundamentalist Revolt of the Modern Age*. San Francisco, 1989.
Lewis, Bernard. *The Arabs in History*. Rev. Ed. New York, 1966.
_____. Editor. *Islam and the Arab World*. New York, 1976.
Martin, Richard C. *Islam: A Cultural Prospective*. Englewood Cliffs, New Jersey, 1982.
Nasr, Seyyed Hossein. *Sufi Essays*. London, 1972.
_____. *Ideals and Realities of Islam*. San Francisco, 1989.
Nicholson, Reynold A. *The Mystics of Islam*. London, 1966.
Pickthall, Muhammad. *The Meaning of the Glorious Koran*. New York, 1953.

Rahmin, Fazlur. *Islam.* Chicago, 1979.

———. "Islam: An Overview." *Encyclopedia of Religion.* Vol. 7. Editor-in-Chief, Mircea Eliade. New York, 1987: 303–322.

Renard, John. *Seven Doors to Islam: Spirituality and the Religious Life of Muslims.* Berkeley, California, 1996.

———. *Windows on the House of Islam: Muslim Sources on Spirituality and Religious Life.* Berkeley, California, 1998.

Rippin, Andrew. *Muslims: Their Religious Beliefs and Practices.* Vol. 2. *The Contemporary Period.* London and New York, 1993.

Savory, R.M. Editor. *Introduction to Islamic Civilization.* Cambridge, England, 1976.

Schacht, Joseph, and C.E. Bosworth. Editors. *The Legacy of Islam.* 2nd Ed. Oxford, England, 1974.

Schimmel, Annemarie. *Mystical Dimensions of Islam.* Chapel Hill, North Carolina, 1975.

Schuon, Frithjof. *Understanding Islam.* San Francisco, 1972.

Shaban, M.A. *Islamic History A.D. 600–750(A.H.132): A New Interpretation.* Cambridge, England, 1971.

Shahid, Irfan. *The Cambridge History of Islam.* Cambridge, 1970.

Smith, Margaret. *Al-Ghazali: The Mystic.* London, 1944.

Stoddart, William. *Sufism.* New York, 1986.

Trimingham, J. Spencer. *The Sufi Orders in Islam.* Oxford, England, 1971.

Watt, W. Montgomery. *Muhammad at Mecca.* Oxford, 1953.

———. *Muhammad at Medina.* Oxford, 1956.

———. *Muhammad: Prophet and Statesman.* Oxford, 1961.

Wellhausen, Julius. *The Arab Kingdom and Its Fall.* London, 1973.

Wolf, Eric R. "The Social Organization of Mecca and the Origins of Islam." *Southwestern Journal of Anthropology* 7 (1951): 329–356.

CHAPTER 13

The New World

The Age of Discovery (1490–1522), the Renaissance (1490–1650), the Scientific Revolution (1545–1794), the Age of Revolutions (1776–1789), the Enlightenment (1670–1800) and the Industrial Revolution (1820–1900)—these terms have come to take on almost epic dimensions in the imaginations of Western historians and scholars. The discoveries, both material and spiritual, that took place between about 1490 and 1900 forever changed the Western world. All of these periods run together and form a mosaic of historical oscillations and undulations. But out of all of these events the most significant for the world history of religions was arguably the discovery of the New World.

Just before dawn on August 3, 1492, three small vessels under the command of an Italian sailor named Christopher Columbus headed westward in search of a new route to the Orient. After some two months at sea, Rodrigo de Triana, a lookout on the Pinta, suddenly cried, "Land!" Columbus assumed that he had found the Spice Islands of Asia, the Indies, and thus named the inhabitants on this land *los Indios*. At that time Europeans generally understood that the world consisted of three continents—Europe, Asia and Africa—all joined to form an *Orbis Terrarum*, Island of the Earth. Geography and history, both influenced by the Catholic Church, proclaimed that God created one world surrounded by mysterious seas of unknown dimension. Ever since Marco Polo's journey to China (1271–1295) Western Europe had been fascinated with the Orient and lured by its riches. Western Europe lacked the exotic raw materials of the Mediterranean world and could not trade with the Orient except by going through the Middle East. Columbus hoped to find a passage by sea to the Orient in order to open up trade for Spain just as Europe was coming out of the old feudal system of economics and government and was moving towards some semblance of a permanent political organization. The interest in trade grew with a mercantile class and the rise of cities — by 1500 one tenth of Europe's population was urban.

The growing towns were situated in important sites. For example, London, Hamburg, Antwerp and Lisbon were built near the mouths of rivers, while Paris, Mainz and Ghent were located near river junctions. While these cities were small by today's comparisons, London had a population of about 50,000 people. Europe's largest city, Constantinople, had 250,000 inhabitants, Paris 200,000, and Ghent 135,000. But these cities were populous for their time, and their link with water destined them to be important trade centers in the future. It would be difficult to understand the emergence of Western universities, art and inventions without the existence of these important cities. But their most important contribution to Western history was economic and, as we shall see, religious.

Columbus never really found what he was looking for. On his third voyage in 1498 he decided to push southward in an attempt to find the Golden Chersonese, the Malay Peninsula. This he felt would certainly provide a passage to the Indian Ocean and the oriental riches which he sought. He in fact landed in Venezuela. The water he found in the Gulf was fresh, not salt, and this puzzled him because Marco Polo had reported that nothing but open sea lay to the south of the Golden Chersonese. Columbus died shortly thereafter, never having understood the true significance of his travels. It was not until much later that a New World was truly discovered. The voyage of Amerigo Vespucci along the coast of South America (1501–02) also proved to be mysterious. He too failed to realize the novelty of the world that he explored. It was not until 1507, with the publication of the *Cosmographiae Introductio,* published by the Academy of St. Dié, that Western Europe recognized that Columbus and Vespucci had discovered a "fourth part" of the world separate from the rest.

As Edmundo O'Gorman has so brilliantly shown, Columbus did not discover America. Columbus never figured out that he had come upon an inhabited world that did not exist even in the imaginations of the people during that time. As he puts it, America had to be invented because it did not fit into the world view of the Western Europeans at that time. Ronald Meek is right when he says that the discovery of the New World had radical consequences by challenging Europe's notions of geography, history and theology. During the time of Columbus and Vespucci, universities were under the auspices of the Catholic Church. Geography, science, astronomy, history and literature were all ultimately subsumed under the umbrella of theology, which, as Aquinas had noted in the thirteenth century, was the "Queen of the sciences." Theology controlled and structured the parameters of all university learning.

With the discovery of a part of the world that was not mentioned in the Bible, and did not exist even in theory, the world view of Western Europeans was shaken to its very foundation. This radical novelty applied both to the inhabitants of the New World and the land itself. Who were these new people? At that time everyone was understood to be a descendant of Adam and Eve, and yet here were people who apparently had never before been encountered.

Other significant matters were going on as well at this time. In 1456 Gutenberg printed the Bible on parchment. Once the secret of paper manufacturing reached the Rhineland and mass production was possible, a growing literate population developed in Western Europe as well.

About 1513 or 1514, a Catholic monk named Martin Luther rediscovered the significance of faith for the Christian life. Drawing from Romans 1:12, "the just live by faith," Martin Luther resuscitated the importance of this doctrine and ultimately founded a new Christian church. For Luther the Epistle to the Romans was "the most important document of the New Testament."

Luther was troubled by what he regarded as a growing immorality in the Catholic Church. But more importantly, Martin Luther was troubled by the emphasis on what he perceived as an emphasis on salvation through works. It occurred to Martin Luther that no matter how well one acted, one could never, because of sin, justify one's salvation in the eyes of God. A truly just God, Luther noted, would grant no one salvation. Thus on October 31, 1517, he affixed his 95 Theses against the Indulgences on the door of the church at the Castle at Wittenberg. The selling of indulgences troubled Luther greatly because some unethical priests had abused the practice and preached that one could obtain permission to sin through the acquisition of indulgences. Luther engaged in bitter debates with the Church for the next several years.

Finally, in 1520, he was ordered to retract his position or be excommunicated. In response he rejected the supremacy of the Pope over the counsels as well as the distinction between clergy and laity in a brilliant manifesto, *To the Christian Nobility of the German Nation*. Two months later he published *On the Babylonian Captivity of the Church* and again attacked the clergy's abuse of the sacraments. Luther accepted only three sacraments: baptism, the Eucharist and confession. Later he renounced confession because it seemed to place too much emphasis on works. Luther found himself constantly confessing his sins because no sooner had he left the confessional booth than his mind would entertain sinful thoughts, creating the need for another confession.

During the Reformation, Luther also brought about another important change in the Church. Aware of the significance of the discovery of the raw goods of the New World for Western European economics, Luther legalized usury for the first time. Interestingly it was not until the discovery of the New World that Christians approved this practice. For 1500 years it was understood that Christian love extended to all persons, even enemies. In the eyes of Christians every human was a brother. As Benjamin Nelson has shown, usury flew in the face of Christian brotherhood and created a universal "otherhood" where each person was an "other," not a "brother."

Usury rests on a more fundamental notion, profit. Not the profit implicit in every exchange — the value gained in acquiring something one needs in exchange for a plentiful item. People all over the world barter and exchange surplus goods for things that they need. That intrinsic profit is very different from the profit generated by usury and later, mass production. During the Axial Age, caravans of goods stretched through urban markets and directly exchanged goods and religious meanings. But the profit generated there was nothing like the profit generated from usury and eventually from mass production during the Industrial Revolution.

Capitalism was also fostered by the Protestant theology of John Calvin. As Max Weber has shown, Calvin stated that God predestined those who were saved. The question arose as to how would one know if one were so chosen. Calvin's answer was that those who were saved would be known through their works. Thus Weber showed how Calvinist Christians worked ever harder in order to prove, at least to themselves, that they were among God's elect. This work ethic also helped launch capitalism and later the Industrial Revolution, all of which had important religious consequences.

In 1543 Nicholas Copernicus published *De Revolutionibus Orbium Coelestium*, in which he posited that the earth revolved around the sun rather than vice versa as had been previously held. Even Martin Luther disagreed with this notion because it flew in the face of biblical accounts. After all, said Luther, Joshua made the sun stand still. Drawing upon Copernicus' ideas and using his telescope, Galileo Galilei (1564–1642) published *Sidereal Messenger* which described his observations of the heavens. Galileo found that the moon's surface was mountainous, not smooth, that the sun's face had dark moving spots and that the sun itself had a monthly axial rotation. But most importantly, Galileo confirmed the Copernican conception of the solar system. These findings were a grave challenge to the established ecclesiastical belief that the sun revolved around the earth. In his *Great Dialogue on the Two Chief Systems of the World, the Ptolemaic and the Copernican*, published in 1632, Galileo constructed a theory of mechanics that was supported by the theory of a moving earth. This challenged Aristotelian physics and was denounced as heretical by the Church. Galileo's observations functioned as a critique of the medieval integration of theology and logic as exemplified by the thought of Thomas Aquinas.

Sir Francis Bacon (1561–1626) also ushered in the new Age of Science. For our purposes Bacon's key development was twofold. First, he called for a new science based on empirical observation and experimentation. Second, and more important, he put scientific observations and empiricism to use pragmatically in order to control nature. The purpose of science, said Bacon, was to manipulate the natural world for human use, thus wedding science to technology in an unprecedented manner which would have far reaching consequences during the Industrial Revolution. The Baconian theory of science as technology had a tremendous impact on the Royal Society of London, which published its *Philosophical Transactions* in 1665, one of the earliest scientific journals. From England Bacon's theories spread throughout Europe. Interestingly, Bacon also championed usury (Northup 127–131).

During the Renaissance, other important scientific discoveries were made which had major impacts on the religious orientation of Western peoples. William Harvey (1578–1657) discovered the circulation of blood, Anton Van Leeuwenhoek (1632–1723) uncovered the existence of microscopic organisms, and Isaac Newton (1642–1727) developed a theory of mechanics and motion which was to become the foundation and model for physical inquiry for more than two centuries. Newton unified existing theories with respect to the movement of bodies. He completed Galileo's work on the science of motion by constructing the general laws of dynamics, and he also discussed the concept of gravity. Of religious significance, Newton's studies produced compelling evidence for the universal scope of the principles of mechanics and undermined, in a persuasive manner, the old medieval belief that terrestrial and celestial bodies operated under different principles.

Reason and Unreason

Side by side with the development of reason and science during the Renaissance was another curious development. We previously discussed how French men who contracted leprosy during the Crusades were placed in leprosariums upon their return to Europe. Lepers were thought to be punished by God. Crusaders contracted leprosy when their faith was not total and their hearts were not pure. In Christendom lepers functioned as spiritual and social outcasts, and leprosariums were built to house these unholy, sinful infidels.

Although leprosariums began to empty in the fifteenth century, the question of leprosariums was not settled until the end of the seventeenth century. What remained longer than leprosy were the underlying values and images attached to the figure of the leper as well as to the meaning of his separation from the rest of society. Although the leper vanished almost from memory, the structures of exclusion persisted. As Michel Foucault notes, "poor vagabonds, criminals and deranged minds would take the part played by the leper" (7).

Reason was elevated to a new level, not only in the sciences but also in philosophy. With the thought of Rene Descartes, reason was exemplified in a new way. During the time of Thomas Aquinas, reason and theology were melded but in a way that preserved the primacy of theology. In the Age of Discovery the primacy of theology gave way and reason became associated with a specifically human order.

Insanity came to be seen as the opposite of reason. The sacred was not dependent on reason and thus could not be controlled by reason— but unreason could be. Thus the sacred was re-created on a level that could be managed by those people in control, and that is precisely what happened to the insane.

The insane had always traditionally wandered around in Western Europe. By wandering they were connected with the religious meanings of the wild and the pilgrimage where one left one's home and went to another place. Along the way one was neither here nor there, and thus foolishness occurred. During the pilgrimage, the domestic structure of the home, where one is able to order things the way one wants to, was given up. In so doing one submitted oneself to a world that one did not control. The insane were constantly wandering. Originally the insane would travel on ships going up and down canals, and the association between the insane and the fluid meaning surrounding water indicated their lack of human orderliness. The Ship of Fools was a strange boat that sailed along the calm rivers of the Rhineland and the Flemish canals. Following the Ship of Fools came carnivals that separated the insane from the rest of society.

The madman, like lepers, reflected, or rather, refracted the negativity of the sacred. Nevertheless, like leprosy, insanity revealed the presence of God. At first the mad were allowed to wander through the streets and were perceived as living in a state of Adamic innocence. The insane manifested the direct impact of God's transcendence on humans. Humans directly touched by God became insane and refracted the "other-worldliness" of the sacred. But eventually the insane, like the lepers, took on the negativity of the sacred and came to be despised as they called into question the human order of Western Europe. The mad reminded the mainstream of the folly of human existence and of the fact of human limitations and death. When the madman laughed, he reproached the arrogance of humanity. Insanity, therefore, critiqued the significance of Western European society. The sheer spectacle of these people proved to be too bothersome for the rational order of the day and thus they were put away. In this action one sees again an attempt on the part of the West to control the sacred and thus create their own world.

The poor, the unemployed, and the insane all found themselves in houses of confinement by the middle of the seventeenth century. Interestingly one out of every hundred inhabitants of the city of Paris was confined somehow. At the end of the eighteenth century in England, Holland, Germany, France, Italy and Spain, John Howard visited hospitals, prisons and jails and noted a common ground among all those who were shut up. By the eighteenth century the hungry also had become a police matter. As Voltaire and Colbert both showed, the police were linked with forcing the weak and poor to work for the rich. As Voltaire put it, "Since you have established yourselves as a people, had you not yet discovered the secret of forcing all the rich to make all the poor work? Are you still ignorant of the first principles of the police?" (Foucault *Madness and Civilization* 46).

The city was and is the "man-made" world *par excellence* and eventually the confinement of those outside the mainstream, like the insane, was extended to beggars and debtors. It is interesting that many early prisons were debtor prisons established by the wealthy in order to require the idle to work. In this connection it is interesting to note that the police functioned as priests with guns who protected the sacred order of the city. The police, who originated in Paris, were hired by the rich and powerful to protect the interest of the wealthy. Etymologically, the police are in charge of the administration of the city. The words "police" and "policy" both are rooted in the Latin *politia*, "civil administration," and Greek *polis* "city." Later, from the medieval Latin *politia*, came the French *police*.

New World

The twentieth-century Western world cannot be understood apart from the events mentioned above. And yet all of the events described pale in comparison to the discovery of the New World. Debates emerged within the Church and the universities in an attempt to make sense of this discovery. One of the most famous Catholic debates occurred in 1550 and was called the "Council of the Fourteen." Commenced by Charles V, this discussion concerned the way in which the inhabitants of the Americas were to be treated. Two influential Spaniards, Sepulveda and Las Casas, gave differing views. Sepulveda spoke first. His position rested on the writings of Oviedo, who took a very negative view of the natives. Sepulveda argued that Native Americans were natural slaves and advocated the policy of *ecomiendaro*, which permitted the Spanish colonists to exploit the natives for economic gain. Furthermore, Sepulveda attempted to justify conquests by violence in order to Christianize the godless heathens.

Las Casas spoke for almost five full days refuting the position of Sepulveda. Trying to show that the natives were a noble people who had beautiful arts and a well developed government, Las Casas stated that the Indians were eager to learn. He also noted that they were quick to accept Christianity. After listening carefully to both sides, the Council finally decided to sanction the position of Sepulveda.

Primitive/Civilized

As Louis Hanke has shown, the most significant aspect of this divergence of views is that the Indian was viewed as either a "dirty dog" or a "noble savage." Charles Long has noted that both positions are based on preconceived notions brought from the Old World which share a common structure — they point to the "otherness" of Native Americans in contrast to Europeans. As ignoble savages, Indians were seen as existing without religion or humanity. As noble savages, Indians were seen as living in a state of Adamic innocence prior to the Fall. As noble savages, the natives lived in a paradisal state. As "negative others," Native Americans were seen as animalistic or, even worse, satanic. Even Las Casas, who argued for the oneness of humanity, anchored his position on the Indians' receptivity to Christianity. Las Casas never simply affirmed Indians as Indians. Although Romantics such as Rosseau approved natives in their own right, they attributed to them a sense of innocence that recalls the Garden of Eden. In all cases Europeans viewed Indians as other than Europeans, that is to say, other than human. Whether noble or ignoble, their humanity was not recognized. Implied here was a superiority on the part of Europeans. As Francis Jennings put it, "The Christian Caucasians of Europe are not only holy and white but also civilized while the pigmented heathens of the distant lands are not only idolatrous and dark but savage" (6).

By the late sixteenth century the English had already begun to describe the relations between Europeans and Indians in terms of a "savage/civility" structure (Quinn 210–213). John Smith astutely saw the economic motivation for early Christian missionary activity when he wrote that the colonists made "religion their color, when their aim was present profit." According to the early English view North America was likened to either the biblical wilderness or Canaan. In 1587, in the *Epistle Dedicatori*, Richard Hakluyt declared that England's mission in the New World was "to recall the savage and pagan to civilitie, to draw the ignorant within the orbit of reason, and to fill with reverence for divinity the godless and the ungodly" (quoted in Taylor 366). Furthermore, Hakluyt wrote that "to posterity no greater glory can be handed down than to conquer the barbarian." According to Hakluyt there was no moral, religious or legal obstacle to the use of force to overcome the "savages" (quoted in Taylor 366).

In 1609 he wrote that undoubtedly it would be best to handle natives gently if possible, but if that will not work, then soldiers should be sent to prepare them "for the preachers." In 1609 Robert Gray, an Anglican, preached and published a widely circulated sermon entitled "A Good Speed to Virginia," which spoke of the promise of the Lord to the children of Israel that they would "cast out the Cannites." Drawing upon Joshua 17:14–18, Gray declared that the English, like the Old Testament Israelites, had become a great people confined to a narrow land. North America properly belonged to the English because the Native Americans partook of the "nature of beasts." Indeed, Gray wrote that because of "their godless ignorance and blasphemous idolatry" the Indians were "worst than those beasts which are of the most wild and savage nature" (quoted in Cave 283).

Similarly Robert Johnson in 1609 wrote that Native Americans were a "wild and savage" people who were neither "Christian nor civil" but lived instead in a "beastly, brutish manner" (Johnson *Nova* 7, 11, 12). Johnson also incorporated the Indians into the biblical story itself. He stated that Indians, the direct descendants of Noah who had provoked the wrath of God 3,000 years earlier at Babel, were under a heavy curse and punishment of God. God had now chosen the English to remove the heavy yoke of bondage from those savages who would accept the Gospel. As he put it, it was the duty of the English to "bring those infidel peoples from worship of Divils to the service of God." The English were to try to lift the savages from their state of ignorance and devil worship to one of civilization and redemption. However, as Robert Gray wrote, if the Indians refused, the English were authorized and even commanded to exterminate the "Idolaters, rather than let them live" (quoted in Cave 286).

Others, such as William Crashaw, denied that the English were authorized to kill those who refused to convert, but this was based on his belief that they were truly inclined "to civilitie and so to religion" (quoted in Cave 287). New England's Puritans added very little to the ideology of civilization as expounded earlier by the Anglican preachers and publicists. Puritans saw North America as England's promised land by claiming a divinely appointed mission to develop the wilderness into a Christian kingdom on earth. Despite the generally unfavorable view of Indians held by Puritans, Puritans by and large denied that they had the right to force Indians off of their land.

Anthony Pagden has argued that, from the twelfth century until the beginning the sixteenth, the term *barbarous*, whatever similar vernacular it might take, had come to stand broadly for all non-Christian peoples and any race which behaved in savage or "uncivil ways" (24).

Greeks of the seventh and sixth centuries, who coined the term *barbarian*, used it simply to mean "foreigner." The Greeks even applied the name barbarian to the Egyptians, whom they respected. During the Middle Ages and the Renaissance the term took on a particularly negative meaning. As Francis Jennings has shown, all attempts to explain the primitive/civilized distinction in rational terms fall short. It is, as he says, "a moral sanction rather than any given combination of social traits susceptible to objective definition. It is a weapon of attack rather than a standard of measurement" (8).

The primitive/civilized structure is imbedded firmly in the consciousness of the West, although at a less than conscious level. Furthermore, it is found at all levels of society, not simply among the learned. Not only does it exist today at the very foundations of capitalism and Anglo-American jurisprudence as we shall see shortly, but it manifests itself at the popular level when, for example, parents and teachers tell children to "stop acting like heathens" or to "eat like civilized people." The president of the United States often makes reference to the "civilized nations of the world." In so doing he embodies the language that was spawned after the discovery of the New World.

Frank Getlein has analyzed two paintings in the late eighteenth and early nineteenth centuries, "The Peaceable Kingdom" by Edward Hicks and "The Death of Jane McCrae" by John Vanderlyn. Hicks' painting shows Indians and Quakers agreeing to a treaty while in the background children sit among wild beasts such as leopards and lions. The paradisal serenity of the scene is obvious and points to the idea that the New World is a second Eden, a virgin land. By contrast, in Vanderlyn's painting, a white woman is about to be brutally tomahawked and scalped by two evil looking Indians. The woman looks noble and innocent as she gazes helplessly at the brutish warriors who are about to do her in. Both views of the New World and its inhabitants are embedded in the European consciousness and both are ideologies—halfway between a mistake and a lie. Furthermore, as Charles Long has noted, both conceptions point to the singularity of their primitiveness, which is more than a description and less than a concept.

At the surface of colonization stood the desire to resuscitate a true Christianity, especially so among the English. John Smith compared America to Eden. The movement west across America became a symbol of spiritual progress. The Anglican William Crashaw wrote, "The God of Israel is ... the God of England." This ideology was soon linked with an archaic solar symbolism. Christians were exhorted to follow the course of the sun to salvation. This westward movement eventuated in the Doctrine of Manifest Destiny, which religiously justified the conquest and conversion of the Native American peoples (Drinnon 232–242). America was seen as a paradise to be Christianized. As Native Americans resisted the conquest, they became demonic beings representative of the biblical wilderness. But although conquest was often couched in Christian terms, it belied a deeper structure of meanings. Francis Jennings' *The Invasion of America* is an excellent book dealing with the relationships between Puritans and Indians in the northeast United States. English Puritans referred to Indians as savages from the beginning. In the late eighteenth century Cotton Mather stated that "the best thing we can do for our Indians is to Anglicize them in all agreeable instances" (quoted in Bowden 136). Similarly John Brainard in the late eighteenth century demonstrated a similar view when he stated, "We do not despise them for their color but for their heathenish temper and practices;... when they become Christians, and behave as becomes such, they shall have the same treatment as white people" (quoted in Bowden 156).

Europeans and European Americans embodied the language of civilization from the earliest days of discovery until the present time. The king of England in Letters Patent issued in 1606 for the colonizing of Virginia urged a mission "which may by the Providence of Almighty God, hereafter tend to the capital glory of His Divine Majesty, in propagating of Christian Religion to such people, as yet live in darkness, in miserable ignorance of the true knowledge and worship of God, and may in time bring the Infidels and Savages living in those parts, to human civility into a settled and quiet capital government" (*Calendar* 48).

The Reverend Samuel Purchas carried on the editing of *The Voyage Narratives* begun by the Reverend Richard Hakluyt. In his long series of narratives entitled *Hakluytus Posthumous or Purchas His Pilgrimes* (1625) Purchas writes that the Indians are

> bad people, having little of Humanitie but shape, ignorant of Civilitie, of arts, of Religion; more brutish then the beasts they hunt, more wild and unmanly then that unmanned wild Countrey which they range rather than inhabite; captivated also to Satans tyranny in foolish pieties, mad impieties, wicked idleness, busie and bloudy wickednesse:... All the rich endowments of Virginia, her Virgin-portion from the creation nothing lessened, are wages for all this worke; God is wisedome having enriched the Savage Countries, that those riches might be attractives for Christian suters, which there may sowe spirituals and reape temporals. (XIX, 232)

Thus Purchas contends that the rich resources of Virginia are God's reward to the English for converting the savages to Christianity.

One English writer put the case this way: "We give the savages what they most need. Civilitie for their bodies, Christianitie for their soules" (quoted in Limerick 10). Cotton Mather in 1702 probably echoed the sentiments of his age when he noted that civilization was more important than conversion: "They must be civilized ere they could be Christianized" (Mather 562).

Adam Smith

Part of the ideology of conquest was the stadial theory of progress, first published by the father of capitalism, Adam Smith. According to the bible of capitalism, *The Wealth of Nations*, man has progressed through four stages successively, each of which corresponds to a subsistence modality — hunting, herding, farming and capitalist commerce. According to Smith, capitalism represents nature's fulfillment of humanity. Smith wrote that capitalists are unquestionably superior to all other peoples, and he was quick to contrast "civilized" gentlemen with the "savages" of the New World.

A society of merchants governed by democracy and oriented by the sciences is a better society, said Smith, than one based on hunting, herding and farming, although he did recognize that the world of commerce presupposed an agricultural surplus. Such a mercantile society, said Smith, is civilized in contrast to the primitives living in other cultures. Smith made much of the difference between civilized and primitive peoples and stated that primitive peoples are important primarily because they provide "raw materials" for the economic growth of Europeans (590). It is important to note that Smith's theory of capitalism drew heavily upon the voyage literature of the Western Europeans (Meek).

For Smith the discovery of the New World and its raw goods was the greatest event in human history. Civilization, said Smith, presupposes the division of labor and the division of labor rests upon humanity's natural tendency to exchange. The propensity to exchange itself was born of the desire for material surplus and wealth which all humans share. Humans, Smith argued, have a natural desire to accumulate economic surplus. Because savages do not desire such material wealth they are not fully human. Thus, Adam Smith should be credited with the general textbook definition of economics which presupposes that human beings intrinsically seek material wealth. In other words humans are inherently greedy. Native Americans, by not sharing in this world view, were seen as less than human and were ripe for economic exploitation.

Anglo Law

The primitive/civilized ideology also plays an important part in Anglo-American jurisprudence. European Americans conquered Native Americans and never accepted them in their own terms. The all out total war of European Americans against the original inhabitants of the Americas was totally unknown to American Indians. Land taking was essential to the building of America, as John Marshall perceived quite clearly in the seminal case of *Johnson v. M'Intosh*. *Johnson v. M'Intosh* remains the basic case in Native American land title law. In writing this opinion, Marshall clearly took up the language of civilization, and in so doing contrasted the colonists with the "fierce savages," the American Indians. Marshall noted that the European "discoverers of America" were eager to acquire lands and that the "character and religion" of Native Americans, in European eyes, justified conquest, especially given the generous European gifts of "civilization and Christianity." Through the Doctrine of Discovery, Marshall held that the colonists held title against all other European nations as well as native inhabitants.

Utilizing Adam Smith's stadial theory of progress, Marshall explained that the court "will not enter into the controversy, whether agriculturists, merchants and manufacturers have a right, on abstract principles, to expel hunters from the territory they possess, or to contract their limits." Instead, Marshall rested Anglo land title in conquest, a title that is "acquired and maintained by force." Marshall's basic point is that the character of American Indian religion justified conquest in light of the "superior genius" of Europeans. Because Native Americans could not be assimilated into civilized humanity, Marshall opined that the fierce savages inevitably had to be conquered by the sword (590). The primitive/civilized structure in *Johnson v. M'Intosh* is obvious, strong and exists to this day.

Nineteenth Century

But it was perhaps in the nineteenth century that the ideology of civilization most powerfully manifested itself in America. Americans, whose numbers were rapidly increasing along with a technology bolstered by the Industrial Revolution, found themselves at odds with the American Indians in almost every conceivable manner, although the federal government's policy in relation to American Indians vacillated between assimilating Indians and crushing them. Indians, in all cases, remained other than the white Europeans. Native American religion was inextricably connected to the land on which they lived. Their land and their religion were so interrelated that one did not exist without the other. Indian ownership of land in common was completely antithetical to the idea of individual property ownership.

One of the last great Anglo-American efforts to destroy Native American religions was brought forth by United States senator Charles L. Dawes, who was himself a liberal. In 1887 Congress passed the General Allotment Act, better known as the Dawes Act. The original Act allotted to each head of household 160 acres and 40 acres to minors. In 1891 this was amended to give 80 acres of agricultural land or 160 acres of grazing land to each Native American. Civilized whites knew enough about traditional Indian religion to know that enactment of the Dawes Act would help destroy tribal heritage and promote assimilation into the mainstream. Said one Indian Affairs Annual Report, "Common property and civilization cannot coexist" (quoted in Loftin 21). Senator Charles Dawes observed that among Indians, "there is no selfishness, which is at the bottom of civilization." The secretary of war, John C. Calhoon, made the following statement to the House of Representatives on December 5, 1818, arguing that Indians must be civilized:

> By a proper combination of force and persuasion, of punishments and rewards, they ought to be brought within the pales of law and civilization.... Our laws and manners ought to supersede their present savage manners and customs.... The land ought to be divided among families; and the idea of individual property in the soil carefully inculcated. (American State Papers II, 183)

Also during this time Native American children were forced to go to Anglo schools. While in school they were forbidden from speaking their native language and were required to dress like whites. The general rules of Indian boarding schools were quite clear.

> All instruction must be in the English language. Pupils must be compelled to converse with each other in English, and should be properly

rebuked or punished for persistent violation of this rule. Every effort should be made to encourage them to abandon their tribal language (Rule 41 of Reservation Boarding Schools, as reported in Annual Report of the Commissioner of Indian Affairs for 1890 CLI).

Also during the late nineteenth century the federal government instituted a policy and then a law prohibiting the practice of Native American traditional religions. Indian agents recognized that the practice of Indian religions prevented their being assimilated into Christianity. In the 1890s government treatment of religions took an even darker turn. Ghost dancers were slaughtered at Wounded Knee in 1890, and in 1892 Pawnee Ghost Dance leaders were arrested in Oklahoma. Also in 1892 the Bureau of Indian Affairs outlawed the Sun Dance religion and banned other ceremonies, which were declared Indian offenses "made punishable by withholding of rations or thirty days imprisonment."

In the early 1880s the secretary of interior wrote to the commissioner of Indian Affairs to "call your attention to what I regard as a great hindrance to the civilization of the Indians, viz., the continuance of the heathenish dances" (quoted in Limerick 11). Teller went on to argue that, "if it is the purpose of the government to civilize the Indians, they must be compelled to desist from the savage and barbarous practices that are calculated to continue them in savagery." Similarly, wrote I.J. Wooten in 1895, "Christianity is the calcium light of civilization, quickens the love of justice and morality and is, above all, the most powerful agent that can be used to obliterate the practice of the degrading superstitious rites of the medicine man held in reverence by all Indians" (quoted in Limerick 12).

In the end, the ideology of civilization proved to be more than the natives could bear. Anglo-Americans used all means necessary to vanquish the Native American occupants of the New World. Although warfare was prominent, European diseases played a larger role in killing American Indians. Native Americans had no immunity to European diseases such as measles, small pox and chicken pox and these diseases probably caused the death of 70 to 90 percent of the native population. In and of itself this had no religious significance, but by the seventeenth century some Americans stated that God had blessed them with the smallpox which they could use to eradicate the demonic Indian. John Winthrop wrote prior to founding Plymouth that God willed that New England would be given to the English by killing "the natives with a miraculous plague" (Forbes II 91) The plague, in fact, was smallpox, chickenpox and measles, which the Puritans believed were sent by God to help clear the land for settlement (Forbes 295).

At the Bay Colony the first Puritan historian described the extermination of the inhabitants by disease as the "wondrous work of the great Jehovah" in order to make room for settlement (quoted in Jameson 48). In 1620 King James had expressed the same sentiment in a statement to the Plymouth Colony in which he declared that God had sent "a Wonderful Plague ... to the utter capital destruction, Devastation, and Depopulation of the whole capital territore" (Eno 274). This view eventually resulted in crude germ warfare through which the United States government would deliberately supply Indian people with smallpox-infested blankets.

Conclusion

In the Enlightenment a reversal of index symbols took place so that science structured and characterized the West's worldview more than religion (Cassirer). Immanuel Kant's "dare to know" captured the spirit of the times. Reason was seen as more primary than religion such that God became a God of reason for a large portion of the population during especially the first half of the Enlightenment (Gay 18).

Then, in the latter period science replaced religion in a dramatic way. As Alexander Pope put it, "The proper study of mankind is man." But the religious impulse did not simply go away despite the hostility of its critics. Religion, in a sense, resided at an almost unconscious level through the ideology of "civilization."

With the emergence of the primitive/civilized program a profound and fundamental change in religion took place. Religiously the ideology of civilization had profound consequences. Up until the discovery of the New World all peoples perceived that God, in some form, was everywhere. It was commonly believed that all human beings had access to the divine. With the emergence of the primitive/civilized ideology that view changed. For the first time in human history some people believed that others were not fully human and had no true gods. By locating the sacred within a particular human community over a discrete period of time, the West attempted to limit God's eternity and universality.

Americans have been busy acting on the world in an unprecedented manner ever since Puritans like Jonathan Edwards first began talking about America as a wilderness which must be developed in order to establish God's kingdom on earth. The world in its wild state as God created it was no longer sacred but became hallowed only through the intervention of human activity and volition. For the first time specifically human powers were seen as divine. Religion was no longer a matter of finding one's place in the sun and recognizing that one lived in a world that one neither created nor sustained. Post-Enlightenment people live in a world that they establish and control. Or do they?

Bibliography
Chapter 13 — The New World

American State Papers. Indian Affairs. 2 vols. Washington, 1832–1934.
Arber, Edward. Editor. *Travels and Works of Captain John Smith.* Vol. 2. Edinburgh, 1910.
Ayto, John. *Dictionary of Word Origins.* New York, 1990.
Beiser, Frederick C. *The Sovereignty of Reason: The Defense of Rationality in the Early English Enlightenment.* Princeton, New Jersey, 1997.
Boorstin, Daniel J. *The Discoverers.* New York, 1983.
Bowden, Henry Warner. *American Indians in Christian Missions: Studies in Cultural Conflict.* Chicago, 1981.
Byrne, James M. *Religion and the Enlightenment: From Descartes to Kant.* Louisville, Kentucky, 1997.
Calendar of State Papers. Col. Series: America and West Indies. 1675–1676, also addenda 1574–1675.
Cassirer, Ernst. *The Philosophy of the Enlightenment.* Princeton, 1951.
Cave, Alfred A. "Canaanites in a Promised Land: The American Indian and the Providential Theory of Empire." *American Indian Quarterly* XII (1988): 277–298.
Chadwick, Owen. *The Popes and European Revolution.* Oxford and New York, 1981.
———. *The Secularization of the European Mind in the Nineteenth Century: The Gifford Lectures in the University of Edinburgh for 1973–4.* Cambridge, England and New York, 1975.
Clark, J.G.D. "New World Origins." *Antiquity* XIV (1940): 128ff.
Commissioner of Indian Affairs Annual Report. Senate Docket 9, 25th Congress, Third Session, 1838.
Crashaw, William. *A New Yeeres Gift to Virginia.* London, 1610, B3–D3.
Dathorne, O.R. *Asian Voyages: Two Thousand Years of Constructing the Other.* Westport, Connecticut, 1996.
Dols, Michael W. *Majnun: The Madman in Medieval Islamic Society.* Oxford, 1992.
Drinnon, Richard. *Facing West: The Metaphysics of Indian-Hating and Empire Building.* Minneapolis, 1980.
Ecks, Diana L. *On Common Ground: World Religions in America.* New York, 1997.
Eliade, Mircea. *A History of Religious Ideas: From Muhammad to the Age of Reforms.* Vol. 3. Trans. A. Hiltebeitel and Diane Apostolos-Cappadona. Chicago, 1985.
Eno, Joel N. "The Puritans in the Indian Lands." *Magazine of History with Notes and Queries* 4 (1906): 274.
Forbes, Alan B. Editor. *Winthrop Papers, 1623–1630.* Boston, 1931.

Foucault, Michel. *Discipline and Punishment: The Birth of the Prison.* Trans. Alan Sheridan. New York, 1979.

_____. *Madness and Civilization: A History of Insanity in the Age of Reason.* Trans. Richard Howard. London, 1967.

Gay, Peter. *The Enlightenment: An Interpretation.* New York and London, 1966.

Getlein, Frank. *The Lure of the Great West.* Wisconsin, 1973.

Goetzman, William H. *New Lands, New Men: America and the Second Great Age of Discovery.* New York, 1986.

Gray, Robert. *A Good Speed to Virginia.* New York, 1937, B1–C3.

Hakluyt, Richard. "Epistle Dedicatori." *Virginia Richly Valued.* London, 1609.

Hanbury-Tenison, Robin. Editor. *The Oxford Book of Exploration.* Oxford and New York, 1993.

Hanke, Lewis. *All Mankind is One: A Study of the Disputation between Bartolome de Las Casas and Juan Gines de Sepulveda in 1550 on the Intellectual and Religious Capacity of the American Indians.* Dekalb, Illinois, 1974.

Harley, J.B., and David Woodward. Editors. *The History of Cartography.* Chicago, 1987.

Hatch, Nathan O. *The Democratization of American Christianity.* New Haven, Connecticut, 1989.

Heelas, Paul. *The New Age Movement: The Celebration of the Self and the Sacralization of Modernity.* Oxford, England, 1996.

Howse, Derek. Editor. *Background to Discovery: Pacific Exploration from Dampier to Cook.* Berkeley, 1990.

Ives, George. *A History of Penal Methods: Criminals, Witches, Lunatics.* Reprint. Montclair, New Jersey, 1970.

Jameson, J. Franklin. Editor. *Johnson's Wonder Working Providence.* New York, 1910.

Johnson v. M'Intosh, 21 U.S. (8 Wheat.) 542 (1823).

Johnson, Robert. *The New Life of Virginia: Declaring the Former Success and Present Estate of that Plantation, Being the Second Part of Nova Britannia.* Peter Force. Editor. *Tracts and Other Papers Relating Principally to the Origin, Settlement, and Progress of the Colonies in North America.* I, No. VII. Gloucester, 1963.

_____. *Nova Britannia: Offering Most Excellent Fruites by Planting in Virginia.* Peter Force. Editor. *Tracts and Other Papers Relating Principally to the Origin, Settlement, and Progress of the Colonies in North America.* I, No. VI. Gloucester, 1963.

Jennings, Francis. *The Invasion of America: Indians, Colonialism and the Cant of Conquest.* Chapel Hill, North Carolina, 1975.

Lamberg-Karlovski, C.C. Editor. *Archeological Thought in America.* Cambridge and New York, 1989.

Limerick, Patricia Nelson. "The Repression of Indian Religious Freedom." *Native American Rights Fund Legal Review* 18 (1993): 9–13.

Loftin, John D. "Anglo-American Jurisprudence in the Native American Tribal Quest for Religious Freedom." *American Indian Culture and Research Journal* 13 (1989): 1–52.

Long, Charles H. "Primitive/Civilized: The Locus of a Problem." *History of Religions* 20 (1980): 43–61.

Marshall, P.J. *The Great Map of Mankind: Perceptions of the New World in the Age of Enlightenment.* Cambridge, Massachusetts, 1982.

Mather, Cotton. *Magnalia Christi Americana.* Vol. 1. Hartford, 1952.

Meek, Ronald. *Social Science and the Ignoble Savage.* Cambridge, 1976.

Morison, Samuel Eliot. *The European Discovery of America: The Southern Voyages,* A.D. *1492–1616.* Oxford, 1971.

Morris, Norval and David J. Rothman. Editors. *The Oxford History of the Prison: The Practice of Punishment in Western Society.* New York and Oxford, 1995.

Neill, Stephen. *A History of Christian Missions.* Harmondsworth, Middlesex, England, 1986.

Nelson, Benjamin N. *The Idea of Usury: From Tribal Brotherhood to Universal Otherhood.* Princeton, 1949.

Northup, Clark. Editor. *The Essays of Francis Bacon.* Boston, 1936.

O'Gorman, Edmundo. *The Invention of America: An Inquiry into the Historical Nature of the New World and the Meaning of its History.* Bloomington, Indiana, 1961.

Pagden, Anthony. *The Fall of Natural Man: The American Indian and the Origins of Comparative Ethnology.* Cambridge, England, 1982.

Parry, J.H. *The Age of Reconnaissance.* Berkeley. California, 1981.

Pearce, Roy Harvey. *Savagism in Civilization: A Study of the Indian in the American Mind.* Baltimore, 1965.

Prucha, Francis Paul. *The Great Father: the United States Government and the American Indians.* Lincoln, 1984.

Purchas, Samuel. *Hakluytus Posthumus or Purchas His Pilgrimes.* 20 Vols. Glasgow, 1906.

Quinn, David. *Set Fair for Roanoke: Voyages and Colonies, 1584–1606.* Chapel Hill, North Carolina, 1985.

Scammell, Geoffrey Vaughn. *The World Encompassed: The First European Maritime Empires, c. 800–1650.* Berkeley, 1981.

_____. *Ships, Oceans and Empire: Studies in European Maritime and Colonial History, 1400–1750.* G.B. Aldershot, and Brookfield. Editors. Vermont, 1995.

Sharp, J.J. *Discovery in the North Atlantic.* Halifax, Nova Scotia, 1991.

Smith, Adam. *An Inquiry into the Nature and Causes of the Wealth of Nations.* New York, 1937.

Taylor, G.A. *The Original Writings and Correspondence of the Two Richard Hakluyts.* Liechtenstein, 1967.

Tiller, Henry. "Report of November 1, 1883." *House Executive Document* 1, Part 5, Vol. 1, 48th Congress, 1 Session, Serial 2190, Pages XX–XXII.

Weber, Max. *The Protestant Ethic and the Spirit of Capitalism.* Trans. Talcott Parsons. New York, 1950.

Wootten, I.J. *Report of the Commissioner of Indian Affairs.* Nevada Agency, 1895.

Index

Abbasids dynasty 222
Abraham 117
Abu Bakr 217, 219, 220
Abu Hureya 31–32
Achilpa 2
Adam and Eve 119, 120
Adena culture 26
Age of Discovery 235
Age of Revolution 235
Agni 88
Agriculture 31–36, 101, 103; origins of 31–32; Syria 33; New Guinea 33; Indian 83
Ainu people 16–17
Akan Ashanti 36
alchemy 180
Ali 220, 221
Alexander the Great 133, 161
Alexandria 203
Allah 216, 225
American Indians 1–47, 215–251
Amitabha Buddhism 182
Analects 169, 170, 171, 172
ancestor worship 102, 105, 107
Ancient Near East 131
Anglicans 244
Anglo law 247
Anguttara Nikaya 148
animals 4–7, 13, 110
Antipas, Herod 196
Aquinas, Thomas 208, 237
Arafat 227
Aranyakas 90–97

Arius 204
Aryans 85
asceticism 148, 156
Athanasius 204
atman 89, 93, 98
Augustine 204, 205
Australopithecus 9
Axial Age 200; confessional religions 136; political order 143
axis mundi 155

Babylonians 128
Bacon, Sir Francis 239
Baghdad 222
Bahai 232
Barabbas 196
Bedouin tribes 220
Bhagavad-Gita 97, 98
Bhakti 98
Bear ceremonialism 16–18
Blackfoot Indians 5
brahman 89, 93, 97, 98
Brahmanas 89–97
Brave Buffalo 1
bronze 101
Buddha 195
Buddhism 134, 139, 144, 181, 232; Four Passing Sights 148, 149; Fire Sermon 149, 151; Nirvana 151, 153; Axial Period 153, 154; Sangha 154–156; asceticism and fertility 156, 157; early Buddhism 157, 158; Mahayana and Hinayana 158, 159; Nagarjuna 159,

160; Tantric 160, 161; decline of Indian Buddhism 161, 162; Maitreya 162, 163

Caesar 202
Caesarea 195
Calvin, John 238
Capernaum 195
capitalism 246–247
Caste system 85
Cave art and paintings 18–20, 23
Chalecedon, Council of 205
Ch'an Buddhism 182
Charlemagne 205
Chaung-Tzu 177–179; story of butterfly dream 178; story of happy fish 178
Cherokee Indians 4, 27, 34, 40, 55
Cheyenne Indians 40
Christianity 138, 143–144, 153, 161, 181, 220, 230 232; life of Jesus 189, 192; Gospel 192–196; resurrection 196, 197; relationship with Judaism 197–201; early Christian life 201; age of martyrs 201–202 Constantine 203–204; Augustine 204–205 Middle Ages 205, 206; church and state 206, 207; crusades 207, 208; Thomas Aquinas 208; chivalry 208, 209 Byzantium, 209
Christians 223
ch'i 110
Childe, V. Gordon 31, 45
China 124, 134, 162; Hsia 102, 103; Shang 103, 105; Chou 105, 107, 167; divination 107, 110; spirit worship 110, 111; creation mythology 111, 113
Chinese Buddhism 181, 183
City of God 204
Chaung-Tzu 180
Chivalry 209
Chou dynasty 167
Chu Hsi 184
chun tzu 170
chung 170, 171
Columbus, Christopher 235–236
commissioner of Indian Affairs 249
Communist Revolution of 1911 112
Confucius 112, 113, 138, 144, 167–174, 195
Constantine 203, 204
Constantinople 210

Copernicus, Nicholas 238
Corinthians, First 200
Council of the Fourteen 242
Crashaw, William 243, 244, 245
Cree Indians 4
Cro-Magnon 10–11, 18
Crow Indians 22, 23, 40
Crusades 207
Cybele-Attis 197
Cyrus the Great 131

dagoba 155
Dakota Indians 7–8
dance 20–21
Darius 132
Dark Ages 205
David 127
Dawes Act *see* General Allotment Act
death and burial 14–16
"The Death of Jane McCrae" 244
Deer Park 154
deus otiosus 35, 87
Deuteronomy 125, 127
Dhammapada 154
dharma 157
Diagram of Extreme Limits *(t'ai-chi tu)* 110
Diocletian 202
Dinka of Africa 37, 38, 39, 40, 42, 43
division of labor 54
docetism 205
Doctrine of Discovery 247
Dogon of Africa 33–34, 45
Dorobo 38
Dravidians 85
dream time 2, 19
Dyaus Pitar 87

Eastern Orthodox Church 209–210
ebiontism 205
Edict of Milan 203
Edwards, Jonathan 251
Egypt 43, 44, 53, 83, 117, 122, 124, 125, 136, 193; Egyptian environment 67–69; Nile River 68–69; Hyksos 68; religion 69–70; sun god 70–72, 76–77, 79; pyramid 72–73; pharoah 73–74, 78; Three Dynasties 74, 75; Old Kingdom 75; Middle Kingdom 76; New Kingdom 76–77; Egyptian medicine 77–78; diseases 79

eight trigrams 109
Enlightenment 235, 250
Ephesians 200
Eucharist 201
Ezekiel 128

faith 123, 200
farming 106, 121, 122
feudalism 209
fiqh 223
fire, origin of 53–54
five relationships 170–171
forgiveness 194

Galileo 189, 195, 238
Galatians 197, 200
Garden of Eden 119
Gautama 147
General Allotment Act (Dawes Act) 248
Genesis 117, 122, 123
Ghandhi, Mohandas 83
al-Ghazzali 230, 231
God of History 126
Golden Chersonese 236
Gray, Robert 243
Great Schism 207
Greeks 244
Gregory VII, Pope 206
Gutenberg 237

hajj 219, 227, 228
Hakluyt, Richard 243
al-Hallaj 231
Han dynasty 174
Han Yu 183
Harappa 83, 84
Harvey, William 239
Hasan al-Basri 230
Havasupai Indians 33
Herod 189
Herodotus 132
Hinduism: creation mythology 87; Vedic deities 87–88; Brahmanas 89–90; Aranyakas 90–97
hijra 218
Holy Roman Emperor, Henry IV 206
Homo Erectus 11–12
Hopewell culture 26–27
Hopi Indians 4, 5, 12, 19, 24, 25, 33, 34, 40, 41, 44
horse sacrifice 86

Hospitalers 209
hsien 180
humans, origin of 9
Huns and Mongols 205
hunting 4–7
husbandry 101, 103

I Ching (Book of Changes) 109
Iman 227
India 101, 124
Indo-European 85
Indus River/Valley 84–85
inipi 2
insanity 240
iron 103
Isaac 123
Isis-Osiris 197
Islam 139, 206; life of Muhammad 215–219, Caliphate 219–220; Quran 224–225; The Five Pillars 225–228; Sunni and Shi'ite 228–230; Sufism 230–232

James, Book of 154, 192, 200
Jaspers, Karl, 131
jen, concept of 169
Jeremiah 127
Jericho 43, 45, 125
Jerusalem 195, 207, 218
Jesus 131, 136, 153–154, 138–139, 189–193, 230
Jews 223
Jibril 225
jihad 224
Job, Book of 36, 62
John, First 200
John, Gospel of 203
John the Baptist 190
Johnson, Robert 243
Joshua, Book of 126
Judaism 55, 181, 197–199; Cain and Abel 120, 121; Noah 121, 122; Abraham 122, 124; the Exodus 124–126, 128; Age of Kings 127, 128; Jewish prophets 128, 141, 142, 143, 190, 195
Julian 204

Ka'ba 216, 219, 227, 228
karma 91–92, 93
Kaska Indians 12
Khadija 216

Kharijites 220
king 104, 153
Kings, Second 3:2–7 123
kingship 55–56, 86, 89, 208–209
knights 209
Kong-kong 112
Krsna 98
Kufa 229
kung-an 183
!Kung Bushman of Africa 8, 20–21
Kwakiutl 3

Land of Canaan 122
Lao Tzu 108, 109, 144, 174–177, 195
Las Casas 242
leprosy 207, 239–241
Levy-Bruhl, Lucién 7
Li 170, 171, 172, 177
Li Lo 183
Li Shan 184
Lotus Sutra 158
love 200
Luke 189–190, 192, 200
Lung Shan 102
Luther, Martin 237
Luttsiang-Shan 184

madrasas 231
Magdalene, Mary 196
Mahabharata 97
Mahavagga 149
Majjhima Nikaya 149
Malay Peninsula 236
Maori 18
Mark, Gospel of 191, 192, 196, 200, 202
Marshack, Alexander 19, 20
Marshall, John 247
Martel, Charles 206, 221
Masai 37, 38, 39, 40
Mather, Cotton 245, 246
Matthew, Gospel of 189, 190, 191, 192, 194, 200
Mauryan empire 134
maya 86–87, 97
Mbuti Pygmies 6, 12
Mecca 215, 216
Melanesia 7, 15
Mesopotamia 43, 44, 67, 68, 69, 75, 83, 117, 118, 119, 124, 136, 140; Tigres and Euphrates rivers 51–52; Sumer 51–52; Ziggurats 52, 54; sciences 56; Sargon 56; Dumuzi (Tammuz) 57; A-ki-til 57; *enuma elish* 58, 59–60, 83 118; *akitu* 58; Lugalzaggizi 58; Anu 58, 63; Ea (Enki) 56, 64; Apsu 58; Tiamat 58–59; Marduk 58–59; Epic of Gilgamesh 60–62; Enlil 63–64
Messiah 193
Metallurgy 43–46, 101, 120, 147
middle way 161
mining 43–46, 120
Mo Tzu 173, 174
Mohenjo-daro 83, 84
moksha 93, 96
Mongols 205
moon 20
Mori'ah 122
Moses 125
Muhammad 215–219, 223, 229, 232
Muhammad, Elijah 231
Muslims 206

Natchez Indians 27
Navajo 41
Nazareth 189
Ndembu 6
Neanderthal 10, 15
Nebuchadnessar 128
Neo-Confucianism 183–184
Neolithic 136, 137, 197; origin of 31–32; relationship to agriculture 32–36; pastoralism 36, 37; concepts of God 37; raiding and sacrifice 38–41; herding symbolism 41–43; pottery, mining and metallurgy 43–46
Nepal 147
New Testament 198, 201
The New World 24–27; discovery of 235; 236, 241, 242; historical developments in Europe following discovery 236–239; ideology of confinement 239–240; primitive/civilized ideology 242–251
Newton, Isaac 239
Nicene Creed 210
nirvana 151, 159, 160
noble savage 242
Northwest Coast Indians 6, 55
Nuer of Africa 36, 37, 38, 39, 40, 41, 43
Numbers 125, 128
Nun 75

oikoumene 136, 203
Ojibwa Indians 34
Ortiz, Alfonso 7
Owner of the Animals 3–4, 13, 17

Paleolithic 102, 106; origin of 1–4; Sky God 3–4; hunting 4–7; origin of language 7–8; human origins 9; origin of tools 9–11; origin of fire 11–13; animal symbolism 13; death and burial 14–16, bear symbolism 16–18; art 18–20; dance 20–21; Shamanism 21–22; ceremonialism 22–24; New World 24–27
P'an Ku 111, 113
Passover 124
Pastoralism: origin of 36–37; Catal Htuyuk 36; sacrifice of oxen 38–41
Paul 198–200
"The Peaceable Kingdom" 244
Peking man 11, 15
Pentateuch 117
Peter, First 154, 201
Pharisees 193
Philippians 200
Pilate, Pontius 196
police 241
Polo, Marco 235
Polycarp of Smyrna 202
Pope, Alexander 250
pottery 43, 101, 103
prana 89
Prajapati 86, 89
prakriti 95
Prehistoric Religions: origin of 1–4; Sky God 3–4; hunting 4–7; origin of language 7–8; human origins 9; origin of tools 9–11; origin of fire 11–13; animal symbolism 13; death and burial 14–16, bear symbolism 16–18; art 18–20; dance 20–21; Shamanism 21–22; ceremonialism 22–24; New World 24–27
primitive/civilized ideology 242–250
Psalms 127
Ptah 75
Purchas, Samuel 245–246
Pure Land Buddhism 182
Puritans 244, 245, 249, 250
Purusa 86, 89, 95

Queen of the Sciences 208
quei 110
Quirinius 193
Qurash 215, 218

Ramadan 227
The Renaissance 235, 239
Roman Empire 135, 137, 193, 197, 201
Roman religion 35

Sahlins, Marshall 35
salat 226
Samkhya 95
samnyasin 96
samsara 94, 159, 160
Samuel, First 127
Samyutta-Nikaya 151
san jiao 184
Sankara 96
Sargon 46, 56
Sassanid Empire 220
Saul 126
Saulteaux Indians 16
sawm 227
Saxons 206
Scientific Revolution 235
Sea of Reeds 124
Sedna 22, 34
Seleucid Empire 133, 134
Sepulveda 242
Sermon on the Mount 192
shahada 225
Shamanism 21–22, 136
Shang-Ti 106
Shar'iat 224, 229
shen 110
shiao 171
Ship of Fools 240
shirk 225, 231
Shiva 88
Soma 88
shu 171
silk 103
Silk Road 132–135, 136, 140, 162, 182, 198, 215, 216, 217, 232
Sioux Indians 1, 40
sky god 3–4
smallpox 249
The Small Perfection of Wisdom Sutra 157–158

Smith, Adam 246–247
Smith, Huston vii
Smith, John 243, 245
Socrates 143
Solomon 127, 128
suf 230
Sun Dance 249
sunnah 221
Sui dynasty 181
sui generis 137

Tao 169, 171, 176, 179, 182
Tao Te Ching 108, 174, 176, 180
Taoism 111, 113, 174–181
te 172
Templars 209
third noble truths, 150
Tiamat 118
Tibet 160
Tien 106
Tseng Dynasty 181
Tu'bal-cain 120
tun wu 183
Turks 222

Upanishads 91–97
ulama 231
Umayyad Dynasty 221, 222, 230
ummah 218, 221
universe, origin of 1
usury 238
Uthman 217, 220

Vedas 85

Venezuela 236
Venus statuettes 18–19
Vespucci, Amerigo 236
vinaya 157
Vishnu 97

wakan tanka 2
Wang Yang-ming 184
The Wealth of Nations 246–247
Weber, Max 238
Wei River 105
wen-ta 183
Wheatley, Paul 32
The Wisdom of the Further Shore Sutra 158
Women 5–7, 18, 32–33
writing 104
wu-wei 175

Yahweh 124, 126
Yang shao 101
Yathrib (Medina) 218
Yellow River 101, 104
Yin Yang 108, 110
Yoga 92–93
Yogacara 160
yung 170

Zahid 230
zakat 227
Zarathustra 131, 133
Zealot 193
Zoroastrianism 133